IRON
IN MY HANDS

dave draper

IRON
IN MY HANDS

DAVE
DRAPER

Foreword by Dan John
On Target Publications, Santa Cruz, California

Iron in My Hands

Dave Draper

Foreword by Dan John

Articles originally published on *davedraper.com*

Copyright © 2016 Dave Draper
Foreword © 2016 Daniel Arthur John

ISBN-13: 978-1-931046-87-9

First printing July 2016

On Target Publications
P O Box 1335
Aptos, California 95001 USA
otpbooks.com

Library of Congress Cataloging-in-Publication Data

Names: Draper, Dave, 1942– author.
Title: Iron in my hands / Dave Draper ; foreword by Dan John.
Description: Santa Cruz, California : On Target Publications, [2016]
Identifiers: LCCN 2016001933 (print) | LCCN 2016010128 (ebook) | ISBN 9781931046879 (pbk.) | ISBN 9781931046862 (epub) | ISBN 9781931046855 (mobi)
Subjects: LCSH: Bodybuilding. | Bodybuilders--United States--Biography.
Classification: LCC GV546.5 .D733 2016 (print) | LCC GV546.5 (ebook) | DDC 613.7/13--dc23
LC record available at http://lccn.loc.gov/2016001933

Also by Dave Draper

Brother Iron, Sister Steel
Iron on My Mind
Your Body Revival

Contents

Foreword

Dave Draper is the Blond Bomber, Mr. Universe, and the childhood hero of legions of bodybuilders and weightlifters. To the envy of many, he shared a pool with Elly May Clampett on the *Beverly Hillbillies* and hung around with Sharon Tate on the Malibu set of *Don't Make Waves*.

But more important, Dave Draper is a poet.

Frankly, when discussing Dave Draper, it's difficult to know where to begin. When reading his writing, one senses sadness and solitude, yet it's filled with joy and appreciation for details. Dave's laser-like focus on detail borders on legend; he's a master craftsman of body, wood and words.

He shapes nature into furniture, words into wisdom and the human body into perfection. His words will live on forever as the voice of sensible training and a lifetime approach to fitness and health.

One can compare Dave's written work to Dylan Thomas's ability to soar from the mundane to the tremendous (and back again) in pieces like *Do Not Go Gentle into That Good Night* or the underappreciated *In My Craft or Sullen Art*.

This is not hyperbole. Dave can take a question from an aging, overweight reader and touch the sky with his answer:

> *This you know: There are no tricks, there are no pressures and there are no deadlines.*
>
> *There is simply working out with intent, feel and focus; sets and reps and poundage to guide you, not to threaten you; hardy work that agrees with your five senses and joints and incentives. Like Einstein said, or was it Zane?, a good workout has rhythm and flow and balance and just enough force.*
>
> *Excessive force breaks the body, the mind, the joy and the spirit.*

If you'll allow me, let me try to explain Dave's writing from the simple title of a work written by my late professor, Leonardo Alishan: *Dancing Barefoot on Broken Glass.* The tension between joy and pain in Alishan's title rings true when capturing the writing of Dave Draper.

> *In pain, there is joy.*
> *In joy, there is pain.*

Understanding this tension brings you to your physical goals, but also the truly important goals of mind and spirit.

Certainly, Dave provides us with workout ideas, exercise progressions and training concepts. He gives us the insights, the clichés and even the proverbs, but always with wink and a nod:

> *Every exercise, every movement, every action should be done with precision and exactness in mind. The focus and thoughtfulness, care and control, even if you're a sloppy mess, are present in your mind and assist you in your overall development.*

Trust me.

Trusting me is like trusting a seeing-eye dog with a monocle and walking stick. Woof.

No one else writes like this. No one else has the life experience, the insights and the intuition.

Trust him.

Dan John
Danjohn.net

Introduction

JUST WHEN YOU THINK you've read all there is to read about lifting weights and building muscle, along comes another 80,000 words echoing in the corners and hallways of the musclehead gym: schemes and routines and hints and tips with the intent to inform, encourage and entertain.

The immediate message: See iron, lift iron.

The ultimate message: Train hard, eat right and be happy.

Don't you just love simple? It's one of the main reasons I chose the sport. No pitcher, no quarterback, no foul ball and no meddlesome referee. Just you and the iron and the rhythmic sounds of action, the grunts and groans and clanks and thuds.

You are your partner, your team, your biggest competitor and your best fan; muscle and might are your favorite goals, with a good pump and burn to accompany you along the way.

And none of it happens without moving a ton of weights, forging countless sets and reps, enduring a pile of aches and maybe some pain, and amassing a stack of stories to tell.

And speaking of stacks of stories to tell, pull up a bench and I'll tell you a few.

dd

1

A Quick Glimpse in the Rearview

IMAGINE A TEN-YEAR-OLD, the youngest in a family of three boys, who inherited threadbare baseballs and ragged mitts and smooth, under-inflated footballs like the sorrowful, unexciting toys they were. Here kid, have fun. I preferred climbing trees, racing through the meadows and scrambling up quarry walls, only to jump into the blue water far below.

Batter up, balls and strikes and touchdowns were not for me.

Now the guy down the street, the big guy who built the tree house for his kid, he lifted weights in his garage after work. I heard him clanging around and saw him lift the bar over his head. Wow! Strong, and he had muscles. He likes it, I could tell. He'd wave when I went by on my bike.

I bought a bar and a small pile of weights from a neighbor for five bucks that summer when school got out. My dad and brothers looked down and nodded as I eagerly slid finger-smashing plates on and off the bar and practiced tightening the red collars with my nifty wrench. Oomph! This was for me.

No one on first, no one in the end zone, no swing, miss and you're out. Just me and my muscles wherever I went.

First it was in the basement in Secaucus and then the garage. Later it was the Y in Newark, the Vic Tanny's in Jersey City, the Health Club in Hackensack and Weider's shipping room in Union City before the Muscle Beach Gym we called the Dungeon in Santa Monica in the spring of '63.

The Dungeon, the creepy basement of a very old hotel, contained the equipment that once withstood and delighted in the sun and salt air of the famous Muscle Beach four blocks west on the Pacific's edge. It was a dark and dreary subterranean reminder of dazzling and wonderful years gone by. You'd think something beautiful and bountiful was struck down and punished for its audacious freshness and strength. In '63, the gym was five years old.

I was twenty-one.

Shoving open the forced-shut door, one of two ten-foot aging guardians, tramping down two flights of stairs and there it was in all its splendor, the Muscle Beach Gym. That is, if you could see the place. It was seventy-five feet wide and 100 feet long and had two strategically placed fifty-watt light bulbs to prevent us from stumbling over the symmetrical arrangement of benches, racks, barbells and dumbbells and pulley apparatus.

There was a water fountain in the far corner and a john in the other corner, and both worked when we needed them. Much of the light (not much) came from two skylights of glass blocks built into the sidewalk of Broadway Avenue above the south wall.

The equipment was handmade by hunky weightlifters, not craftsmen. Lumber from construction sites was slammed together by approximating eyes and big hammers and nails. Stout pipes held the iron plates and were wildly welded in place to serve as dumbbells from fifteen to 150 pounds. Pulleys were free-hanging, six-inch contrivances with ample lengths of cable to hoist any weight at the command of the lifter.

Oddly, the underground arena didn't have a foul smell and it maintained the same agreeable temperature year round. A few twelve by twelve tiles remained on the concrete floor, paint had long faded, was peeling or exposed crumbling plaster.

One mirror hung, a tarnished, unframed four-by-five-foot chip of glass, which seemed too old and too tired to reflect an image. Why it remained the years I was there is a mystery. We had to peer, squint and study its content and, alas, give up as nothing recognizable was offered.

There were never more than ten guys in the gym at any time, only one woman I can recall. The scene I just described is pitiful, but it tells of the best gym I ever trained in. These were the moments before the first seismic shift took place.

My next stop was Joe Gold's. The concrete was still wet, must have been spring or fall of 1966. Coincidentally, as Joe was building his famous Gold's gym, the Dungeon was shutting down and moving to a storefront across the street. The hotel was slated for demolition. They put up a parking lot.

Joe and his long-time buds, including Zabo Kozewski, did much of the construction. The gym was as simple as a structure could be, an approximately 50' × 100' × 20' rectangle made of cinder blocks and a wood roof. Open the front door and look out and there was Main Street, a block from the ocean. Inside were all the appropriate and perfect bars and dumbbells to soothe and develop a musclehead's body, mind and soul—thick-handled and pristine, solid and bold, clean, visible, handy.

And look! Large and polished mirrors on every wall.

3

The benches were made of rugged steel, designed and constructed by Joe in his garage at the end of a cul-de-sac a mile away. The pulleys were oversized for smooth sailing and mounted on gigantic frameworks for multiple purposes. Everything had its space, just enough, not too much. Light zoomed in from skylights and front windows by day and fluorescents by night. Showers and a restroom were in the back, above the teensy parking area.

The arena was set for building muscle and might, and the atmosphere and attitude followed. There were no greats walking the floor and no hotshots greedily consuming the mirrors. Guys and a few gals pushed the iron with basic purity, hard work and mature passion.

Joe Gold was a very good man and was always the adult in the room. Neither jerks nor loudmouths were allowed, thus respectable behavior was integrated.

There was quiet before the storm.

2

As Fast as You Can, but Don't Hurry

It's Monday morning and you drag yourself out of bed. This is the day of the week you gather the responsibilities you dumped on Friday and ignored on Saturday and Sunday. You load them on your shoulders before standing upright, taking a shower or having breakfast. The neglected duties and tasks can wait no longer. Guilt, anxiety and urgency—unlikable companions—assist you in the deed.

The weight is not light, nor is it desirable, and it takes a few minutes to find your legs and collect your spirits. As you focus and find success in a few mundane chores—brushing your teeth (job well done), pulling on your clothes (got that right), pouring the first cup of coffee (hardly a splash)—the burden lightens and the sky brightens.

Today is the first day of the rest of my life. The streets are alive with the sound of music. Dribble. You grab your keys, wallet and necessary gear, and head out the door.

Tuesdays are better because Monday is over. You made it unscathed and had a decent workout to top things off. The latter, insignificant to your colleagues, is the thing that mattered most. Without the workout, Mondays wouldn't have a chance. You'd remain in bed curled up in a ball until the day was gone.

Furthermore, Tuesday is the day you train arms. That would be biceps and triceps with enough midsection to soothe the soul and rattle the six-pack. Let's hear it for barbell curls and pulley pushdowns, dumbbell incline curls and dips. Ah, life ain't so bad. Contract, extend, grunt, concentric, eccentric, focus.

The appetite takes an upswing by Wednesday, which is good because force feeding every three hours is like a weird self-imposed torture. Oh, no . . . It's the scrapping of tuna and the dripping of water day after day . . . I'll talk, I'll talk. Still an uphill climb, but the day has hope.

You feel emboldened upon arising on Wednesday, jumping out of bed early after a night of sound sleep. You have a sure grip on this thing called life, and you know why they say only the strong survive. You lean back in the kitchen chair as a second cup of coffee warms your hands. What shall I do today that's daring? Won't take any crap from anybody, that's for certain.

Squats during lunch hour sound like an adventure. Go heavy and hard, with the thrust of a freighter. Make those plates clatter and clang. Dump the bar in the rack with a crash. Wrap up the routine with leg curls and extensions and calves, and be out the door and down the stairs before the echo of metal grows faint.

The afternoon's a breeze. You attend your work, however tedious or difficult it might be, with efficiency and high spirits.

Everything is light after moving several tons of iron; everything is simple. Colors are brighter, sounds more acute and what might otherwise be annoying is almost entertaining.

You wallow in patience, lose yourself in concentration and see humor where stress generally abounds. Somebody keyed you car. Ha! Get this: He goes home and can't open the front door because his key is jammed with your custom candy-apple-red paint. Ha! You're in stitches.

Man, do you sleep Wednesday night, and Thursday arrives right on time too. Good morning, world. Race ya to the top of the mountain. Too late, already been there! You have places to go and things to do, a job and responsibilities. The weekend is almost here and you don't want to be caught in a lurch. Three down, two to go, and today you work on deadlifts. Maybe have extra carbs for lunch and train late afternoon—the body's better prepared, stronger.

You realize every day is distinct, unpredictable and unique, and you're responding to mute social conditioning when you define the day by what day of the week it is. You hate to confine yourself to rules of habit, but sometimes that's the way the game works. Go for it, what the heck. Nobody's looking.

You do the same thing with your training, once you pass the ABCs. Sufficient order is necessary—guidelines, routine. You have days you work arms and days you work legs or shoulders, and there are certain exercises you practice to bring about the desired effects. But within any workout you need plenty of room to allow your imagination and instincts, desires and needs to take control. That's the best part about training, the joy of it: to express yourself according to your personality and ability while achieving your purpose.

You arrive at the gym and find the Thursday mood is circulating the equipment. Faces are less somber and more hopeful than those displayed on Monday. The gym and the workouts soften anxious features by distracting, humbling and fulfilling the trainees early in the week. And as the week rolls by, zeal and good cheer accompany the guys and gals as they walk through the front door.

The weights are moved with gusto. They jingle, jangle and clang like *musico de grande improviso.*

And so we come to Friday. Up in the morning and you count your blessings as you prepare to leave your castle: four super workouts this week and one more on the way, the job, my loving family, tuna, good health, farmer walks . . . and you're out the door. Similarly, other iron enthusiasts thank God for beer, the pickup, the dog, the ole' man, waterproof eyeliner and strapless training tops.

Fatigue is evident, but strength and drive are sustained by the promise of the weekend. When the mind is willing and the body squirms, you recall the accomplishments behind you and imagine the joy and relief ahead. You continue your commitment to good and right in your work and communication, each step taking you closer to that Friday workout. It's the best.

It's the best, not because of records set, pump achieved or workload accomplished, but because of the feel of the steel, the awareness of exertion, the goodness of the cause, your presence in the gym and those around you, the clang and clamor and atmosphere, the successes and failures and fulfillment.

Each rep is a charge, every set is a blast. It's Friday.

The weekend is the weekend. Except for those occasions when overtime hours and household chores extend the workweek, there are two extra days of life for sleeping in, watching sports, going to the lake, playing with the kids, praising God, visiting family and friends, going to a concert or just plain collapsing.

Of course, there's always the gym . . . in case you missed a workout or simply miss working out. Word has it there are a few crazies in the weightlifting department.

A large number of fitness and muscle-building enthusiasts depend on Saturday and Sunday for their primary workouts, Monday through Friday being crowded with, as if it were possible, more important things.

You move time around like chess pieces, training when you want, as long as you want. The hard work and time invested in the gym feel like genuine recreation, a healthy diversion or a productive pastime, and less like an obligation, punishment or forced labor.

What freedom you have! Freedom to vote, speak, worship and work out—work out any day of the week, any way you want and wherever you can. All you need is a purpose, some barbells and dumbbells, a little knowledge, a lot of heart and plenty of guts.

From these basic ingredients great bodies, minds and souls are built.

3

The Only Way Is Up

WHY ARE YOU DOWNHEARTED, oh, my soul?

You're in a slump. We all have them, the valleys of our lives, those regrettable times when nothing goes right, contentment and achievement are vague memories, and future expectations of either are doubtful.

It's not one thing in particular that knocks you out of whack; it's an accumulation of things. The world is falling apart at the seams. Your immediate surroundings are maddening—traffic, weather, leaky roof, potholes, bills, the sameness of things. And the gym is not the answer as it should be, but is part of the problem—the weights are heavy, the joints ache, there's no pump; the sweatpants are tight in the waist, t-shirt is baggy in the shoulders . . . lousy attitude and lousy mirrors.

Eating junk or taking a day off—common approaches to manage the mess—only make it worse. Negativity spawns negativity and you tire in attempts to raise your heavy spirits.

Sometimes you've gotta let go and be still. This does not mean give up or give in; it means stay tight and hold on, look and listen. It's called being strong and courageous, confident, hopeful, patient, disciplined, slightly desperate and a little mad.

This is tougher than we think. Look what we're dealing with.

The world situation: Who can fix it? We've been trying forever, here we are today and it's still a beautiful mess. Still, our individual participation is vital. Don't do anything to make it worse, and maintain a positive and productive atmosphere around you. Contribute where you can with your talents, knowledge, awareness and energy, and recognize in your head and heart that you're doing just that. You count. You influence your surroundings far more than you realize. Your smile can light up a room; your glare can darken it.

Imagine what your laughter can accomplish right about now. Earthshaking.

The local situation: it's called daily living. We all face it, endure it and cope with it. Now is the time to recall we have also loved it, applauded it and could not get our fill of it. The road is winding and rough, and then it's a highway. There's the storm and there's the calm, the steep climb and the mountain's peak. One cannot be without the other, you note, if you're paying attention.

Here it comes again. Breathe deep; grab on, hold tight and go with the flow. Look up; observe, learn and grow. This too will pass.

The training situation: before we talk about the gym and the iron, throw a net around your diet and pull it in. When folks get blue, they head to the fridge for ice cream. If that doesn't work, they're into the kitchen for cookies. The phone is the next source for sausage pizza from Luigi's Italian Hut. Finally, it's the family, the family car and The Swedish Smorgy across town. All you can eat, $6.99.

Eating lots of garbage to chase a mean attitude is like adding dry timber to a raging forest fire. Stay cool. No littering.

The gym situation: ah, the only place you have control. Even when the weights are virtually bolted to the floor, you have control. You can practice exhilarating isometrics, exertion with no apparent purpose other than pure exertion. Deeply rewarding and downright fun, pain with no relief. That, indeed, is the worst scenario I can think of. You've gotta give the old-timers a lot of credit, pushing and straining and groaning without movement, pump or achievement—only trembling and deep, dark, silent pain.

Mercy, it's gotta get better from here.

A light bulb goes on. Let's move light weights, since the heavy weights won't go. We have nothing to lose and everything to gain. We are in the grips of a slump and the only thing standing in the way is the towering, unquenchable ego—a hairy monster with a big stomach and a little brain. The intellect tells us muscle in motion under resistance stimulates tissue growth and adds to the entire system's health and well-being. Common sense and experience tell us not every day is triumphant. And the Good Book tells us there is a season for everything, reaping and sowing, pumping and burning.

Today, it's light weights with focus on form and muscle stimulation; high burning reps rather than low power reps; feeling, discovering and enjoying instead of intense exertion, maximum concentration and critical pain.

The path to accomplishment is not always straight and clearly defined. Sometimes the traveler, if savvy, will abandon the ordinary trail to circumvent perceived obstacles. He might, for expedience, try a direction less frequently chosen. Or, the rascal might go left instead of right simply because he wishes to—for the freedom and fun of it.

Sometimes eager steps forward are steps too many, steps backward or steps into the abyss. Where one day heavy weights engender hypertrophy, another day they may engender injury. Squats today, as duly prescribed, might overload the knee or back if the lifter is unfocused and out of touch.

If you don't have the desire, brain fuel, mettle, oomph or heart to blast it, make a series of snaps, crackles and pops. They're less explosive and get the job done. They tickle and tease and are entertaining. What have you got to lose this day already in question?

The years in the gym and under the iron have a way of wearing you down. To carry on you must be inventive and half crazy. A worn-down lifter no one can tolerate, neither the lifter himself nor those within a stone's throw. Worn-down lifters, like those tossed stones, become pebbles, then sand and grit, and finally dust. I'm allergic to dust. Dust makes me sneeze. It's time to improvise.

Anything goes when creative, half-crazed lifters combine exercises, or movements, as they prefer to call them now, and execute them with continuity. They know how to blend two or more exercises so they become one; they know intimately the affinity and purpose of the movements. They sense them as elements in the formation of a compound (H_2O), spare words in a command (Just Do It), notes in a catchy tune (do, re, me, fatso, la, ti, do).

I once wrote a set of slumpbusters, ten favorite exercise combinations that entertain and blast, change direction, challenge the norm, save time, get to the point and build muscles.

Thirty years, maybe fifty, have gone by since they were first installed and practiced. Like bread crumbs to the hungry, let me toss out another pinch of even-less-likely combinations.

Why? Because you're hungry and they work; you're half-crazy and why not.

1. Close-handed under-grip pulldowns supersetted with dips—extraordinary extension supersetted with extraordinary compression

14

It's Friday, leg day, and you're finished. You worked arms and upper body two days ago, ran and did midsection yesterday, and won't train again till Monday. You're beginning to feel lonely, a faint sign of withdrawals. That tic in your right eye and the tremor of the lower lip confirm your fears. Your fix has not been satisfied, something's missing, you're not done here. You need more, just a little more: a clever, yet simple combination to fill the hollow within.

This blend of pulling and pushing works the whole upper body. It can be practiced by itself for a very short workout and, if done with sufficient intensity, can replace a long, hard day at the gym when time has fallen off the earth's surface. The pulldown simulates a chin up, working the biceps fully (great for improving chinning ability for enthusiasts still lacking chinning status), guarantees a strong grip, grabs hold of the lats mightily and engages the serratus. And there's more abdominal work in the action than you would believe, as indicated by the pain of strain in the torso the next day.

The dips, as directed by body position, work the tris and shoulders and back and pecs. But you knew that. You also knew you would get a great pump.

5 supersets, rep range 12, 10, 8, 6

I generally start with a moderate weight for higher repetitions and add weight each set, getting lower repetitions as the weight increases. Pace and all-out effort vary with mood, need, energy and fatigue level.

2. Press behind neck (PBN) supersetted with pulldown behind neck

This is a satisfying combination of exercises when you've been craving that wide, V-shape feeling all day long. Legs needed to be worked and you did your duty valiantly, squats and their accompaniments, but now you deserve a reward, a prize, a thrill.

The PBN is not for the fainthearted. It requires substance, practice and finesse, but the payoff is heavy duty—thick deltoids, thick upper back. Grip and focus are everything (along with all the other stuff—back support, body position, steady motion, exact muscle engagement, complete extension and contraction). However, if you feel a pinch, these are not for you. I love them, but they can cause problems for some people.

The pulldown is best performed facing away from the apparatus, allowing distance from the overhead pulley. You want to achieve a smooth and tight contraction in the upper back without the interference of your head or unwisely shifting your head forward to permit the bar's tight and energized passage. Tugging (contracting and pumping) the bar into place as if repeating overhead biceps poses for an audience of approving fans is the proper way to execute this exercise. Have fun. Listen to that crowd going wild!

5 supersets, rep range 12, 10, 8, 6

So who said these would be revolutionary? It's not the movements and their combinations; it's the lifter and the performance.

I have more crumbs, but I've run outta time and space and readers. Besides, the wind's up. Gonna grab my wings and hit the air.

4

Vigorously and Without Doubt

LOST TIME IS NOT found again.

Young Bob Dylan penned those words generations ago, harmonica in hand and guitar by his side. He then sang the lean prose with a tormented voice in one of his incriminations on life. A person of fewer wounds might say time is lost forever when the timekeeper does nothing to correct it. I say time is not lost but only misplaced—to be replaced by understanding and time-saving lessons.

Try putting the last two revisions to music and you know why Dylan stuck to his prose and became a shining star.

"Who cares?" you ask. "Let's build strong muscles and get ripped."

Finally, somebody with a head on his shoulders. The time we thought we lost by trying this training principle or that diet has served to teach us, entertain us, sustain our interest, carry us forward, fill a storehouse with experience, strengthen character and humble our souls. The unbearable slow-rep methodology, the excruciating 100-rep-per-set squat technique, that sardine-and-grapefruit diet or those toasty soybean cauliflower casseroles had far more meaning than we thought—little benefit, no reward, but lotsa meaning.

We've experienced, we've learned, we've grown, we're moving on.

The road is clear, my grip is tight. No more lost, misplaced, replaced or wasted time. In fact, I don't wear a watch, nor do I have a calendar hanging over my desk. I live for the moment. I'm free.

Freedom means doing whatever you want, whenever you want, without restraint or interference . . . Excuse me, my beeper just went off. This'll only take a sec.

> *Yes, hi . . . a quart of milk and a loaf of bread, return the book to the library, pick up the dry cleaning before five, check the PO box, stop at Triple A for maps, grab some cardboard boxes from the Safeway dumpster, don't forget the prescription at the pharmacy, a sack of cement from ACE Hardware for the deck project . . . What deck project? Is that all?*

I want a large Quiznos' sub and a Big Swiggy.

Freedom in training means proceeding confidently with your urges—long-laid plans and recent discoveries—and with current trends and recommended techniques. If you're going to do them, do them well. Perform them with confidence, practice them with devotion, execute them with spirit. Anything of value that exists in your spectrum of schemes will be gained only by hard work and committed application.

One more thing; keep your eyes wide open. It's essential.

Training with doubt is training imprisonment. With every set and rep, you question what good it will do, where it will take you and what it will produce. No clear image emerges as you sit in your solitary confinement. You apply effort with restraint as suspicion confines you. You work out in shackles; your spirits are bound. Training passion and workout joy are stifled, strangled by uncertainty and reserve.

I can paint a pretty grim picture when I want to make a point. Sometimes I go overboard and get depressed. No worries, I stand in a corner pounding my chest and repeat "Huge and ripped, huge and ripped" until the negativity drips from my body like snake venom. Works every time.

Doubt must be arrested and replaced with assertion and exhilaration. A confident state of mind must be chosen and adopted, and then practiced and proven. You've got to believe in what you're doing, knowing that if what you're doing isn't exactly right, it will still promote discovery, learning and growth.

It's difficult to determine which training program is the best and most effective to satisfy your needs at any given time. These needs include—separately if not all at once—muscle size, density, shape, definition, quality, might, swiftness, endurance and health. So you reference your experience, observations, conversations and the written word found in books, magazines and web pages, and you formulate a scheme.

Oh, yeah, right. No problemo, Charlie Brown. Bull's-eye, on the money and perfecto mundo. Information, like candy at the dime store, is abundant and nauseating, and an overload will give you a bellyache.

Remember: Stick to the basics, and you'll never get sick.

The new plan works until the novelty wears off. I don't even want to begin to speculate how short-lived a workout love affair lasts in this day and age. We're an odd mob—capricious, impatient, expectant, greedy, naive, indoctrinated and spoiled.

Two, three weeks tops, and we're discouraged, depressed and desperate . . . Rats!

According to my calculations, research and dreams, I shoulda yada yada . . . but instead, I'm nada yada yada.

Doubt is as sure as the rising sun, or more appropriately, the cold winter fog, the dark midnight gloom. Remove the stumbling block, and replace it with a springboard. This is your game, your track and field, your platform.

Not every plan we put forward is precise or without fault. Stick to the plan. Make a few bold adjustments, substitute the bar with dumbbells, modify the rep scheme, apply intensity where you're able and reservation where you must.

Reduce the pace, increase the weight. Be strong, don't doubt, go hard. Wondering is permissible—nothing wrong with a little curiosity. But the doubt, the duct tape around the eyes and mouth, hands and feet—that must be removed.

When I was little kid, all I did was chin-ups, pushups and dips and ran and rode my bike. No plan, urges only. No sets and reps, all I could do, plus a little more was sufficient. No deep motives, strong muscles were plenty.

No time limit, forever would do.

That might not be the advice a coach or parent would pass on to a sprouting youngster, but I wouldn't change it for all the muscle in the gym. Grab on, hold tight and go, go, go—a great phase in discovering oneself, exercise, muscle and might. This will pass, change will come, but not till the deed is done.

Sometimes we try to fix a thing that ain't broke, and ruin it forever.

Another time in my life when I was a big kid (this can be most any time since I was a little kid), I'd walk into the gym with limited forethought, grab any iron that got in my way, lift it purposefully and intensely for ninety minutes and walk out refreshed, advanced and complete. The movements were like pieces in a jigsaw puzzle; they fit together smoothly, swift and sweet. Doubt did not enter the gym with me. I had plenty, but I left it at the door like a pair of muddy boots.

Those were very good years. The question is, like the chicken and the egg, were they very good years because I didn't doubt, or because I didn't doubt were they very good years?

Today, as an older kid standing amid a different sport of giants from the giant factory, doubt dots the landscape while I deal with the variables that accompany time, age and the ages. There must be a better word for *doubt*, in that we have collectively taken a stand against the disagreeable companion. Let's call it deception. Better yet, the Bible refers to the devil as the great deceiver; let's call doubt the devil. Doubt, deception, Satan—mankind's archenemies.

The variables of time and age fall from the sky like small meteorites. They are infrequent, dense and peculiar. They can be damaging, and they certainly get our attention. Don't you love it when I get outer-spacey and scientific? The meteorites represent arthritis, pain of injury, muscle tears, limited range of motion, loopy hormones, swollen joints, tendonitis, weakness and fatigue. These factors add new challenge (ha!) to the once simple, constructive and entertaining sport of building muscle and might.

Some say they remove the challenge and spoil the sport, reducing it to the ongoing struggle for another day. Wow! Take these bums outside the camp walls and put them out of their misery. They've gone from doubt to discouragement to hopelessness to goodbye-cruel-world.

Never! We are here to save souls. Take the motley crew to the gym, immerse them in exercise, smother them with encouragement and restore their deflated training zeal.

Injury is a savvy instructor; pain is a smart cautionary signal, and limitations are boundaries that direct and margins to exceed. They are tough training partners that respond positively to exercise performed vigorously and without doubt. I like that: vigorously and without doubt.

I could go on and on, but I'd go alone.

5

Where Do Little Girls Come From?

I'VE BEEN THINKING ABOUT the recent passion for kettlebells and wondered where we went wrong in the grounding purity of true weight training. Kettlebells don't speak—they emit screeches and howls. Barbells and dumbbells whistle and sing and tell us truths long hidden; they growl and snarl and never whimper.

Perhaps I'm a little harsh on kettlebell exercise as I've been unable to get even the lightest bomb-like thingy over my head without taking out a wall, a lamp or a pedestrian. They're wrecking balls in my wayward mitts. I'd practice if I had the nerve, more space, a building to demolish . . . or better liability insurance.

So when asked to prescribe a routine for a young girl at the gym, the frightening round, black mechanisms concentrated with gravity were not mentioned. I went with bittersweet barbells, dumbbells and resistance machines and free body movements.

At twenty, cute as a button and with no bodyfat, she seemed slightly bored. I narrowed the training challenge to five functional and complementary exercises.

Actually, I wasn't asked to prescribe anything. There I was with one more set of triceps before wrapping up my workout, when I observed the red-haired beauty executing a set of seated lat pulls. I thought about—within the brief instant I allow for extraneous thinking while engaged in serious weight training—how lucky she was. She's about perfect, as young girls are, and all she needs to do is regularly and cheerfully nurture her mind, body and soul with a modest amount of challenging exercise, and then eat sensibly.

Guys, of course, must push the iron and lift the steel till it clatters, thuds, crashes and rusts. They must never miss a workout, and each session must surpass the former in power and yield, or else. They must eat protein frequently and closely watch the carbs. They must build muscle strength, shape, size, density and hardness as they lose fat and get ripped. They must fight the dead-end temptation to use weird, felonious chemicals and every awful ingredient on the market that "assures lightning-fast gains as you sleep."

At the end of the day, Red looks great and Spike looks desperate.

Okay, okay, what's the routine I devised for my new friend of the female persuasion? After she completed her set of seated low lat rows, our meeting and conversation went something like this: She was now reclining on the bench like it was a cushy lounge, twirling her water bottle and staring at the ceiling.

I asked her if she liked the gym and training and lifting weights. Her eyes lit up. She said she loved it, it was relaxing, and she once had a personal trainer. I asked if she had a routine she followed— she admitted she needed one but was just doing what she pleased these days. I then commented on the lat row, saying it was one of the best exercises because it worked many muscles from head to toe and contributed to whole body strength, function and shape.

I was now entering murky waters. Could she take exercise advice from a Neanderthal? I continued to explore the possibilities by applauding her desire to train, her good fortune to have the world before her, and her great combination of quality muscle and lack of bodyfat.

"So many young women have imponderable obstacles to overcome before they can begin to look like you, and here you are. Can I make some suggestions on the performance of this exercise so you can gain all it has to offer?"

I knew she'd say yes. I evoke pity when I'm on my knees with clasped hands exhorting, "You need to know the truth, child."

I told her about the importance of a full-forward action to engage the lower back (structural strength and health), the thoughtful pull as the entire length of the lats (very appealing) is brought into play, along with the forearm and biceps muscles (useful and adorable), and, at the peak of the movement, the chest out and the back arched in upper-back contraction (develops dynamic posture and musculature) and a most sensational feeling. The return action, smooth and focused, is an integral part of the movement.

Three sets of ten reps with eighty-percent exertion and virtuous form are just right. She agreed.

Her boyfriend cruised into the picture, a twenty-five-year-old, 200-pound six-footer who can lift a house, a small garage and the surrounding trees.

"She has eleven-percent bodyfat," he declared. No doubt. We exchanged remarks of envy and the unfairness of life, quickly pointing out she probably couldn't rebuild an engine from the block up.

"The really neat thing is you only need five exercises plus some cardio to achieve the sun, moon and stars," I said, "whereas, Mountain Man here needs that many for each bodypart."

She laughed while Mountain and I just stared glumly. Reality sucks.

"Would you like to know what I would do, if I were you?"

I was bound to tell her and gave no pause for her to reply. She could have left the building and I would have told the wall.

"Five exercises, three sets of each for ten reps with moderate to daring exertion, of the following exercises in the following order after warming up with variable intensity on the bike. The bike will serve as your leg conditioning for the first month, and then we'll add squats. They're a riot."

1. Thirty-degree-incline dumbbell press—*works upper chest, front delt and tris*

2. Stiff-arm dumbbell pullover—*works lats, minor pec, some bis, tris and abs*

3. Seated lat row—*works lower and upper back, lat line, forearm, grip and bis and core*

4. Machine dips leaning forward—*works shoulders, upper back, chest and tris*

5. Standing barbell curl, with a touch of thrust—*works biceps, forearms and grip, plus those plentiful whole-body supportive muscles engage when a thoughtful thrust is added, a pinch of salt to the stew*

I'll spare you the details, but I gave her the original Bomber spiel about discipline, patience, perseverance, resolve and motivation, until she packed her gear and headed for the door.

"But wait, there's more," I yelped as she hurried across the parking lot.

"Protein, lotsa protein . . ."

Her car screeched around the corner, down the block and out of sight.

"See ya . . . Red . . ."

I didn't say a word about airplanes, the sky and flying high. Next time.

6

Rehabbing Injuries: Superman, Super Girl and Me

I SAT IN THE WAITING ROOM of an out-patient surgery clinic, bemused by the piles of magazines placed for the entertainment of the clientele. Magazines have never been a hot item in my frugal life, and there were enough in this one space to have consumed an acre of trees. What a colossal waste of money and resources, I thought. I could buy a double In-n-Out burger—protein style—and a large milk for the price of a *Field and Stream* or *Vanity Fair*.

There were weeklies, monthlies and quarterlies about teens, women, the glamorous, the overweight, camping, race cars, hiking, Hollywood, baseball, football, mechanics, software, movies, millionaires, the economy and home-making—nothing about muscle building or getting ripped. I stood and was about to protest when a family of three—Mom, Dad and daughter—hurried in and beat me to the receptionist's desk. Rats!

I'm an adult. I'll survive. I found a tattered *Superman* comic in the children's corner and settled in for a good read. My antenna for incoming data remained up and active just in case.

As Superman was about to thwart a major attack on a nuclear facility by stuffing terrorists into a tank of radioactive waste and burying it in the center of the earth, I overheard that the girl accompanied by her parents was being admitted for substantial ankle surgery. Poor kid, just nineteen. She'd been a competitive athlete all her life—running, jumping, kicking and scoring—and the games had taken a toll. Payback at an early age, heartbreak and pain and loss of ability.

Her mom and dad, now waiting in the holding area, shared her story with another set of parents in similar circumstances. I tuned in my secret new Superman listening powers. At least the parents were deeply sympathetic and not the insensitive whackos who drive their kids to the edge, over the precipice and finally to the grim operating room.

My kid's scar's bigger than your kid's scar!

As the parents bonded, exchanging the details of the procedures proposed by the attending physicians, I recalled the gloom of my own not-too-different encounters with the scalpel. It's never a delightful experience. After the shock and awe of the injury, there are the pain and realities of disability, the cessation of zealous training and the mounting disappointments: the doctor visits, the diagnosis, the recommended treatment, the second opinion and the surgery date.

Then, there's the anticipation of the dreaded day during which you learn the meaning of aloneness.

And just when it becomes too much, there's the long, dark moment when you stand before the door that separates you from your warm, colorful world and the cold world of black and white and sharp metallic silver, thick with the hideous and foreboding smell of disinfectant where very serious and mysterious things happen.

Mom says, "Our college girl will train in the rain and run in the sun and race in place till red in the face, this day, every season with undying reason."

Her dad confesses, "She catches balls tossed in her direction, or slugs them sightless with bold connection. She steals them, too, the lane, the puck and the base, and never comes in last, winning first place."

In my corner and to myself I add, "She's a star, a champ, poetry in motion whose life has been altered, emotional commotion."

It's been twenty minutes. How long do these tests take? I've got things to do. I'm hungry.

I'm sitting on a little crayon-marked tabletop encircled by little crayon-marked chairs, studying *Superman*. The comic's not as big or as exciting as it used to be, it seems to me. Besides, Ronnie Coleman makes Superman look like a shrimp. I'm growing up. I'd use an adult chair, if there was one available. The fix-it business is good today.

I think of the young athlete heading under the knife, the trials of life and the tests we endure, and gradually see the bright light that transcends the darkest darkness. She's a heroine now, smiling radiantly, who's more than won a race; she's overcome defeat.

Her mom and dad, each slumped in resignation holding their favorite magazines, stare at the glossy pages selling glamour, pleasure cruises and a black high-speed Porsche. They don't see what I see.

I wait. It takes eyes to see or the light grows dim. At the first opportunity I wiggle my way between the pair and introduce myself as a concerned parent "with grandchildren of my own.

Yes, indeed. I couldn't help but notice the young lady's plight and overhear your conversations."

That I'm a snoop and like to meddle in other peoples' hardships did not come up.

They are sufficiently bored and become interested in my paternal concern. They know enough about life to realize the impact of the trauma on their precious daughter, but have not exactly regarded it as an opportunity to embrace, nurture, fully experience and appreciate.

I certainly do not mention the idiom, "That which does not kill you makes you stronger," and dare not say at this moment, "God has a plan for your little girl." But I do give them my positive point of view, the view of someone who knows battle, but is outside this particular war zone.

I rambled on. She walked into the procedure room an hour ago and will be wheeled out in another two. The procedure room is a nifty term for the sterile place where they cut, drill holes, scrape bone, replace, reshape and reattach tendons and ligaments. The first days are up in the air as pain, novelty, initial recovery and adjustment occur in a slowly clarifying haze. Rest and recovery are consuming.

From the onset, certainly, she must be offered loving care, but more than that alone, the hope and suggestion of advancement— physically and mentally—as she strives to overcome the setbacks thrust upon her. Trials are difficult; they are also the precursors of inspiration. They slow us down, that we may prepare to go faster and further. They sidetrack us, that we may find the true way.

Here's a frightening, all-too-familiar scenario to accompany the load of the injury, the surgery and the recovery: a weak person sits idly as the wound takes its own time to repair. They eat and watch TV (the obvious distractions), grow sorrowful, cynical, lazy and fat. I shudder at the sound of my words, saying them intentionally to provoke the parents. They shake their heads emphatically, "Not our girl."

That's the response I was hoping for, staunch rejection of my disturbing portrait.

If I were her, I'd be as active as possible as soon as possible. If the nonambulatory days turn into weeks, I'd beg, borrow or steal a wheelchair, a walker, a crutch or a cane and get to the gym. There I'd learn to hoist my body safely and effectively, as I visited various machines for full-on resistance training. This is not only externally fortifying; the determination and discipline exhibited under duress are self-inspiring, self-stimulating and internally constructive.

One comes to know one's self as few individuals do when battling the odds, an awesome achievement to complement life.

There's a movement for every muscle group, right down to that well-protected ankle. And with the administration of wisely chosen exercises, the accompanying oxygen- and nutrient-packed blood flow and the positive attitude fueling the whole wonderful process, the mind and body will enjoy accelerated repair and development.

The fields and courts, the team and teammates, the practices and games and the balls of various shapes and sizes can wait. The champ's in training.

And muscle grows strong and injuries heal fast when the athlete is eating right. This is an easy one. A smart athlete eats smaller, balanced meals regularly throughout the day with an accent on high-protein foods. She'll ingest enough nutrient-high carbs from fresh salads, vegetables and fruit and useful, non-greasy fats offering plenty of essential fatty acids. That means no junk food, fries, sugar and pop, Pop. Fact is, the entire family will sparkle from practicing the simple plan . . . but you knew that.

33

Here's my card. You might suggest the young gazelle meet me at the wilds of the gym when she's ready. I may be an old bear, but I can clear a tidy path in the right direction for her. You two can tag along, too, if you'd like.

Do either of you fly; are you afraid of heights? I have an imaginary bomber parked outside if you're interested in taking to the sky. My friends and I do it all the time.

There's no way like up.

7
Muscles and Fitness: Today, Tomorrow and Forever

WHAT'S AN AARP, OR RATHER, where is Aarp? The first time I heard the word without the option of ignoring it was earlier this year when a man rang the house and announced he was calling regarding Aarp.

He sounded pleasant and sincere. I didn't want to be rude or dismissive, so I said, "Cool. Isn't that a seaport in northeastern New Zealand?"

He said no. I shot back, "It's a small furry animal native to the planes of Australia."

I was sure it had something to do with the down-under. It's always good to display your intelligence and savvy to strangers calling on your home phone . . . keeps 'em off balance.

He said no, again.

"An affliction not unlike belching and similar to hiccups," I persisted. I was into it.

Upon discovering aarp was not an animal, place or thing, but AARP, the huge association of Americans over the age of fifty, I automatically said, "I gave at the office."

Wrong again. The gentleman was contacting me to arrange a personal interview with the organization's staff writer. I was invited to appear in AARP's colorful monthly magazine, "a short personal profile, Mr. Draper, with you offering fitness advice to America's maturing adults."

I blinked. Not *GQ*, not *Men's Fitness, On Fitness* or *Muscle and Fitness, IronMan* or *Muscle Digest*. Not TDM, Today's Dashing Male.

I maturely yet hesitantly concluded we all age sometime; I might as well give it a shot. "Sure," I said with magnanimity and courage and an imperceptible quiver in my voice, "I can do that. Over fifty, huh?"

Well, bombers, the article is done and they sent a two-man photography team from LA to complete the photo layout. We provided them with stacks of old stuff, but "we want shots of Mr. Draper today, as if breathing on the very pages."

I did what I could to prepare for the photo session, which was nothing other than fret, grieve, worry, stress and groan. Twenty-four hours is not much notice to a bodybuilder, thanks. They—whose names were Mike and Ben—arrived late morning and were setting up lights when I walked into The Weightroom. Laree was shopping the mall and sports shops for undersized tank tops without logos for me and something besides jeans with holes for her.

Weeks ago we offered to save AARP time and money by shooting the needed pictures ourselves. "Laree can handle a camera like Earnhardt can handle a car."

They saw through my scheme and said thanks, but no thanks. These old folks are sharper than I thought.

The day was fun; we worked hard, shared the experience with two neat pros and never flinched after two hours at the gym with me looking goofy under the lights and two hours like gophers in the redwoods around our house. You survive a thing and rejoice. Thank God!

But the larger thing to survive is the publication of the pictures before a potential audience of twenty-three million. Will they—the photos—be a horror show, a small wrinkly embarrassment, or simply another achy day in the acquiescing world of aging under pressure . . . and the lens of a camera?

The day of reckoning is the first week of October when the magazine floods the mail. I'll be on an oil rig off the coast of Venezuela.

There's an upside to the catastrophe. Though I have not read the article, it was written by a talented *Newsday* writer who does a fine job of gathering words and telling a story. Of the 23,000,000 AARP members receiving the magazine in the mail, perhaps half will get it all the way into the house. Of that 11.5 mil, another half will skim it. Of that five-plus million, a few will stumble across the grinning image of an old muscle guy and think, "Hey, I know that dude. That's what's-his-name. I thought he was younger."

And, finally, a small handful will read the words, grasp the message and put it into practice. The world is saved one life at a time.

Another upside: If one out of 100,000 begin to hang at davedraper.com, we'll have a whopping 230 additional bombers to soar, glide and consort with. We've gotta think big. I won't even consider what it could mean if a few ingest the contents of *Brother Iron* or a tub of Bomber Blend: renewed life, energy, health, purpose and longevity.

We'll welcome the AARP visitors warmly and offer them an understandable and seductive digest of the essentials to good health, muscle and might as one enters the wonderful world of iron exercise. Let's face it, it's the same stuff we know and practice regularly and have been since we were little squirts . . . of sorts.

And we'll encourage and inspire them because that's what we as a group of high flyers do best.

Well, so much for aging; back to where we belong: staying young. Aging is for those who sit around and think of yesterday while today is passing them by. Aging happens when the weights rust and gather dust in the garage, basement or under the bed, out of sight and mind.

Those who sit on couches and recliners with their fists in bowls of something gooey and chewy are aging, not those whose hands are full of dumbbells and barbells, and whose mouths are full of protein. The latter are growing, learning and gaining, grinning and scheming.

Look out! I'm coming up from the rear and passing you on the outside . . . the inside . . . over your head.

So much for moving on; my mind has done a loop and is back on the fifty-plus track. "What," I ask myself, "is the most compelling challenge facing those heartened individuals interested in getting in shape? Is it setting a goal? No, the goal is already there—getting in shape.

Of course, it takes on various forms and descriptions: losing weight, gaining muscle, increasing strength, looking and feeling fit, and improving cardio efficiency and general health. And at the onset, each aim is approached the same: exercise, eat right and be positive . . . and strong, cheerful, thankful, focused and so on.

Is it patience? Teens have a patience problem. They're taught to expect what they want, now; even less-than-mature adults fall for that line of bull. Patience is established by this stage of the game, or it certainly should be.

Perhaps that's the big problem, that many think this life thing is just a game. He who dies with the most toys wins. Eat, live and be merry for tomorrow you shall die. Life is a roll of the dice. Win or come in last.

No, I don't think so. Those who stagger past the fifty-year line seldom declare life is a game. They might put on a good show, shoulder pads in place, but the smudges, bruises and fatigue register the seriousness of the matter. Age has a way of humbling life's participants.

Is it the exercise? Nah! An exercise program is simple and enjoyable when introduced with spirit and encouragement and empathy. We've got those goods in the palms of our hands, and the possessive words—we and our—includes you and me. This is a bombing expedition, you know, not a one-man sweep. Exercise and time will present a low stumbling block, but we'll drag them over it as they give it their best willing effort.

On three, oomph! Now you've got it. Again. One, two, three . . . ugh! You're lookin' good.

How about discipline and guts? I'm always fumbling for these keys to success and I'm not alone. We seem to lose them running frantically from our responsibilities and obligations. Time does temper us, and hopefully the two keys are fastened securely to our wrists with equally tempered chain.

What, then, is the foremost problem? I'm concerned about perseverance, old-fashioned stick-to-itiveness: the will to push the iron, lift the steel and carry the load beyond today, tomorrow and the next.

Too often the sharp image of the goal fades before a real impression is achieved. The mind's eye wanders and the grand intentions slip. A day between training—exercise and smart eating—becomes a week. A week becomes two.

Without consistency the goal is never grasped.

This sounds like a physical thing—and it is—but it's more a mind-and-soul thing, and a matter of friendly persuasion and education and inspiration. They must learn to fly and see the sky. We can do this, they can do this, and together we shall.

Another idea would be offering free trips to Bermuda to those who fill out our Bomber's Miles in the Sky form and send in a before-and-after picture (untouched by Photoshop), along with a ten-dollar bill.

Is ten bucks enough, too much?

8

Muscles, Time and Moving On

It has recently occurred to me that I'm not as young as I used to be. And I have a sneaky suspicion you may be experiencing a similar awakening, sudden and stunning in its arrival.

Well, it's about time. Youth gets to be old after a while.

Getting older is a real test of one's humor (I got a D–), especially upon discovering there's nothing funny about it. But we're comics and clowns and we joke about our looming frailty, lumpiness and fussiness, and laugh (not of the rolling-in-the-aisles variety, more like a snicker) at the iron-headed irony.

The symptoms of time's inexorable passing are pesky and less than kind. I offer my observations for your examination.

- I can't get out of bed in the morning without an hour's notice.

- The elbows and knees grow, biceps and thighs shrink.

- And if I could hear, I'd swear the former squeak.

- Skin gathers like wise guys on street corners and sags like sails after a storm.

- The entire body glows with pain and the light keeps me awake at night.

- Energy goes south, endurance goes north and fatigue hangs in there.

- If the gas reserves in my gut could fuel my car, I could drive non-stop forever.

- Upon entering the gym, I immediately look for a place to sit.

- Aerobic exercise is out of the question as the equipment is up a flight of stairs.

- Loading and unloading the leg press has become my primary back workout.

- I keep a training log to remind me what bodypart I'm working.

- I tie a string to the log and attach that to my wrist.

- My doc assures me that working out no longer aids my muscles, but counting the sets and reps is good for mental acuity and helps me resist senility.

- Lately I prefer to train in a cardigan sweater, Dockers and deck shoes.

- I'm seriously eyeing a polished hardwood cane with a nickel-plated eagle head handle—quite dapper. And handy.

Ugh, I sound like I'm ninety, going on a hundred. Life is and always will be filled with adventures to dare, challenges to overcome, battles to be won and goodness and peace to be sought, protected and propagated. One day we awaken and we're all grown up, plus more.

What does one do? Some laugh, some cry, some adapt, some deny. How about you—what about me?

As for me . . .

I'm constantly modifying my training intensity. These are experiments only—I greet each new year with steady and persistent training, minus the last-rep ultimatum. The reason for this is multifold: aching is fine, but last-rep pain is downright mean and I need a break; the training pace will increase and, I suspect, my mood will improve; change is always good and the letting-go is a test of courage; I might reverse some injury trends and signs of overtraining. Besides, there's a season for every activity under heaven. 'Tis the season.

This is a more substantial alteration than most of us realize. As I write these words and review the prospects, I feel a sense of relief and hope, curiosity . . . and doubt. Withdrawing effort is not a common approach for me. Am I caving in or am I being strong? Is this a sign of decline or an indication of maturity and wisdom? Will I welcome the change or return to the safety of similitude? Will I regenerate and grow, or will I weaken and diminish?

Love it or hate it, do it or die?

Though I enjoy and respect them all, I don't want to become a mild-mannered trainee who upon completing a set turns to a mate and demonstrates a golf swing or continues applauding Congressional bipartisanship, or returns to a paperback, undistracted.

Hypertrophy depends on the last almighty repetition, the final insane quivering contraction of muscle against its will and capacity, the entering of that timeless space where pain dissolves into white silence and mountains are moved. Only then, I have been told by bold and solid sources, do we grow and become more.

You're witnessing the intense period of evaluation I undergo before making a life-altering decision. No rocks are left unturned. Friends think I should get a job, a hobby or treatments.

Not I, I'm done. Monday I'll put my brilliant method into operation.

Just as we're cautioned never to say never, so it follows we should forego declaring, "So it will be." My aim is to train according to my relative fluctuating influences—mood, energy, time—with three tantalizing modifications: reduce the sets per exercise from five to four, eliminate the last-rep of maximum effort and insert the high-rep training principle (HRT) where and when inspired.

A quick review of the Drape's Over-Sixty Four-Day-a-Week Routine:

- *Monday—chest, back and shoulders;*

- *Tuesday—biceps, triceps and lats;*

- *Wednesday—legs;*

- *Thursday—off;*

- *Friday—total-body combination;*

- *Saturday and Sunday—off*

The total sets per workout are a bit over thirty, in the rep ranges of six to fifteen, plus midsection. Each workout takes ninety to 120 concentrated minutes, the pace governed by body limitations and the controversial last-rep max output.

In an attempt to enjoy and appreciate the perceived advantages of the revision in training intensity, I'll perform four rather than five working sets of each choice exercise—the fifth set can be brutal and apprehensive. This will have a valuable mind-freeing effect and allow me to focus more deliberately and determinedly on each rep and set and every nuance of movement.

This way we make the most of the action with less time and physical and mental energy expenditure. Eliminating the extreme last-rep output saves exhausting time, enables quicker recovery and, thus, efficiently improves the workload pace.

In both occasions, pain and extended training turmoil are reduced without loss of muscle-building effect . . . or so we hope and will discover. A month should provide sufficient evidence to make a determination.

Now, to satisfy the need to pounce on the body and beat it within a hair-breadth of its life, I shall apply high-rep training (that HRT sounds like "hurt") to the final set of those exercises that are unfortunate enough to gain my attention.

Only now, as I add this third accommodation, am I relieved and feel a sense of raw animal control.

Installing the scheme should be quick 'n easy. You may have noted I didn't call this trailblazing training modification a "routine." Routines are something we read in muscle magazines or books on the subject. I intentionally avoided the term "program," as programs are offered by schools, institutions and coaches. The word "workout" is not accurate, a workout being something we do systematically between entering and leaving the gym. "Plan" would suffice if it didn't sound so ordinary. Proper and important folks reference their exercise endeavor as a "schedule," which sounds like time has bitten them in the butt and won't let go.

Schemes, however, are devised by the crafty, the clever and cunning.

Based on scrutiny and computed instincts, I've removed something from one place and with a wink of the eye inserted another thing. Here I minimized, and there I maximized. Careful wording and phrasing—last-rep max, modify, extended training turmoil—further enhance the sound and appearance of my, if you'll excuse the triteness, plan.

Quick 'n easy sounds simple. They are, in fact, like flying a bomber, quick 'n easy in action, but skill- and courage-demanding in application.

Waste no time. Be wise and of strong heart. Take to the sky without fault or delay. It's another fine day, my friends.

9

About Us and the Things We Do

THE DAYS, THEY GO BY. Monday will always be Monday, blue as a bruise. Tuesday is chest-and-back day, the only way you can identify that everyday day, give it distinction. Wednesday is the day in the middle of the week, and the center of things is generally agreeable. Thursday offers hope, as most of the work week is complete and tomorrow is Friday. Yes! Friday is Friday, a rainbow of colors if you plan to paint it. And where there's a rainbow, there's a pot of gold: the weekend, Saturday and Sunday.

Greet each day with a hug and a pat on the back—better yet, make that a bear hug and a slap on the back. Recognize them or not, they are some of the best friends you've got, but here today and gone tomorrow.

The days are separate and distinct, yet there are times when they follow each other like soup cans on an assembly line. Hum, clink, clink. You count the cans as they wobble by, bored and thankless. Hum, clink, clink.

Suddenly and without notice, the machinery stops and the doors are thrown open to cold winds and the rush of traffic. Soup cans resemble scrap metal as they pile up one on top of the other. Urgency fills the air and things must be done. Catch a plane, consult a lawyer, stop the bleeding or console the grieving. You adapt and, as always, wish you'd been grateful when you had the time. Instead, you're grateful now, the best you can do.

These are exciting days, filled with hope, inspiration and encouragement. The days of production, enlightenment and achievement—the winning days—consume us on momentous occasions and leave us spinning. They seem too good to be true, so we forego appreciation and anticipate their ends.

Or, convinced we deserve them, we bask in their glory as if they'll never end. Hum, clink, clink . . . Soup's on, cream of celery, your favorite.

We're learning, day by day. Thank heaven for weightlifting and muscle building. We're able to make every day a special day. Once past the front counter and along the dumbbell rack, we can finesse our training into a fulfilling challenge or an engaging game: a skillful sport, an uplifting activity or a delightful diversion.

Soup-can days and days of eruption and disruption can be transformed into entertaining, productive and healing days.

Does your workout seep into your work day, or does your work day seep into your workout? Do you succumb to the follies of life, or do they become dust under your strong, lengthy strides? Are you hampered by momentary intrusions, halted by daily obstacles or propelled by the power of a vigorous spirit, mind and body?

Where you have control, take control: exercise and eat right! Training rules, and you're the law. It's the stabilizer when your foothold slips, the fortifier when plans are laid to waste, the friend you know amid strangers, the oxygen and fruit of life in a barren place.

Exercise and fitness are not options. They're essentials.

Hard to recognize and easy to forget, your training and the things it affords keep you standing when others fall, pressing on when others retreat and smiling when others sneer.

We hear it all the time: I don't have time to go to the gym— the kids, the job, the man. I know; it's tough. We grow weary and hope wavers, our bones ache and time scatters, the barbells are heavy and stuck to the floor.

Poor baby! Give up. What's the use? Get plasma and recall the good old days during halftime and station breaks. What's in the fridge?

We don't lose our health and strength; we throw it away. We don't slide out of condition; we're tossed out for lack of participation. Fitness is not lost; it's squandered like thankless treasure. Our muscles don't get soft; they evacuate. Strength moves out when the stomach moves in, and stamina checks out while we're sleeping . . . on the couch in the middle of the day.

Sorry! You've been deserted.

No man is an island, though I sometimes see myself as a weed patch adrift in the swamp of life.

It is with this lighthearted attitude I proceed day by day, noble in purpose and gallant in pursuit. I'm alert (whazat?), always aware of my surroundings (where the heck am I?) and observe my neighbor without judgment (whatta dope!). I gather understanding from experience (a bum pushing a shopping cart along the streets) and learn through my mistakes (working feverishly on my doctorate).

Independent, unfettered, untroubled and free, that's me. I obey the law most of the time because most laws are good most of the time. Where there is law, there is order; where there is order, we prevail; where there is chaos, we fail.

I watch, I see, I glean and I apply. I avoid convention and the way of the masses, unless, of course, they work. Too often they are too ordinary to be worthy: round pegs for round holes, square pegs for square holes and so on. Not for this mutt.

I derived this sense of direction from my mom and dad, good people who put a roof over my head and pointed me forward. Now this is not the worst method to prepare a kid for the future. Thanks, Ma. To spoil and offer no direction is by far the most frightening tactic of all. The "Have iPod, Will Travel" generation causes me to wonder, doubt and lose my breath.

Life is serious, we're on the line and the enemy surrounds us; projectiles fly, the bandits want our things and the ERs are full; kids are without heroes and heroes are without kids; the wrongs pile up on the backs of the weak and downtrodden; the rich get richer and leaders speak with forked tongues or are misunderstood.

Ah, but consider the gym with its metal and geometry—circles, arcs, straight lines and angles—and pure sounds of crash, squeak, clank and thud. The gym offers force and pain and relief. It provides challenge and struggle and satisfaction.

Stress doesn't have a chance; like weeds, it's pulled and burned for fuel.

Athletes, wiseguys, cool dudes and sweethearts of every age gather around piles of dead weight to be taunted and proven, purified and invigorated, strengthened and liberated. No one loses, everyone gains.

Problems are poured into vats of toil beneath the heat of presses, deadlifts and squats. The smell of evaporating woe is invigorating, intoxicating. The occasional groan you hear, honest and provoking, is a song of delight, an ode to desire, a one-syllable poem filling the air.

All else is silence or rock 'n roll.

10
Training: Love It or Hate It

WHERE DO WE GO from here? We've taken a bite out of the year and the taste is good. There's time to think and act before we devour the spring and reach for the summer. I don't want to stuff my face with the best time of the year and not savor the moments, anticipate them, welcome them, delight in them, make the best of them. I dare not waste them.

You can tell when people are over forty, fifty or sixty years old. We occasionally ponder time's passing, wanting to slow it down, re-do it or go back from whence we came—our youth, twenties, thirties, anything but old. Me? I just want to store time in a jar and release it as I cruise along.

Let the good times roll. Train hard, eat right, be strong.

Here are a few related questions directed to those who exercise regularly.

Do you dread your training?

I remember when I passed the point of no return. The small heap of weights in the yard, at the end of the bed or in the basement gained my attention and followed me around, a warm, fuzzy pup I couldn't ignore. We played, he grew and so did I. One day, as I sought competition, I noticed my faithful pup had become a fleabag mongrel. We played no more—we fought. Warriors refusing to lose, we respected each other and shared the good fight.

The gym floor often became the battlefield.

Do you love the deed?

Never have I not loved the idea of weightlifting. The practice itself holds other experiences. The early attempts to move the iron are novel and exciting, curious and mysterious and inventive. Continued applications of force against steel yields rewards that multiply and are most desirable.

Don't you love the pump, muscular growth and regular increases in strength, the designing of workouts, their smooth execution and that last engaging rep?

Obstacles and plateaus are leveled by cannons; they test the body, mind and soul. Enduring them lifts us to new levels of completeness: physical, mental and spiritual. Who among us doesn't appreciate endurance and its plentiful fruits?

Appreciation borders on love.

Beyond the early days of play, struggle and the horizon of plateaus, we one day—sooner or later—come to the tantalizing engagement of muscle and might, the tuneful rhythm of exercise and pace, the slow release of doubt and fear, and the gratefulness for our time and place amid the steel.

As if these delights were not enough, there are more: the comfort of expression and freedom and the understanding born of discipline and purpose, compromise and patience, no matter the abundance or scarcity indwelling your bones.

These joys are difficult to distinguish from love.

Is your exercise time an obligation, a responsibility?

Why not? Obligation and responsibility develop strong people. Strong people undertake obligations and responsibilities. One's strength and health is a responsibility, a major responsibility, and largely a neglected one. Look around you and what do you see? Seven out of ten feel neither obligated nor responsible for their strength and health, shape or well-being. We all lose, we all pay and it doesn't stop at their waistlines.

For you and for me, our exercise is an obligation, one we embrace with open arms as it streamlines our lives. And, I suspect, the iron is far more than responsibility alone. By itself, responsibility is a chore, and chores can get old and redundant, imitated and boring, lifeless and bitter.

Our workouts must never take on the characteristics of a chore, lest we become an image of what we do.

Is your training a habit, a blank, going through the motions without emotion?

Good habits are very good. In the door, to the weights, sets and reps, sweat and strain, hi, goodbye, out the door and home. The workout doesn't have to be a production, a ceremony, a major project. Just do it.

It's the emotionless blanks who need a nudge. I know people like that. They're zombies walking heavily through the gym with their arms extended, mouths open and their eyes like galvanized quarters.

"Take me to your exit."

From the stationary bike, magazine in hand, they make a lap around the gym floor before sitting on the leg extension for an extended length of time, thinking of cookies. If only we could inspire them to grasp a barbell, dumbbell and pulley. They would come alive, their vacant eyes would see and they'd grunt audibly with their once-silent mouths.

Nice sneakers, though . . . clean, snappy. Cool iPod.

Is your time on the gym floor recreation, playtime and talk time?

Nothing wrong with a little fun, mixing business with pleasure and a few friendly words with your buds and chums. Intermingling is healthy, supportive and fulfilling. I know some hard trainers who can carry on meaningful conversations throughout their workouts with tacit nods, grunts and a few key words.

I seldom feel alone or abandoned in the gym, in a crowd or at the solitary crack of dawn. I don't have much to say and I do have a lot to do. But there are some who enter the gym, look about earnestly, as if seeking inner training direction, and adroitly zero in on a sucker, the most likely to respond to grandiose conversation. Sports are a favorite (bearable), opposite sex is in the top five (pitiable) and politics slither in like a venomous snake (deplorable).

Just leave the magazine in the rack and the cell phone in the locker room. This is a gym. Starbucks is down the street.

That doesn't mean you can't have fun. Feel the steel.

Are your workouts a preparation for other sports?

Some of us remember when team coaches forbade weight training, an unhealthy pursuit by warped minds. Today, almost every superior athlete engages in the activity to enhance athletic ability.

Sport-specific weight training is an integral part of professional pre-season training, and the champs work out year-round.

General conditioning readies the average person for everyday sports participation from hiking and climbing to golf and tennis. It also serves to ready us for the impact of the day: racing on the freeway, running down the street, participating in a full-body contact at the mall, scrimmaging at the office, sliding into the parking lot, stressing and straining at home and chasing the kids.

Train hard, play hard.

Do you skip workouts without disappointment or guilt or total collapse?

Did you pause to think about the answer? Or did you say with assurance (indignation, perhaps), "I don't skip workouts."

The answer is usually somewhere in between. We all miss workouts. Life has a way of inconveniencing us from time to time, demanding our attention. Family, job, TV, weddings, funerals—it's always something. One postponed training session is tolerable, two is unmentionable, three threatens sudden implosion and four borders on death by firing squad. Five, they seize the spouse, kids and dog, and, six, the western hemisphere is vaporized. No seven . . . no . . . none!

If you don't agree, I can't help you. You're doomed.

Are those hours and days of the week with the iron a passion?

If you don't know what passion is, go on to the next question. You don't need passion to exercise; ordinary interest, common sense and responsibility will do just fine. But to train vigorously, enjoy it and develop serious muscle and might, passion is essential.

Passion is the inner fervor, the burning desire, the lust-less love, the insatiable zeal that causes the lifter to lift beyond limit, to train when the castle walls are burning and to grin as the bar bends on his back and crumbles his shoulders. The passionate trainer never misses a workout, even when she should. One more set leads to another, one more rep to another, and another.

Passion is one degree short of obsession. Obsession is a disease; passion is love.

Do you train and leave it in the gym, or do you pack it up and take it with you?

I've actually seen people leaving the gym as if nothing had happened. They're fresh and bright and smell good. Not staggering, not red-eyed, no bruises, no gasping.

"You forget your high-heel sneakers, Sue?" I ask under my breath, hunched in the dark corner by the rusting metal, sagging bars and cobwebs.

Training? I take it with me. Can't just leave it there after all that blood, sweat and tears . . . nobody else wants it. We're inseparable. A wise person needs good companionship, a buddy with whom to share all things, delights, despairs, wins and losses. I guess training and the iron come 'round full circle after all the years—follows me like that pup I can't ignore.

I hear thunder overhead, the rumble of bombers in the clear blue sky. No time to waste. I'm headed to the gym to prepare for takeoff.

Save me some air, bombers.

11

What You Did Is Who You Is

It's late spring, a favorite time of the year, and you've resurrected your entire summer wardrobe. A fabulous fashion display—shorts, T-shirts and tank tops, most of them threadbare.

You play hard. And you face the naked truth.

The stretch of warm and sunny days ahead presents pleasure or panic, depending on the shape you're in. You knew last winter this day would roll around. You anticipated it eagerly and hopefully. You prepared for it as the spring approached. You made lists, scheduled time, set goals, renewed your gym membership and stocked tuna and water.

Winter dragged by as winters do: fireplace and holidays, down jackets and the slippery slopes. Tell me: Did your workouts get the big chill and your diet the cold shoulder? Did your arms minimize and your abs maximize as the temperatures dropped and the sun flopped? Do the garbage and the groceries and the baby weigh a ton, and does a flight of stairs look like the Rocky Mountains?

Did you eat smart and exercise—despite the wind, cold, gloom and layers of clothing? If you did, you are one of humanity's special cool CATS (Characters Against TV and Snacking).

Or did you retire to the comfort of copious food and a cushioned shelter? You'll know by the shape your shape is in. You are, perhaps, an honorary member of society's—*Warning: The following language is graphic and may not be suitable for human consumption*—porkulent PIGS (People Intentionally Growing Stomachs).

What you do is who you are, or, more precisely, what you did is who you is.

There's still hope for those who—through neglect, irresponsibility, laziness, ignorance, foolishness, lameness or apathy—have failed to apply their fitness disciplines throughout the past year. And some of you have endured life's subtle difficulties—coma, solitary confinement, traction, amnesia, uncontrollable bleeding, seizures and delirium—and exercise and smart eating have not topped your priority list. It happens. It's Life.

Take heart! It's not too late; it's never too late.

I have 10 commandments for you. You may call them suggestions.

First, a disclaimer: You've heard them all before. That's okay! Obviously you forgot them. You've also heard the sharp directives: do not smoke, do not speed, do not litter, danger ahead, slow down and stop. How about, don't lie, don't cheat, don't steal and love your neighbor? They're good. They work. They're keepers.

Let's go over them one more time.

1. Dispose of the troublesome food around your digs; soft drinks, sweets and salty, fatty treats top the list. They are

mocking you, controlling you, diminishing and hurting you. Toss them!

2. Balance your meals to suit your needs with your favorite proteins, carbs and fats. You can't go wrong with forty percent of your calories from protein, thirty percent from nutritious carbs and the remaining thirty from essential fats. The less sugar and grease you ingest, the better. The more living and whole foods you consume, the better.

3. Eat five or six small meals regularly throughout the day to support your ongoing need for energy fuel (carbohydrates and fats), ingredients for daily metabolic functions (vitamins, minerals, micronutrients, enzymes), material for tissue growth and repair (proteins) and much more.

4. Start each day with a simple breakfast to greet the morning's demands with strength and high spirits. Eat every three to four hours to fortify your system and your activity. Planning to gain weight, add a meal. Hoping to lose weight, limit your meals to three a day, and make them count. Eating sensibly reduces hunger, eliminating the need and desire to consume out-of-control, fat-inducing and poorly assimilated larger meals.

5. Have fresh water handy for regular and generous consumption. It purifies, restores, energizes, harmonizes, mobilizes and—this part's amazing—quenches thirst.

6. The value of protein supplementation cannot be disregarded. Supplemental fortification can add to your well-being and your body's ability to build muscle and might. Wise supplementation can save you time and money. Wild supplementation can drive you to the poorhouse.

7. Restate your training goals and purposes. Review your nutritional scheme and exercise regime. It helps to know what you're doing, where you're going and why. Get a clue, Lou.

8. If you've never visited davedraper.com, there's a huge amount of training and nutritional information at your fingertips. It's simple and straightforward, tried and true. Have fun, snoop around, discover, learn and grow. Go to the front page and click on any subject that catches your eye, rings a bell or grabs you by the wagging tail and won't let go.

    If you've been at this for three, five or eight years, you've matured and grown. You know where to go. The basics remain. Nothing's changed, nothing's cancelled, nothing's new. But more bright-and-shining tips, hints and encouraging experiences have been added regularly. This is a reminder to dig in.

9. I'll sneak this one in here where offenders will least expect it. Do you smoke? How can you, with all you know about life and love and the pursuit of happiness? Sure it's a tough battle to confront. So are emphysema, cancer, hardened arteries, accelerated aging, incessant coughing, an ashen, wrinkled face, shortness of breath and impeded muscle growth. Most cigarette habits cost something like $600 a month, or $7,200 yearly (protein powder, gym membership and a pair of sneakers, shorts and a t-shirt . . . and a retirement account).

    Cigarettes also stink. Be strong and courageous, healthy and happy. Stop.

    While I'm at it, do you drink excessively or do drugs? These common, everyday social habits are tearing us apart. Development ceases, destruction commences. The body is beaten, the mind is wasted, thoughts are scattered, emotions are abused, character is shredded and the spirit wanders aimlessly. Forget muscle and might, health and wealth, family and friends, joy and contentment. You have alcohol and its companions instead. Live life. Stop.

10. About exercise: has it been a while? You still have your membership, but the gym went belly-up at the end of last year (and you know the feeling). The weights you've collected since high school in '76 have transformed into an unrecognizable, fuzzy pile of rust stashed under the dismantled go-cart with a lawnmower engine in the right rear corner of the garage. Your Weider Wall Charts were buried in the earthquake of '89, along with your wrist roller and a water bottle.

Yes, we all have good reasons why our training is not on track, but our training must be done.

It doesn't have to be elaborate. Walking works. Walking uphill works better. Walking swiftly wearing a weighted vest and weights in hand works best. Running is faster.

The first step is the hardest; the first rep is the toughest. Pick a handful of favorite coordinated exercises and practice them with order, good form, enthusiastic pace, bomber assurance, steady focus and true aim. Once you start, keep your eye on your goals and don't stop.

If you do nothing else, do this: alternate the following short and simple workouts throughout the week with committed, unbridled might.

Supersetting is suggested after a brief, injury-preventing warm up.

Workout One

30-degree incline dumbbell press and seated lat row

(4, 5, 6 sets × 8, 10, 12 reps)

Workout Two

Squat and deadlift

(4, 5, 6 sets × 8, 10, 12 reps)

Workout Three

Standing, incline or alternate dumbbell curl with dips

(4, 5, 6 sets × 8, 10, 12 reps)

Throw in some cardio of choice (rumor has it brisk walking works), and do some leg raises and calf work throughout the days, weeks and months.

This approach is designed for those who don't have an approach, and when arranging one is unlikely. The combinations are almost primitive; they're unsophisticated, glitter-free, borderline dumb, nearly crude and indescribably fun.

They are, also, absolutely effective if you have a heart and soul and adhere to the other sensible suggestions listed previously.

Drop it in first gear and floor it.

12
Observations Worth Forgetting

You SEE SOME NEW FACES on the gym floor. Flyers have been posted on vehicles in the neighborhood announcing a six-week membership for $49. It's a deal; even if you don't use it, you can honestly say you made a valid effort.

From the looks of things—soft and round—this line of thinking works for lots of folks.

The recent-most toilers-in-iron have a few things in common, besides their noticeable out-of-shapeness. They've been in a gym before, but they forgot what to do there. Suddenly the bars, bells and gadgets, swell body-shaping ideas on a flyer, are before them in stark and heavy reality, and they all look the same.

These people walk about tentatively and anxiously. Displaying knitted brows and darting eyes, they touch the equipment with curiosity and suspicion like dogs sniffing a stranger's hand. To bite or not to bite—you can almost hear them pant, growl and whimper.

This piece looks familiar, they mumble, their lips moving imperceptibly as they give a sidelong glance at the instructions decaled on a vertical upright: Heavy Duty Squat Rack. *Hmmm, that sounds like a dandy. I'll start here.*

You glance in their direction, your eyes meet and they quickly look away, as if they were caught stealing or cheating or lying, scratching their bottoms or talking to themselves.

This is when I, too, avert my eyes, make a scary face, emit a guttural sound and grasp the nearest weighted device. Bombing, blasting, bursting.

I'm not the type to smile broadly and offer assistance. I've practiced that routine in the past and received a frosty reception, total rejection or abysmal defeat. I tried my best. I recall the gals looking at me like I was a creep (*Hey, babe, you train here often?*) or the guys ignoring me like I was a jerk (*Hey, fathead, you're doing that exercise wrong!*). Kids, I could tell, wanted to be left alone (*Hey, runt, if you're going to lift weights, do it in the corner*).

No, thank you. No more Mister Nice Guy. I'm looking out for numero uno.

A bulky guy bumps into me, plodding wearily through the gym, back door to front counter, like he left his jackhammer to cool off in his truck. *Surely this fellow is here to purchase a refreshing drink and be on his way*, I say to myself. Good work is hard to find, as are good workers. He smells like a tool shed and I hope he leaves quickly.

I'm not intolerant or judgmental or a snob; it's just that you've got to separate the gym from the detritus of the outside world. The guy's shedding and polluting and slogging.

A short length of chain in hand, I'm modifying the extension of a cable on the pulley system to suit my needs. I like things just right—smooth, well fit, effective—and take the extra step to achieve it. I look up, and—sprawled on the most sought-after bench press in all his unshaven, unwashed, shabby greasiness—is Buster

Trashpockets. I'm wondering, is he on his way out, lost, drunk or a potential member in good standing evaluating the equipment?

I don't think a grown man should have the crack of his butt showing three inches above the waist of his baggy pants. Call me old fashioned. In fact no one over two gets away with that in my book. And now we have this fiftyish dude immodestly straddling a weight tree as he selects his next pair of clanky plates.

Say it ain't so. He's working out. And he seems to leave smudges and litter and a stinky cloud wherever he goes.

This is a tough situation. You say something, and you're the jerk. Say nothing, and Stinko walks. The sixteen-year-old baby-sitting the gym is, well, sixteen years old. 'Huh' and 'wha' are his common responses to most circumstances. I'm on my own.

Stretched longwise across five spaces in the peapod parking lot is a worn pickup hooked to a worn trailer loaded with worn tires and other worn stuff. No space remains for arriving muscle-builders unless they walk, ride bikes or crawl. Grrr . . . I'm mad.

Of course, I bring his attention to the parking situation and he vehemently and selfishly defends his position.

"Where else am I going to park?"

I say something less than diplomatic—respect and responsibility are my theme today—and he grouses like a grouse. Others look on: Draper's on a rampage.

Having vented, I return to my workout. Maybe he's gotten the message that he doesn't own the joint. Maybe he'll develop a sense of respect and responsibility as he develops his muscle and strength. These go hand in hand. Maybe next visit he'll rake 'n wash 'n drip-dry before he soils the gym and repulses the trainees around him. Sensibility and cleanliness often accompany disci-plined lifters. Maybe he'll become a hairdresser, a professor or a politician . . . the mayor.

Oops! Another new guy, tattoos covering every inch of exposed skin. His head is shaved and he's wearing a tank top and knee-length shorts. He's a kid becoming a man, and he's loading a bar with plates.

Man-kids with tattoos do that a lot, I notice. Swagger in (*I'm cool*) and before warming up, pile on the plates to match the one-rep max on the best day of his life when he was twenty pounds heavier and had the football team to spot him. I picture the bar coming down with a crunch and a groan, and he meekly restores his manhood as the bar is pulled from his chest by the center, two fullbacks and a cheerleader. He floods that end of the gym with excuses that fall to the floor as quickly as his bench press. Ho, hum. Seen it all before.

I watch stealthily from my hunched position by peering through the jungle of gym equipment and see his reflection in a mirror. I'm a secret agent man. Mad Dog grabs the weight and knocks out twelve perfect reps. My eyes glaze over and I feel like an ass. He walks my way. Oh, no . . . hope he's not mad.

After a long swig from the water fountain, the black-and-blue, dash-of-red-and-green-and-flesh-colored dude says, "Hi, my name is Dean. I trained here when I was young, Mr. Draper. You look better than ever. You helped me with my bench press. How are you?"

I knew there was something special about the remarkable young gentleman the moment I saw him march onto the floor and confidently address the equipment—years of dedicated training the right way.

"I see your workouts have paid off, Dean."

"I joined the Marines back then and just returned from fifteen months in Iraq. Not a whole lot of time to lift, Sir. Thought I'd get in some training before going back. The weights get heavy fast, Sir," he said as I nodded.

Call me a dope.

Not to change the subject, but who's that, another new face? She looks familiar. That's the gal who won the Miss Santa Cruz and Iron Woman contest in 2005, I'm sure of it. Never forget that athletic muscularity and stunning shape, a rare combination. Same strong jawbone. Has a reputation for training like an animal, but you can tell by looking even if you didn't know. Muscle density is a dead giveaway, and the totality of the muscular development. She knows her way around a gym.

Oh, she wants to talk to me. Cool, but I'm a very busy and serious man loading and unloading his Olympic bar, a pro at work. No time for small talk. She's all smiles as she says, "Excuse me. May I ask a favor?" Here we go again.

"Yes, I'm Dave Draper," I say, dead sure.

"Hi, I'm Tilly and I'm looking for the Santa Cruz Smoke Club. It's around here somewhere. Have you heard of it?" she asks, dead serious.

The SCSC provides prescription marijuana to the county's suffering residents.

I stare at her, but I don't see her. My shoulders slide down to my butt. I'm confused, dumbfounded, disappointed . . . odd looking.

"Yes, it's in the next building over," I point to a wall.

"What about your workouts, Tilly? What's that you say? You've never been in a gym before? You're not into sports? You're a paralegal? I see," I say.

"You should try it, Til. It's far out. Like, you'll dig it. Heavy."

I go to the gym to strengthen my body, mind and soul. Today I am completely unraveled, unwired and disconnected. No more wise, crystal-clear observations, Draper. Lighten up, loosen up, be cool, chill out.

The gym is many things, a good place to work stuff out.

13

The Times They Are A-Changin'

THE AUTO HAS COME A long way since the Model-T. Bigger, stronger, faster and far too many: on the roads, at the intersections, in garages, on lots for sale and in backyards rusting away. It seemed like a good idea at the time.

Gyms are not much different. There were barbells and dumbbells, benches, racks and pulleys, also very good ideas. And then came along bigger, stronger, faster and far too many: on the corner, in the mall, down the boulevard and in the towering office building, with contraptions to do the same things the solid steel did, except the steel did it better.

New, advanced and state-of-the-art machines are constantly available to the naïve and undiscerning consumer and the optimistic, obliging gym owner who is also going broke: "I'll take a barbell, a dumbbell and a bench, and throw in a dozen treadmills, stair-steppers, ellipticals and stationary bikes with the built-in TVs and stereo sound systems."

Nothing builds muscle and strength better than basic barbells and dumbbells and benches plus a handy milk crate, a few blocks of wood and some bars for dips and chins. Add desire, enthusiasm and improvisation, and you're in the bodybuilding business . . . make that bodybuilding heaven.

There are some odd rules and regulations musclebuilders are pressed to apply these days, along with the impossible selection of highly advanced (cough cough) technical equipment. Many of these come from people who research and write for muscle-building mags, I guess, and have visited a 24-Hour or Bally's gym to get an up-close, firsthand and in-depth feel for their subject matter. Some are even technically legit.

Here's a good one: don't train for more than sixty minutes or your body will go into catabolism and destroy muscle tissue.

Oh that my brothers and sisters would or could train an hour a day, what a fine world this would be. Health and fitness would abound, discipline and self-esteem would define our characters. There'd be less crime and more civility, less apathy and more excitement.

If you're in good shape to begin with—not undermuscled, round as a beer barrel and health-impaired—an hour a day is swell. But who do you know who is in shape to begin with?

It's a good idea, science in a nutshell: inflammation, over-training, rise in cortisol, decrease in testosterone. But do any serious bodybuilders who are so inclined believe they can build a serious body lifting weights one hour a day? It takes that long to get warmed up, focused and rolling. Then there are the sets and reps and strain and pain and overload and hypertrophy, a slug of water and a deep breath and a towel across the brow, hello and goodbye.

Isn't a sixty-minute-max a generalization? Are we all the same? What about muscle structure and body chemistry, training methods and intensities, rest and ability to recuperate, nutritional support, power of the mind and lifestyles? Goals?

Here's another beauty: exercise one bodypart a day for maximum muscular growth.

Cute idea for kids messing around in the backyard with water-filled plastic weights (or that mysterious person who's in good shape to begin with), but not for lifters interested in building serious muscle and strength sometime soon.

Bombing and blasting is old fashioned—like hard work—and went out of style in the '60s and '70s. Training with a personal trainer is very popular these days. What happened to focus and thinking on your own? Have these evaporated with personal responsibility and serenity?

I know, I know. A little background music is harmonic and companionable, and a little direction and encouragement from a sturdy guide is often priceless.

Alas, I suppose I'm just a stubborn ole' mountain goat, though I prefer to think of myself as a lone wolf, a solitary shark in deep waters, a soaring eagle on high, a camouflaged stealth warrior.

The modern training recommendation list grows: change your routine frequently.

What are we talking about, underwear and socks or TV channels? Frequent modifications work for those who have lifted forever, have built some impressive muscle and know the path they walk. But changing a routine before it's provided maximum performance, insistent overload and subsequent hypertrophy is like spitting out gum before the flavor's gone.

You've got to chomp on that iron and steel like a juicy, meaty bone. Savor it.

And be careful, warn the rule makers, don't eat too much protein: a gram of protein per pound of bodyweight is far more than you'll need. Your liver, kidneys, heart and molars are in danger.

I'm sure a gram a pound is far more than you'll need if your body receives isolated amino acids in prescribed doses according to your exact requirements regularly throughout the day and it perfectly assimilates that which is provided.

But the body doesn't. It goes to the inner pool of ingredients and grabs what it needs, when it needs it, if it's there, and utilizes it as best as it is able. The bigger the pool, the better the choices and chances to fulfill the demand. What's left over provides exercise and recuperation fuel, or is cleverly dumped.

Spare the protein, starve the muscle.

The only thing that outdoes the iffy training ideas offered is the profusion of at-home training equipment available through TV infomercials. If I'd had known building abs was so easy and quick, I'd have started ten minutes ago, or chosen something more challenging, like painting by numbers.

Moms and dads, brothers and sisters, you can sit on this comfy collapsible cushion available in designer colors and lean to the left and lean to the right repeatedly for two minutes and develop as many abs as you want as soon as you can. Just make your selection on the digital AbMore DialRite. It works!

There are decent at-home resistance training units on the market that will build moderate muscle and strength, and they are growing in reputation and popularity. I believe they're catching on over the years, as they are refined and advertised, and as gyms are turning into large zoos on the other side of town . . . with more and more gadgets, glitter and salespeople and less parking.

Training at home has great appeal, but the neighborhood gym—with iron and steel—is ideal. Maybe they, like the retro cars—Mustang Fastback, PT Cruiser, VW Bug, the boxy Element—will make a comeback. Or, like old styles replaced before their popularity or usefulness were realized or consummated, Big Jack's Barbell Club will reopen.

Some things we never outlive: blue jeans, hot dogs, ice-cream cones, tee shirts, sneakers, tattoos, Snickers. How about the neighborhood gym? Just a thought!

Curious times: Gold's Gyms are continuing to undergo a corporate revamping, and The Man is committed to extinguishing any and all evidence of hardcore training from their premises. Their infamous Venice Headquarters is continually buffed and bleached as we pump and burn. Wall murals and muscle-bound staff are enduring modification, or eradication, at the hands of housepainters and the corporate firing squad.

World Gym headquarters is under new ownership and the Marina del Rey marquee gym closed its doors. What happens to the band of originals and old timers who have congregated, commiserated and joyfully toiled on the concrete slabs of these establishments over these long years? Some of them are as old as the sand on the nearby Muscle Beach and twice as gritty. Do they fade away like a western sunset, or roll on like the Pacific's everlasting waves?

And what about the rumor I hear down at the old courthouse that Bally filed for bankruptcy?

Bowflex, anyone? Chins and dips? Pushups and isometrics? Jogging in place?

I prefer not to end my bold and decisive thesis with questions. Thus, assume your position behind the controls and ready your crew for takeoff. This is not a simulated effort. This is an authentic procedure upon which lives are dependent. If anyone needs to go to the potty, do it now. No chewing gum. No whispering. No passing notes around. Anyone caught misbehaving will not get cookies and protein when the mission is over.

14

Muscle Blasts from the Past

Yes, I, too, watch the news. I urgently apply the remote control, looking for the best spin of the latest catastrophes while adding my own dopey remarks as if they mattered. My comments are thoughtful and substantial: he's a bum, she's a jerk, that's a lie, they're all thieves, politicians should be imprisoned and so on.

In truth, daily events are part of the reason many of us work out with zeal. Muscles, strength and fitness topped the list early on, but the gnawing stresses of the times have many of us at the gym's door looking for sanity and relief.

A good gym is a way-station, a refuge, a place of your own to lick your wounds or prepare you for the good race tomorrow. The field, the track, your garage or the gym is where you cleanse, restructure, restore inside and out—no miracles, no magic, no kidding. You forgive, you forget, you remove the thorns, you ease the pain, you count your blessings like reps and sets. You become reunited with yourself as a friend who's worthy, and those around you know you better and enjoy you more. Life is good for a long time.

Do not go one week without two workouts. Ever. These can be the minutes that save you from the dreaded muscular disease, The Gap.

You've heard of The Gap, haven't you—an unmanageable malfunctioning of the disciplinary tract, which leads to the deterioration of the walls of the will? Some folks have been known to succumb to the wretched disorder for months, losing muscle tone and gaining a tire around the middle.

Mild discontent, guilt, irritability and sloping shoulders accompany The Gap. Loss of energy and stamina are not uncommon, and binge eating has been observed among serious Gap sufferers.

Some seasons pressure us to limit our exercise schemes, and obliging the pressure is natural and right. Summer vacations and winter holidays beg for time off. Be aware and recognize the safe and friendly boundaries of maintenance training, and faithfully heed them until the more favorable times when you can blast it with hungry might. Failure to do so leads to despicable consequences. Prevention is easier than the cure.

My creed goes something like this: keep it simple, stick to the basics, train consistently with enthusiasm and intensity, use logic, be creative and intuitive, be confident in your applications, be happy and deal with your misery. Be real. Stop fussing.

There are absolutely no secrets. Nothing's new. Collect the necessary information and get to work. The clutter of intelligence, the waste of words describing a simple thing, the superior heaps of decaying mental rubbish surrounding the notion of exercise and sensible eating is maddening. Why, there are people who have read so much they think they actually know something.

The learning's not in the reading, it's in the doing.

It's not uncommon for me to refer to the unhealthy and unfit condition of society as a reflection of its apathy, complacency and ignorance. My references are not insensitive comments on the undesirable fitness level of the people on the streets. They are not condemnations but instructive pleas to set the dormant into motion. They are not intended to ridicule the overweight but rather to stir the sleeping.

They call the weak to strength with no tone of mocking in the voice. The mocking, rather, is in the ear.

Exercising and eating right prepare us for the tough days ahead. Exercise is a constructive diversion that relaxes and reduces stress, strengthens the body, mind and spirit, establishes confidence, builds brother- and sisterhood, adds considerably to the resources of the country and prepares it to win the good fight.

You've heard my sermon before: exercise and eat right for good. It's not clever or original, profound or poetic, but it's exact.

Today, more than ever, we need to be exercising, at home, on the streets, at the park or in the gym. I'm a gym rat, and for those who frequent such entertaining places, I have composed five short workouts that are music to the ears.

Some days we rock and some days we roll and some days we hum a tune to ourselves, and the beat goes on and on. The workouts are immediate, to the point and effective for focusing hazy and roving minds and stimulating weary bodies when performance levels are low and we're out-of-key. Call them sing-alongs, metal harmonies, humming and clanging or the noisy, snappy rhythms to keep the mood up and creativity afloat without expectation, crescendo or maximum performance.

Sing-alongs are harmonious superset combinations that stray from the norm yet retain integrity. Supersetting is a style of training where two or more exercises that complement each other are performed one after the other to enhance training output. This multi-set training not only condenses workout time, but it also considerably increases productivity.

Robust metallic harmonies are designed for temporary use (a day, a week), but can be modified to fit into your regular training schedule if they feel right. Because they're novel, they're fresh to the mind, fresh to the body.

With some exceptions, the jangling combinations listed here can be performed using the pyramid system of reps and weight, or an 8–10 rep range using a moderate fixed weight. Four sets of any slumpbuster is a minimum. If you're pumping and having fun, take it up to seven. One combination, if pushed, might be enough to maintain your well-being and connection with the gym. Two combos can be mixed according to your needs, desire and energy.

I must admit, I've been singing less and groaning more these days (R 'n R can be exasperating). Don't get me wrong; I appreciate groaning and similar expressions of man-against-steel, but a concert of groaning is like a dirge.

Hence, the simple spontaneous supersets:

- Floor-to-ceiling, one-arm dumbbell clean—a common dumbbell movement practiced with a common dumbbell. The alternating, left-right performance simulates supersetting. Hold onto a rack, position your body stably and dig in. Start light and consider whole body engagement. You learn as you go. I taught myself, so can you teach yourself. This is a test.

- Flat dumbbell press and seated bent-over row—same pair of dumbbells; they never leave your hands until the combination is complete. You know how to do flat dumbbell presses, right? Good. At the end of the set, sit upright and place the dumbbells on your thighs; position yourself at the very end of the bench, bend over and allow the dumbbells to extend to the floor without touching. Swell. Take a few deep breaths, focus and pull the weights from a forward, hanging position to a mid- to upper-back position with tight contraction and determined might. Feel the cooperative relief and burn and pump. Six reps will do nicely.

I do a similar extended-set combination with seated dumbbell alternate curls.

- My favorite extended set combination—a high-rep (25–35), multi-position movement—I practice these to warm up the torso, engage the triceps at various sites, work the serratus and lats and generally stimulate the system. It's an instinctive exercise; that is, it depends on your attention on muscle engagement and on methodically exhausting the system of muscles engaged.

Start with your standard pulley-pushdowns with a moderate weight to assure twelve powerful yet isolated reps. Do them. Now stagger your legs, one behind the other, lean into the apparatus and perform another five eager reps from a handle-high position to a locked-out position before you. This action is done with the honest aid of your thrusting body.

Focus on this performance as we go beyond one or two simple muscle groups and involve numerous connected regions. We expand muscle recruitment, maximize their output, cause them to stretch and co-work and burn and pump—indications of healthy overload, a fertile soil for hypertrophy, a.k.a. muscle growth.

There's more: The heart and lungs are getting a run for their money; the grip is working overtime. And there is, of course, rhythm.

Now, reposition the stagger-step away from the pulley system and allow your arms to extend and your body to stretch out without losing cable resistance. You're leaning forward and balanced by your grasp on the cable handle.

From this neutral placement, draw the handle downward, simulating a stiffarm-pullover action. Lats and serratus and the underside of the tris are desperately at work with the remaining muscle strength and endurance you have. Another five reps. Almost done.

Return to your starting position, if you can remember it, hold the handle close to your torso and perform five or ten isolated rope tucks to recruit the final fibers of your abdominal area. There. Don't you feel better now?

Four or five sets are required, depending on needs and desire. Vary reps according to fatigue. This stuff is meant to be fun as well as productive.

Night is closing in and it's time to fold up the wings.

15

Muscle Talk
for the Humble

I THOUGHT BECAUSE I'M a hardcore professional with the sand of Muscle Beach under his fingernails and the stripes of dungeon dwelling across his back, visitors of davedraper.com would be a gnarly mob with their own brand of iron wear and tear. We're bombers, after all.

Not necessarily so, Joe. Think again, Ben.

It seems there are more untested, runway-bound bombers wandering our pages, reading the newsletter, lurking the forum and sending email messages than you can rattle a plate at. To many, designing a routine is rocket science, implementing one is like crossing the Alps on a goat.

Obviously, they've come to the right place for the right reasons. For most it has been a while since they exerted themselves—high school or college, and before marriage, kids, job and assorted bulges. They just need a little direction and encouragement.

Considering this startling observation, a few basic training principles might be in order for the rusty and out-of-touch, the clueless and ill-informed, the tired and the wasted.

We'll all benefit. It's good to return to the faded, dog-eared pages of our training logs to rediscover and uncover, to remind and recall. There's light in the darkness, brilliance in the shadows. We find truth, wonder and creativity in faded memories.

The most direct way to build muscle and strength is to lift weights consistently and with effort. That's rule number one. It's wise to have a simple plan and execute it consistently and with effort. That's rule number two.

How basic can it get? Two rules: lift weights and have a plan. Two precepts: work hard and be consistent.

Designing a plan—routine, workout, program, scheme, methodology—is not rocket science as presumed by some; it's a notch above a no-brainer. Let's face it, if this pursuit took brains, I'd be picking up trash on the interstate.

Begin by asking yourself the following fundamental questions:

What do I know about the subject—zero, vaguely familiar, at the intermediate level, former trainee?

What do I want to accomplish? What are my goals?

How much of myself am I willing to invest: time, resources and energy?

Where, when and with what will I exercise?

Finally, will I? Or is this where our little experiment ends?

More questions will arise now that you've initiated the conversation. Some will be tough, some silly. They'll be bound in the mind and body, the heart and the soul. They will perplex you, frustrate you and drive you up a wall. Be strong. The answers will lead you to success and fulfillment, or bowling, beer and the couch.

Step one: Imagine the body as a collection of separate and basic—yet interrelated—bodyparts or muscle groups. They are the chest region, the back, shoulders, biceps, triceps, midsection and legs.

Step two: For each muscle group there are relatively specific exercises for their development.

Side note: No exercise recruits one muscle without engaging closely associated and attached muscles. Here's where we exercise our common sense, as well as our sinew. Muscles and systems of muscles are connected. This is cool to know, encouraging and technically important. We're getting more pump and burn for every set and rep we perform.

Step three: Determine and list the various simple exercises for the muscle groups by inventing, inquiring, reading or observing.
    Here's a quick rundown of the basics to satisfy today's needs:

> **Chest region**—*Flat bench press, incline barbell press, flat and incline dumbbell press, decline press, cable crossover or pec-deck, flat or incline fly, pushups, dips*

> **Back**—*Deadlift, stiff and bent-leg, bent-over barbell row, dumbbell row, seated lat row, variations of cable pulldowns, pullovers*

> **Shoulder**—*Barbell press and dumbbell press, standing, on flat bench or various degrees of incline, lateral raises—front, side, rear, upright rows, pushups and dips*

Biceps—*Standing barbell curl, dumbbell curl—standing, seated, incline and alternate, thumbs-up curl, reverse curl, straight bar or bent-bar*

Triceps—*Lying or standing triceps extensions with a bar or dumbbells, narrow-grip bench press, pulley pushdown, behind-the-neck pulley extension, dips, dumbbell kickbacks*

Midsection—*Crunches, leg-raise, hanging leg-raise, rope tucks, hyperextensions*

Legs—*Leg extensions, leg curl, squat, lunge, leg press, calf raise*

The list is sufficient because we're not compiling material for The Official Unabridged Encyclopedia of Muscle Building.

Step four: Choose one or more exercises from the lists to design a routine to match your needs—your goals, purposes and ambitions, desires and level of development.

I've got an idea (jaws drop, lightning flashes, thunder rumbles). Because I'm already in the pilot's seat and have my hands on the controls, I'll piece together an assortment of workouts of diverse levels and present comments along the way.

As we're limited in space, time, capabilities and attention span, the exercise will be named and not described. Help me and yourself by using your common sense and imagination, two more of our great resources too seldom exercised. Let's begin.

No equipment? FEW is for you (Freehand Exercise Works).

Freehand pushups, dips and chins, running and planks are hard to beat for building an entire body. They are simple and healthy, and can be practiced and developed right here, right now with a little resourcefulness and no equipment.

Raw, freestyle training is instructive, insightful, demanding and friendly. It encourages improvisation, stimulates the instincts, pumps the muscles, shapes and strengthens them and brings you close to the action.

These movements get you going, take you there and keep you there.

At first, play—push, pull, experiment, stretch, strain, entertain—with the freehand moves to get to know them, the form, the degrees of exertion, what muscles are involved, where you're strong and where you're weak, and uncover any perceived injuries or limitations.

This testing and inspecting will prepare and strengthen your muscles and insertions, familiarize you with the concept of routine training, provide comfort and confidence in the pursuit, and excite your discipline.

Workman, know your job, know your tools.

Here's a plan once you're ready, Freddy. For you too, Betty Sue.

1. Run and jump whenever you get the urge, kids. Run or bike ten to fifteen minutes every other day, adults. Daily walking works wonders for you youngsters with long histories. Determine your own comfort zone and go. You're in motion and that's an accomplishment. Devotion advances as your fitness advances.

2. Practice your planks at the beginning of your workout sessions for a warm-up, or at the end for completeness. Lately, I switch between the before and after placements according to desire, energy or time. Whatever works for you works best, as long as you don't skip them.

3. Pushups are considered an ordinary exercise, almost cliché. Do not under-evaluate their power and potential. The movement involves the whole body from the fingertips to the toes,

and when practiced with correct form and a focus on developing muscle and not on counting wild and explosive reps to collect numbers, pushups are a substantial body builder.

4. Similarly, dips and chins—whether done with the assist of a platform or under one's own power—are simple exercises, valuable muscle builders, shapers and conditioners by themselves or when included in a weight-advanced workout. To the point of annoyance and possibly nausea, I underscore focus on exercise execution and muscle engagement.

5. Eventually, an orderly program of the freehand movements is wise. Personal law and order prevents chaos, encourages proper performance and defines your input and output. They improve discipline.

Once you've established a working relationship with the exercises, here are some simple outlines:

- *Perform a set of each exercise to maximum repetitions every day, five days a week.*

- *Or do two or three sets of each to maximum reps every other day.*

- *Try four sets of pushups to max on day one, four sets of wide-grip chins on day two, four sets of dips on day three, four sets of close-grip chins on day four and rest two days. Run every other day and do midsection every other day according to time and desire.*

- *Do a push exercise followed by a pull exercise (a.k.a. supersetting), as follows:*

  1. *Pushup and wide-grip chin—2–4 sets × max reps*
  2. *Dip and close-grip chin—2–4 sets × max reps*

Arrange the combinations over a weekly period (alternating combinations, mixing and practicing every other day). Support all this with running, walking and midsection every other day according to time and desire.

Freehand exercise, smart eating and right living builds strong men and women from feeble girls and boys.

Here's one of my favorite standards for the early trainee. You've seen it before; it must be good. I like the scheme because it works for me (and Arnold and Zane and Franco and Katz and Sergio and Lee and Zabo and Reeves and Cutler) when time is short, I'm unfocused, on the road or between solid workout regimens. It's complete, smoothly overlaps muscle groups and has muscle appeal, push-pull rhythm and pumping excitement.

Try this three alternate days a week with cardio and midsection when you please (which doesn't mean never, Bub):

Muscle Builder 101-A

- *Medium wide bench press—chest and associated muscles (front delt, triceps, related upper-body mass)*

- *Wide-grip pulldown—lats and associated muscles (biceps, minor pec, related upper-body mass)*

- *Standing barbell curl—biceps, forearm and grip (plus whole-body musculature—including midsection and legs by assisting the minor thrusting action and stabilization)*

- *Freehand or machine dips—triceps, pecs, deltoids, upper back and abs*

- *Walking lunges—legs*

Sets and reps depend on the lifter's status:

- 1 set of 10 reps for the total beginner
- 2 sets of 10 reps for the same lifter in 4 to 6 workouts
- 3 sets of 8–10 reps in a month
- 4–5 sets of reps of choice for bombers when the need arises

Look out for low-flying objects. Crash landings are not uncommon this time of year—shorter days, colder temperatures, holidays on the prowl, sniffles, the lure of the fireplace and hot toddies.

Take your time before it's too late.

16
Our Great Truth Test

LIFE IS SHORT, the days are swift, but the moments of doubt are long. *How are we progressing?* we ask in accord. The inquiry is universal, multifaceted and pervasive; the answer a wonder.

I have constructed a test of one question to determine the attributes and advancement of regular bombers—a clever device to spotlight the curiosity and resolve the mystery of how are we doing.

You load sixteen ton and what do you get?

A) Huge and ripped
B) Another day older
C) Deeper in debt
D) A sore back
E) Fulfillment
F) Pleasure

Choose one. The answer you select reveals
your inner being—your character.

A) Optimistic B) Realistic C) Pessimistic
D) Pathetic E) Simplistic F) Sadistic

I enjoy and appreciate impromptu quizzes, don't you? They keep us alert and on our toes. And they say we're all muscles and no brains. Ha! Fooled 'em again, airheads.

So, how'd ya do?

Yeah, I know. Lotta Ds! But, hey, we try hard. We train hard. We blast it!

Let's move on to more stirring things, like the spoon in your morning coffee or the local weather or a year-end challenge.

Business of the day:

I, the Bomber, have been unanimously selected as your friendly challenge checker. My records show many of you have signed an annual challenge. Good for you! I deem this act courageous, constructive and wise . . . and binding.

A quick review of the current data, however, indicates certain weak-kneed challengers are negligent in providing regular progress reports. This is a breach of commitment and must be confronted. My duty as checker is to remind you, encourage you, persuade, stimulate or threaten you to revive your goals and enthusiastically attend them.

I implore you to work with me that we might resolve this troubling issue posthaste. Select the approach that is appropriate to your particular needs. Be bold, choose them all.

1. **Tough approach**

   We take this personally. We are a serious mob. We have little patience. We know where you live.

If I were you, here's what I'd do: think of your kids, spouses, lovers, friends and pets and possessions. Either the iron goes up or you're going down.

Note: This methodology is iffy and seldom requested. We contract out to an east coast firm.

2. **Practical approach**

   Think of the importance of your challenge and what it has to offer: health and strength, honor and long life. Consider the consequences if you don't participate as pledged: guilt and disappointment, lost days and wasted weeks, pudginess and vulnerability, stoutness and inadequacy.

   Our training is integral to our well-being and deserves special attention. You know it, it's a fact of life and you endorse it highly. It must be done and any postponement is costly and counterproductive, feeble and destructive. Lift that iron, drop the junk food and move like a lean machine, jellybean.

3. **Loving approach**

   I know exactly how you feel, friend. Lifting weights, eating right and being conservative and disciplined in your living habits can be a real drag. The payoffs are grand, but the payments are often downright painful, troublesome and tedious. It's during these trying moments of discouragement and discomfort when our character and courage—our core strengths—are created, defined and engaged.

   We press on or we falter, step forward or stumble backward, reach ahead or rest on our broadening haunches. I cannot relax and enjoy life if I let go. Only when I grasp life, the precious gift, am I strong and deserving, relieved of stress and at peace with the moment.

A short and sweet workout today, one that stimulates the mind and muscle and soul, is the perfect workout. Tomorrow it will bear legs, the next day wings and the day after, air beneath those wings as they spread wide and far. You're soaring.

4. **Casual approach**

What's the big fuss? We can all use a challenge to brighten our spirits and sharpen our egos and tone our bods. Go to the gym, lift a few weights, ride the stationary bike and watch the tube. Meet new friends, dig up some action and talk about sports between sets and reps.

Blast it on occasion when your hormones line up like soldiers on the front line. Cool! What a relief! Before you know it, it's time for a steam, Jim Beam.

About food: don't eat the whole pizza and drink the last beer. Get rid of the soda and dump the chips. You don't need 'em and you won't miss 'em if they're not staring you in the face. Up the protein and lower the sugar and greasy fat; take a protein supplement, drink more water, throw in some pop-top tuna fasts when you feel mean and nasty, and smile as the days go by and the fat evaporates and the strength grows and the muscle tones.

Relax. It's what happens, man. It works.

5. **Desperate approach**

Pssst! Hey you, listen up. We don't have much time. You've gotta do your challenge now before it's too late. The end of the year is coming fast and you're gonna be a mess if you don't start blasting it—today. Blasting works!! And, if you don't move now, you won't move again.

Remember last year? You stopped training and gained twenty-two pounds in twenty-two days; your gym membership lapsed and they dismissed you from the bowling team for tossing the ball from your seat . . . missed the lane, missed the gutter, hit the rent-a-cop.

It's now or never. Delay and die, go now or go home. Bomb it or explode.

6. Zero approach

Why bother, who needs it—the cop-out—withdrawals.

What's it all mean? You go to the gym like a faithful cleric, you lift weights like a big gorilla, you eat like a starving canary, you sacrifice like a shrouded monk and you get hit by lightning like a hapless limb in a vast forest.

You struggle with the weights through the summer and gain ten pounds. You catch the flu in the winter and lose fifteen. That was encouraging—let's do it again.

No one enjoys dieting, sacrificing and denying, but it must be done if you're going to lose the excessive twenty-five to fifty pounds of fat (who can tell anymore?). Swell. Life stops for an endless season of hefting and hoisting, spinning and chinning and vegetables, fresh fruits and teensy portions of fish and chicken and, oh, more water.

We get a little touchy when the blood sugar is low and the iron is heavy and the sinew is soft and time is wasting and the thrill is gone.

Those are your choices, loyal warriors. I leave you with a few final hints or insights or viewpoints that might sufficiently confuse you. There's order in confusion.

Sometimes challenges work best when you keep them a secret all to yourself—you and your inner partner. You whisper, you coax and coddle.

Sometimes they work best when you set them on cruise control and disregard assessment and scrutiny. Let them be. They happen.

Sometimes you've got to carefully share and examine them, press and stretch them to make them work. A little help from your friends can't hurt.

Sometimes they work best when you move them to center stage with confidence, under the spotlight for everyone to see. There they are in all their nakedness for observation and comment and criticism. Way to go.

Get huge and ripped, or lean and mean, or big and strong, or trim and shapely, or thick and powerful, or light and tight, or fast and flexible.

Just get it going now.

17

Lower the Anchor, Don't Drop the Iron

THE NEATEST THING ABOUT being cheap, selfish and poor is you don't worry much about Christmas or birthday shopping: just do enough to keep out of serious trouble. I've got it down to one present, something to enjoy, like a new toilet bowl to replace the cracked one. Or installing a hot-water heater . . . hanging a back door with hinges and a lock . . . removing the tarp and patching the roof.

Did you ever wonder what the rich do with all their dough? I'm talking about overpaid greedy and sneaky politicians, Hollywood stars, athletic champions, big-time corporate CEOs, old money or rich and stoned drug lords.

The rest of us have a little house and a big mortgage, a little car and big gas tank, little mouths and big food bills. We shop at Wal-Mart once a year for underwear, socks and jeans. I'm not complaining; I'm rich like you're rich. But there's money collecting in off-shore bank accounts like garbage in landfills, and floating in the air like lost energy as good people work and dream, grope and plod, starve and die.

Give us a sturdy bench and some dumbbells, a stack of sets and a heap of reps and we're as happy as pigs in sh—er—sheep grazing on a lush and sunny hillside amid wildflowers and songbirds in the early spring. That doesn't make us simple and dumb. I was thinking more like thrilled and thankful . . . healthy and wise. I'd go on, but I don't want to drive you crazy. You'll grab a big stick and commence swinging, "Stop it, Draper, we don't want to hear another word about discipline and commitment, persistence and self-assurance. Take that, and that . . . I'll give you patience and satisfaction!" Smack, whack, bam!

All right, already. I get the message. How about huge and ripped?

Speaking of huge and ripped, when was the last time either of those adorable qualities seriously crossed your mind? I know. Gets rough out there sometimes. Staying afloat is enough.

But that shouldn't discourage us from throwing a life raft over the side and paddling around the less-choppy waters near the hull. There's a lot to be learned and accomplished when you're loose and adrift. Floating is restful and sufficiently stimulating. You can look and see, observe and feel.

You can lower the anchor, but don't drop the iron.

Short and frisky workouts can be delightful if you'll allow yourself the treat (my workouts are seldom what one would call treats). The all-or-nothing attitude is admirable, but can prevent you from entering the gym until the seas have calmed, and heaven knows when that may be. Sometimes it's late summer before you get the ole' tub afloat and—glub, glub—on its way.

If you dare paddle hard and far, you can view what kind of craft you are. Are you a cruise ship or a battleship, a destroyer or a sport-fishing vessel? Maybe you picture a barge. Is that you, a barge carrying garbage down the river to a distant landfill, seagulls flying in squawking rages about your hull? That old self-image needs work. Think tugboat.

Mixing metaphors, I see myself as an aircraft carrier, its decks trimmed with bombers and other stout-winged craft. I don't fly . . . I float. No more wars for me . . . more like a monument, though I still do some dive bombing. Beats being a tanker . . . cargo ships cower. I'm imposing alongside ferryboats. I can take the Queen Mary . . . not as cute as a yacht, but taller. I miss being a B-29. Where's my hangar?

Let's stop for a moment. (Stop? When are ya gonna start?)

I'm concerned about the barges plodding the waterways. Often a barge is not a barge, but an exaggerated impression of oneself. We all feel like barges after a few days of eating like barbarians. Real or perceived, the only prevention of the disaster is to stop it before it occurs. Willpower and, ironically, guts are the resources we must call upon—now and not tomorrow.

That was quick; my computer quivered and smoked. I no sooner mentioned willpower and everyone but you and me pressed the delete key and commenced surfing YouTube. They'll be back in a few months with weak limbs, long stories and looming shadows. And I was about to save them from the sorrowful blues indulgence and indolence, puffy twins in deed and performance.

What are the forces so strong that compel a person to compromise health and well-being for a shot of pleasure, a slug of enjoyment or a slice of delight? How weak is our constitution? Of what crumbly material are we made? Shame on us, we who are in control of our acts and actions—and we are.

I'll take the tuna, thanks. Skip training? Drop the iron? No way! I refuse to pay the price. I pay too much at the pump, cringe too much before the mirror, lose too much on the bench press, bear too much guilt during the layoff—the lost time—and suffer too much pain after the return.

Remember the Gap.

It's as real and deadly as the devil, the boogie man and that pale, mottled guy with the chainsaw. Don't let it get a foothold; prevent its first breath and beat it down with a kettlebell, a slump-buster or the surge of your personal challenge.

"It's only time," you say.

No, it's more substantial than that. It's a brick, a building block, as sound as concrete or hardened earth. It's either set with mortar and sweat and design, or it's misplaced, absent integrity, purpose and cohesion. Upon such a foundation no structure will rise, no building will stand, no authentic bomber reside.

You can regroup, repair the damage, regain lost ground, restore abandoned resources, revive stalled energy and replace stolen and mislaid personal remnants. It's not too late, it's never too late. From a distance no one will know the difference. Only you.

In the morning, at the crack of dawn, when the runway is clear and you're still restless from a night of lost sleep, listen to the hum of the engine, the whir of the propeller and the sound of your heartbeat.

As soon as you get the signal, the urge, the call from the tower, get that pulsing beast off the ground and in the air.

18
Windy Skies Lift Us Higher and Higher

Why would I go to the gym on a day when the roads are flooded and the skies are black? Because it's there, that's why. And, of course, I can't stand the guilt when I miss a workout. I'm insecure; I don't have another life; I could lose my pump; I'd waste away; I'd miss the self-inflicted pain and sacrifice, abuse and hardship. My nose would grow.

Take me to the rack.

I wasn't alone, I saw upon entering the back door. The usual faces, a tad dour in expression, were there to greet me. Actually, they didn't greet me; they barely noticed another madman had crossed the threshold. I was just one more shadow, emitting a groan and in whose blue-grey wake plates of iron clanged. Mondays have a quality all their own.

Here we go again.

The world is a circle of many sharp corners, beyond which are prizes and surprises amid a few choices. What'll it be today, Draper: chest and back, and enough gut to keep the pouch away? Sounds familiar . . . didn't I just do that stunning combination? What's today? Oh, yeah, Monday . . . how could I forget?

Monday, Monday. Look at all the happy faces.

Shoulders and arms have a more appealing ring, some front presses supersetted with sidearm lateral raises. Not! The shoulders feel less like cannonballs and more like golf balls this soggy, sunless day. Maybe arm training is the solution: biceps, triceps and forearms, with hanging leg raises just to be sociable.

Any alert bomber has noticed legs are not mentioned in the repertoire of possible muscle groups to attack. Mondays and legs no longer go together, a recently established condition. One does not attack legs; legs are an attack. Think Tuesday, when the troops are entrenched; or Wednesday, when reinforcements have arrived; or Thursday, when there's possible air support; or Friday, maybe there'll be a truce. Saturdays are, naturally, for recreation.

Sundays are for rest.

Arms—arm workouts—are tough and mean, but they are not exhausting. They are precise, interesting, oddly enjoyable and not ponderous. They are demanding, but not foreboding. They are a relatively small muscle group—nothing personal—requiring less oxygen and demanding less blood flow. Good pump, nice burn, small fatigue footprint.

Arms it is.

Unloading my gym bag of necessary gear (no small task), I sit near the glass exit doors and peer at the rain mixed with hail pelting the car tops. Hypnotic. The shelter that is the gym feels welcome and comfortable. Let it pour, I say with relief and conviction, we need it. I'll hoist the iron and build more muscle.

My mind wanders, ever on a journey to seek, discover, uncover and surpass (delay, procrastinate, daydream and hallucinate).

Hmm . . . I postulate: When does a bodybuilder know when he's achieved maximum muscular bodyweight?

"Never, never, never," is my immediate reaction, "Never, I tell you! Never!"

My first response is, "When they roll you into the gym, oxygen mask affixed to your face and an IV delivering life-sustaining fluids, when you can't distinguish a barbell from a dumbbell."

A second thought, vaguely related to the first, is when the crashing sound you hear overhead is dirt piling upon your coffin. That's admittedly kinda grim . . . a little dark.

The answers keep rolling in: when, at five foot, nine inches and 290 veiny pounds, you can't tie your sneakers because your abdominals bundle against your striated quadriceps, preventing you from reaching their laces. Don't you hate that?

Finally (I promise), when in a pool, should you stop swimming, you sink to the bottom with such swiftness and force as to shatter the tile, poke a hole in the earth's surface and cause the water to gush out.

Thinking is getting me nowhere, a fact I accepted long ago. I'm stalling, it's obvious. I've already drunk half my post-workout Bomber Blend and I've yet to lift a weight. That's why God devised wrist curls. You can do them using a bar left on a bench with no added plates while you sit with minimum movement and you can call that warming up. They set the course, start the motion, initiate the blood flow, produce a pump, excite a burn, exact focus and engender profound thought—one, two, three, four . . . er . . . five . . . um . . . seven . . . ate.

Grasp, release, extend fingers, stretch, hold briefly, roll up, contract, hold briefly, release, extend hunky bar and you are on your way down the tarmac and picking up speed. The sky is before you, altitude unknown.

One rep, one set, one day at a time, as they say at AA (Altitude Achievers) meeting in hangars across the countryside.

First set completed, you're invested and the purpose is defined. Familiarity takes over and the weights are systematically added. The next set is tougher (good) and meaner (loving it). During the third set, the urge to superset is roused as you pull steadily upon the throttle. The power no longer comes from local sources, but from biceps, shoulder and back muscles and distant places—the temples, the teeth and bottoms of the feet. The body shudders with strain and need and urgency.

You're training. Iron and might fuse, sound fades, time ceases, the day falls away. That's the way it works, bombers. Trust it.

When confronted with trouble, grasp the bar, grip the steel and push and pull with growing might. The offender—disinterest—vanishes like heartache when one's true love returns.

The real answer to the very real question—when do you, a bodybuilder, know when you've achieved your maximum muscular bodyweight?—is yet unanswered and worth recalling.

Perhaps, the answer is after an intense year (or ten) of worthy and devoted training and eating well. How's that for specific and scientific and conclusive? We here at the Huge Ripped Raw Muscle Clinic do not submit truths without thorough research and understanding.

Another answer, less glib and about as accurate, is when you're mature in your assessments, have read and applied every solid principle gleaned from *davedraper.com* over a two-year period and your progress has come to an apparent halt.

Note: Apparent halts have nothing to do with real halts. Halts in muscle-building do not exist if one is consistent in bomber weightlifting.

Progress is forever.

In our healthiest and most productive muscle building years, we have a set-weight we reach, a bodyweight at which we no longer build muscle according to our structure and chemistry, genetics and metabolism. Who knows what this bodyweight is? We push hard, yet we stop proceeding. That's that.

That's it. That's all she wrote.

Or is it? The authentic musclehead pushes harder, longer, smarter, more and again. He ekes out muscle like water from the great stones in the deserts of Moses. Unparalleled faith and hope, courage and patience hath he.

Little things are happening all the time, a small improvement here, a minor alteration there, something lost, yet something gained; time goes by, maturity reaps muscle hardness and increased delineation, age is acquired, yet under-worked muscles respond to renewed and deliberate action.

Bodyweight is difficult to maintain, up or down; energy and muscle endurance come and go, but muscle-building wisdom rises.

At 100, we'll still be seeking improvement and observing the positive chaos hither and thither in our wild dreams. Looky here, a new vein emerging across my lower right intercostal.

It's no dream I fly with the wind. You know that. We share the same sky; it's written on our wings.

19
Ah, the Good Old Days

I REMEMBER WHEN WEIGHTS were seventeen cents a pound, I grew like a weed and muscle aches were some sort of mystery my parents grumbled about.

Recollection is an inevitable, involuntary and necessary process. It can be profitable, instructive, entertaining, insightful and painfully dull. And recollections—memories—can be ominous: Guilt, fear and doubt are not infrequently lurking in their shadows.

Occasionally, I'll purposefully recall the past to awaken my brain, arouse my wits, stir my thoughts and put current events into perspective. Besides, wandering the halls of days gone-by can be plain fun, snoozy and musey. I compare then to now to determine what's next. However, when the moon is out-of-round and its smile faded, retrospection leads to introspection, and often to disappointment and bewilderment.

Less than a smile, my past during those periods resembles an edge-of-town junkyard littered with crumpled chassis, dismantled engines, threadbare tires and rusting fenders. Battered witnesses stand clutching the far side of the fence to stare inward. Imagined voices from the deteriorating images call out as a mob: whatta bum, getta job, grow up, what's it all mean, lift and shut up.

My blissful journey of innocent wonder started when I was ten years old with a heap of battered weights totaling 100 pounds. At ten, 100 pounds sounds serious, grown-up, impressive, huge and worldly.

You heard it all before, but what the heck: There they lay in my designated space on the bedroom floor, dumb, heavy and inert. While my brothers stepped over the dense and confined mess, I crawled under it, into it. I proceeded to haul the clattering and merciless load everywhere I went, like it was treasure, food and shelter, a matter of life and death, the Holy Grail. Perhaps companionship—he ain't heavy, he's my brother.

Soon enough I was eighteen and the Newark YMCA was my first introduction to working out in a gym. Ha! It was actually an afterthought crammed into a space adjacent to the boiler room and clogged with Olympic bars and benches from a defunct detention center. Order was non-existent, and neither form nor focus were encouraged: Grab 'n hoist was the preferred MO. Move the iron, heft and toss it.

I learned something right in learning everything wrong.

When I benched 400 the first time, I was nineteen and training at the far end of a snazzy Vic Tanny's in Jersey City. The place looked more like a tawdry madam's house than a gym, with red carpeting and chrome weights and mirror-covered walls and ceilings and strange electrical devices that wriggled and vibrated various puffy bodyparts. A few of the occupants—trendy rascals—wore leotards and tights.

And me, fresh from the Elizabeth Y with its plumbers, carpenters and cops, sweaty T-shirts, BO and expletives, splinters, leaky pipes and cold steel.

Anyhow, I pressed the chrome bar adorned with eighteen shiny twenty-pound plates (biggest in the house and gathered from all corners), two tens and a pair of cutesy chrome collars. The contrivance was silly and unwieldy and the racks upon which it balanced were spindly chrome attached tentatively to a bench upholstered in gold-flecked plastic. I could hear the tinkle of weights amid the muzak in the background.

I considered asking for a spot, but the consequences of the request, should it be accepted, were unimaginable. Better alone than assisted by a dapper dude with trembling hands clasped over his tightly shut eyes. I warmed up, paced, peered out the second-story windows at the sparkling nightlife of Journal Square, pawed and sucked in air like a rhino and knocked out one good rep. Nobody cared. Better that way.

It's all history now, in a nutshell where it belongs.

Nevertheless, next stop, new job, another phase, the warehouse of Weider Barbell Company, alongside Leroy Colbert—you remember Leroy—for seated dumbbell alternate curls and overhead triceps extensions.

A brief stint in Hackensack at American Health Studios precluded a flight destined for LA and the doorstep of Muscle Beach Gym, a.k.a. the Dungeon, the home I'd been looking for.

Good day, sunshine. Hello, Southern California, 1963.

My second outstanding recollection of bench pressing four plates and change—440, if my shaggy, braggy memory serves me well—was shortly before dawn in the dim yellow light of the silent, empty, grim and wonderful Muscle Beach Dungeon. I stared at the bent bar long after the clang of the last plate had ceased. What a stark contrast to the perky atmosphere 3,000 miles east and six months earlier.

The clearly homemade-in-the-USA wooden bench had no shortage of splinters and wobbles and incorrect body-accommo-dating measurements—low to the ground, wide as an ironing board with short, precarious uprights. No padding.

First attempt, after numbing doubt, resulted in the ever-popular, noisy and embarrassing survival movement—slowly tipping the bar to the right and then swiftly tipping to the left, a graceless method of unloading the bar of excess plates. Slam bam.

Second attempt, after self-castigation and vigorous rib-rub-bing, the bar now bent convincingly across the chest, was rotated from the sternum to the hips, where movement ceased, and I was forced against all laws of physics and degrees of tolerable pain, to sit upright and maneuver the deadly iron from my lap to the floor several light-years away. I saw stars.

Third attempt, after unacceptable thoughts of failure under the bar and unbearable images of ascending the gym steps in defeat, I blew out one honest rep. At the same moment, early-morning strongman Steve Merjanian emerged from the sunlit Netherlands above and greeted me with cheers, "What's up, Drapes?"

Not much, Steve.

What elevated the weight is beyond me: muscle and might, power of the mind, fearful emotion, peaking energies, dumb luck, resident ghosts, coincidence, or the right combination of them all? Go figure.

Three years and a lifetime later, Joe Gold, the Maestro, opened the original Gold's Gym, and I merged and evolved—for good and evil—with the '60s. A few contests and a few hoorays and a few years and a few beers and it's off to Central California and a few World Gyms. They come and they go, they came and they went, along with fifteen or twenty years.

Growing up is hard to do, and lifting weights apparently slows down the process.

I've never met a muscle builder who isn't part kid, the better part. Some try to fake it—me man, me woman—but it's a bust when they get that last rep or an outstanding pump, and break spontaneously into hulky pirouettes across the gym floor, howling incoherently something like, who's ya momma now, or I'm cool, I'm bad. I think it's healthy and hopeful . . . endearing and authentic . . . and dumb.

I feel like a kid at times, playing with a bunch of scrappy toys worn out by years of rough-housing. Duct tape works wonders to hold loose ends together, and most wear and tear gets by with a coat of rust-resistant paint or a shot of lubricant. Occasionally, some damaged parts have to be fixed by a pro.

"There ya go, Bomber, good as new." Thanks, Doc.

Alas, some nifty bits and pieces are beyond repair and will be missed: wheels fall off, wing missing, stuffing sticking out. You know, the usual. But that doesn't mean we can't play and have fun. Kids become increasingly inventive and clever as they grow older.

I go to the gym in an hour, dragging my wagon of toys bumpity-bump. No wings, no wheels, just air and high hopes. Ready for change, ready for the fundamentals.

20

Travels with the Secret Unknown Stranger in Disguise

I FOUND MIKE'S MUSCLE HOUSE on Main Street squeezed between a dry cleaner and a travel agency. From the looks of the faded overhead sign, Mike has been there for a long time. Good for Mike and his loyal band of muscleheads. We need more Mikes across the nation. It was my turn to hoist some iron in allegiance.

Not wanting to be recognized and endure the flattering yet tedious questions, stares and adulation, I entered the doors disguised as myself. It worked. Early afternoon, the gym floor was near empty and no one paid attention to the old balding guy wearing a shabby House of Pain T-shirt, who walked like a Chester and wrestled with thirty-five-pound dumbbells.

Rats! And I shaved my arms and pumped up in the parking lot before entering the House. Are these people from another planet, time zone or sport? It is I, The Bomb, DD, the Drapes, the Golden Warrior, El Mondo Man, World's Strongest Youth.

I took advantage of the anonymity and observed the half-dozen or so lifters at work. Varying levels of development, they—Ms. Hiphop, Billy D. Boll, Chuck Truck, Ima Newbie and Jason Latspred—all appeared to be on autopilot. Robots in action: Address weight, assume grip, raise, lower, raise, lower, raise, lower (up to seven on scale of difficulty), replace weight, release grip, turn and walk away.

"Hmm," I said to myself secretly, as I paused to breathe upon completion of a frenzied clash with a pair of resistant dumbbells. I patted my iron opponents on their backsides (guy stuff), grunting and nodding my approval. "Hmm," I repeated.

Don't my iron colleagues get it? This is not a factory. We are not building computers or appliances; we are building strong, shapely muscle and vibrant health.

I was waiting for a buzzer to sound and everyone to grab a bench for a coffee break, which would have been fine with me. I would join them: cream 'n sugar and one of those cheese Danish, thanks. And then it occurred to me: It's not them, it's the time of year, the no-zone—no pump, no burn, no drive, no focus, no smile, no desire, no last rep. No enthusiasm.

Muscle fans, we are in that mundane, insipid period between grey winter and pastel spring. My temporary training partners, though sadly uninformed individuals not hip to the classic body-building scene, are no strangers to the gym. They have the appearance of being attentive musclebuilders at one time or another—last summer or early fall, no doubt.

They are the remnant of a vital force that has diminished since the end of last year. They are the Muscle House survivors on their last legs awaiting renewal, replenishment, support and supplies from the cavalry . . . or heaven above, Calvary.

They're hanging in, running on empty.

Autopilot is better than no pilot or winter storage in a damp, lifeless hangar. I see it at my home gym and feel it in my own bones. Roll the hulk onto the gym floor, crank it over once or twice (putt, sputter) and flick the switch to automatic. Just keep the thing going, gain some air, flutter and land without crashing. Chug, chug, rumble . . . Not every workout is like that. Just a few, really. But they seem to permeate the entire season, the off-season, that time between blasting and bombing.

Once you've trained hard and with purpose, anything less seems mild, almost meaningless by comparison. Preparing for and pushing the very last conceivable rep in every anguishing set throughout a cycle of furious, growth-oriented workouts requires extraordinary resources and courage and motivation.

Nine on the difficulty scale is exponentially more than seven. Seven is a faint tremor; nine is San Francisco 1906 all over again.

Nine is also the only way to grow, some will argue, unless you take the underground. Be careful. It's dark down there.

Good thing for the off-season, or we might burn out entirely—no rest for the body, mind and soul. Our muscles and joints would collapse, our minds implode and our souls grow hungry. Perhaps we need to adopt an off-season training attitude, a willful and purposeful stepping back and thus eliminate the guilt of performing sub-grade workouts for months on end, or skipping them periodically because they're so dang undesirable.

Such stress is painful, discouraging and catabolic. Straight poison.

Many of you are way ahead of me. I'm one of those driven slobs who doesn't know the difference between too much and not enough. As long as the weights are within the county line and I'm conscious, I think I should lift them—hard. Pop, there goes another rotator cuff.

You, of course, have built-in behavior mechanisms that are not overrun by faulty hyper-psychosomatic engines, a.k.a. bean brains. *Excuse me. Are you using that Olympic bar? I gotta have that Olympic bar! Gimme the freaking bar!! Let go.*

Thank the stars above, it's nearly spring. I'm not ready to develop an off-season training attitude. It'll take most of the summer to put that delusion together and make it real. I have one dubious thing in my favor, however. I'll be an aged citizen by the time summer rolls around and slowing down will be that much more feasible, realistic and absolutely necessary . . . attractive, even. I suspect the only reason I train as hard as I do (clang, oomph)—besides an ego the size (and constitution) of a dirigible—is my loyal flight crew and bombardiers. I keep going to keep them going. Or is it the other way around?

Thank you. Our little conversation has inspired me. Starting tomorrow I shall engage my first of a series of reduced workouts. Truth is, the timing is right. Easily and often, professionals in any sport lose perspective. Playing becomes fanatical, winning becomes obsessive and pressing on past the finish line becomes neurotic.

I have been spared of these sick fixations, yet I find myself somewhat preoccupied with muscle building and weight training on infrequent occasions. I count passing cars on boulevards like sets and reps; I consider the body composition of people shopping in the market; I guess what a guy standing at an ATM might bench press if he had to, or what she might look like in a bikini . . . that one strictly from the wholesome point of view of a contest judge, naturally.

I've long fought the notion of modified training, since the day I returned to the gym after a dinky heart bypass. I rumbled onward, underwent months of EDTA chelation to further my arterial health (or not), followed my nose and restored myself, albeit at a lighter bodyweight, and have come to the conclusion that less bodywork is better for this less-than-pristine pickup truck.

I can do more, but it only wears me rather than repairs me. I ain't dumb, I ain't. It's gonna be tough, bombers, but I must restrain myself, rather than strain myself.

No more forced reps, no more five-set supersets, no more extended sets. I tried these modifications in my last upper-torso workout and reduced wear and tear by twenty-five percent without minimizing the muscle training effectiveness.

I'm sure of it. I am robo-man with built-in calculating software . . . very cool applications. I'm thinking of getting an iPod, if I can figure the gizmo out.

The ninety-percent output and the fifth of five supersets are the heavy hitters, formerly responsible for maximum muscle gains (hardness, shape, vascularity, definition). Today such intensity is harmful: The heart mutters, joints swell and ache, muscles cry for mercy and fatigue consumes the body and settles in the marrow of the bones.

A trip to the gym must not be a dreaded event, a dreadful experience. It can and ought to be a joy, uplifting and fulfilling.

Now he tells us. You mean I can remove the tacks from my sneakers and the barbed wire from my underwear?

Over sixty-five? Bomb and blast sensibly. Till then, get to the gym on time, every time, and eat right always. And don't park in my spot. Just kidding. Park anywhere you like.

21

Where Were You in the Day?

EACH OF US HAS A STORY TO TELL, whether we're fourteen or forty, eighteen or eighty. Many are complicated but not one is simple. Some are packed, not one is empty. Every one is worth telling, but few are heard. Our stories are our own.

Do you have a favorite tale from your oft-vague life story, one that stirs you and retains its drama and emotion, its colors, scents and sounds?

Of course you do, if you think for a second. You're not sure anyone wants to hear it, yet you recall it and relive it from time to time. I, too, have such a favorite recollection from my dizzy life. Ordinary is its most outstanding feature.

Life is largely composed of ordinary stories and somebody's got to tell them.

If you stood on the corner of 4th and Broadway in Santa Monica fifty-some years ago, looked north toward Wilshire Boulevard in the early morning and spotted a big young dude with blond hair lumbering in your general direction, chances are it was me. If this guy had East Coast stamped on his forehead and carried a motley gym bag and was clueless, you should bet on it.

Dum-dee-dum . . .

"Hey mista . . . ya know weah da dungeon is?"

You win . . . that was me. Who else would be searching for a dark, smelly subterranean dungeon at the crack of dawn within a short walk of the alluring Pacific Palisades? Who else sounded like a Jersey hood on the run? It was June of 1963 when I arrived at LAX seeking muscle and might.

George Eifferman, later to become a good friend, picked me up at the budding LA airport, dropped me off at my temporary warehouse digs *(couch is in the back . . . it's getting late . . . see ya bright and early)* and gave me the low-down on the Muscle Beach Gym. He called it the Dungeon, said it was four blocks away and the door was always open. I was to make myself at home.

Just as he described it, the door was one of a set of two: sky blue, very tall and dragged when I pulled on it. I was in, and there I stayed until the gym moved in '66.

You stepped in, dragged the door shut in chilly weather or at the night's end and immediately descended fourteen broad steps, turned right and descended another eight in the opposite direction. You've arrived: A basement, no windows, little light, less cheer, tons of weight and gobs of atmosphere. Ready? About-face, walk ten feet, turn ninety degrees left and walk fifteen paces to the locker room, a.k.a. the Trap.

Deteriorating twelve by twelve reddish-brown floor tiles shift and scrunch occasionally beneath your feet.

It was two weeks before I dared enter that dank inner sanctum. It required hardening of the heart, a gathering of courage, much risk and a little madness to step fully into the grimy trap. It took another week to chance the shower, and this only after observing my new friend, Mike Bondura (ex-Navy), penetrate the murky cubicle morning after morning and emerge alive, well and clean. Forty-watt light bulbs have their advantages: failing to cast generous light and reveal the details of one's surroundings.

The place was large and a proper choice of locations after the city councilmen and women required the original beach version of Muscle Beach to relocate the broad-shouldered nuisance "somewhere else, not upon our white sands for all to see." It was also dim and grim.

White gone gray covered the crumbling plaster walls, and half a dozen strategically placed pillars the size of Roman columns held up the place. Other than three or four scattered sixty-watt incandescents, the only light that illuminated the Dungeon, was a four-by-twenty-foot stretch of block-glass skylight inserted in the Broadway Avenue sidewalk above the far wall. That light was silver-white and harsh and abundant, but only when the California sun was high in the sky.

Beneath the skylight were two twelve-by-twelve lifting platforms, grains of Muscle Beach sand still scrunched between layers of hard rubber. Drop a marble and it would roll to the center, where heavy iron was regularly and mercilessly dumped for decades. The designated lifting areas no longer gathered crowds of admiring onlookers. Rather, you could sit upon a reclaimed section of discarded, over-stuffed movie-theater seats arranged at the subterranean platform's edge and doze off.

No one would notice, no one would care.

Pausing at the keyboard (computer, not piano) during my recollections, I plotted the length of the Dungeon, counting thirty easy paces, or seventy-five feet, in my mind's eye. Who's gonna argue a foot or two or ten? And the width amounted to twenty-five paces, maybe sixty feet. The ample height of fifteen feet floor to ceiling forgave the Dungeon its dungeon-ness, accenting the sense of space—room to reach, to stretch, to expand, to groan and grow.

The temperature was always sixty-eight degrees, no matter what time of day or year. And the smell was as consistent: foul with moldy mustiness and the tang of sweat, but well mixed with oxygen and clean ocean air. Sensory adjustments were painless and quick; you could see, breathe and feel, and in silence most anytime.

Joy is found in strange places.

Opposite the front door and clinging to the wall at a forty-five-degree angle was a second staircase that opened to the rear parking lot. A narrow, thin-stepped contraption, it sagged in the middle and threatened to collapse should it be disturbed. Those who chose this dilapidated structure to enter (or escape) used it only once, knowing they had pushed their luck. Beneath the ill-stacked stairway was a small mystery room behind a crooked, time-stained yellow door.

Alone one morning, which was often the case, I managed to stir up some endorphins with a volley of press-behind-necks supersetted with side-arm laterals. I pulled a slug of water from the corroded water fountain near the entry to this ominous mystery room. Feeling pumped and dangerous, I yanked the door open to expose broken wood furnishings, cracked ceramic toilet fixtures, lightless lampshades and framed pictures of someone's long-silent family—all covered in deathlike dust, damp, moldy and thick as cotton. Spiders and rats (and spirits, I'm sure) retreated in startled wisps. Imprisoned for decades, the dust and stink and blackness fought to escape its confines. I shut the door with lightning swiftness, not my place to release voiceless yet hysterical captives from the past.

Most of the gym's equipment was handmade and clustered in one quarter of the cavernous basement. Overhead stood five stories of old hotel and rented rooms and aging occupants in total ignorance of the activities below. We could lift and win and lose and die and no one would care, especially those tipping shots of cheap booze in the saloon above the squat rack. Diluted whiskey and warm beer dripped from the soggy overhead plaster to form a puddle beneath the nasty oversized rack.

One slip too many and you're an alcoholic.

I loved the dumbbells (tens to 150s) that sat on splintery two by tens supported by milk crates—this was back when milk crates were milk crates. They comprised plates from every manufacturer collected by every musclehead in Southern California, and they were welded together in handy heaps resembling . . . well . . . dumbbells. They rattled and pinched and made a monkey of you one day and a strongman in time, if you persisted.

The benches were bulky and perilous and less attractive, and were pieced together by the same guys who welded the dumbbells . . . and repaired the leaky pipes, hung the front door and decorated the mystery room.

There must have been a sale on sky-blue paint at the local hardware sometime around moving day. The only color in the gym was the blue of the benches and the red splotch of their oilcloth coverings. Two movable flat benches, two bench presses, one incline bench, one steep-incline bench, one preacher curl and one beer-soaked squat rack—what more could an authentic musclehead ask for, besides a pump and burn and a weekly unemployment check?

Other bare necessities included a chinning bar and a set of dipping bars made of galvanized pipe and covered with layers of chalk, an overhead pulley setup for free-swinging plate-loaded cable pulldowns, and a long cable and pulley for seated lat rows—these, the most primitive and effective back-builders in the world.

Oh, and one mobile hunk of mirror broken from a larger hunk served anyone who needed to see himself.

There was the homey touch: a couch in a serene area where no equipment but a crudely crafted Roman chair and a scored tumbling mat bursting at the seams were tastefully arranged—ambiance and modern art. The couch was of the stained and contagious variety you'd hastily circumvent in any frightening alley. At the inside edge of the left front leg, my training partner and I hid our chalk. Only we knew it was there.

That's about it. The rest of the place was strewn with Olympic bars of varying degrees of curvature and malfunction and plates that never bent or broke.

Impression, imperfection and improvising were the Dungeon's foremost muscle-building features.

Not to mention Zabo, Dick Dubois, Armand Tanny, Gene Shuey, Sam Martin, Peanuts West, Hugo Labra, Joe Gold, Artie Zeller, Chuck Collras, Chet Yorton, George Eifferman, Reg Lewis, Dick Sweet, Zeus and Thor . . .

Time to head for the modern gym to inflate and ignite, pump and burn, soar and fly.

22

Draper Financials, Inc.— Invest in Iron and Steel

I'M STILL BREATHING HEAVILY after today's workout. It's Sunday and, as it occasionally happens, I zipped to the gym, trained without interruption and zipped home. I flowed. Were I a poet, I'd compose a rhyme. As it is, I'm a musclehead and will make a tuna salad instead.

The workout was the right length (from here to there—sixty solid minutes) with matching effort (enough—no more, no less) and worked the regions of the body needing most attention (the bottoms of the feet to the top of the head).

Were I a songwriter, I'd write a love song. Instead, I whistled a happy tune as I rounded the bend for home.

That was my third workout in five days, a noticeable achievement on the scale of recuperation, one worthy of a seven or eight. Low energy, nagging soreness, muscle fatigue or apathy: carelessness, a tinge of dread or an unfavorable seeking of comfort and distraction has limited me to a couple of workouts a week for more than a month, they of a necessarily compromised structure.

Were I a magician, I'd pull health, wealth and happiness from my hat. As it is, I'm a dinged warrior snagging cool breezes that flow beneath my wings.

The most outstanding feature of the whole affair was that I wanted to go to the gym. I didn't go because I had to go, it was on my agenda or I needed to as part of my recovery. Neither did I go because of the silent urgency presented by chronic guilt, nor the casualness that accompanies the attitude "I'm in the area and have nothing else to do; why not jingle the iron?"

When's the last time we entertained the lattermost urge, the one of carefree looseness? I think I was twelve.

I wanted to go to enjoy myself amid the neat, pure and orderly environment of benches and racks, the productive and positive atmosphere that is weight training. The clink, clank and clunk of metal against metal and metal against man are familiar sounds, safe and healing. Applying myself to the deed of moving the prescribed harmonic objects of force was systemically appealing. The action of the body, its muscle and mechanics and the focus and will to attend their motion became essential to the moment.

There are jiggers of joy in the processes and I was thirsty.

How much weight, how many sets or reps—these weren't important; thus they did not blur the way. Is it or was it more and better than previous workouts? Who cares? I want to do what I do now: feel it, observe it, enjoy it. Striving, driving to excel has its value, but to me today it would be destructive. Being where I am is where I want to be. I'm free from the past and the future. I'm here, now. I'm me . . . I am . . .

Zen Man!

Baloney! I want to be twenty-something and a ripped 240 having just completed reps with 400 on the bench. And I wouldn't mind a tall stack of cash. Alas, we move on by the grace of God.

By all gauges at hand, I'm on the mend.

I wish I could say that of the world around me, the very same world around you. If I had money I'd really be bummed. As it is, I hold my breath and onto my socks when I fill up at the pump, and I no longer cut the crust from a slice of bread.

Bombers, now is the time to pay particular attention to the resources around us. Fixing what is broken starts in our own backyards, with our own tongues, our compassion for everything and everyone around us, and with our vigilance and ready action.

Do we need another reason to take care of our health, our bodies and our minds? Think survival of the fittest and our influence on those around us.

Train regularly, eat right, be responsible, be respectful, be generous, be aware and be happy.

I continue to see the ever-present bellies and the sloth, the smokes and the drugs, the hypocrisy and PC and lies, and it's clear why we're in a mess. Morals are in the tank, God's in outer space and too many hands are in empty pockets. Heads are down, shoulders are slumped, cell phones grow from ears as circles are worn by pacing footsteps. *Hellooo . . . is anybody there?*

You want to invest in a sure thing? Iron and steel, muscle and might. No risk. You control your investment and watch it grow. No middleman, no broker, no cons, no portfolio. Just you and your iron, anywhere, anytime. You can carry a gym bag for personal items of assurance.

I entered the gym with uncontained glee, evident by the broad smile across my mug. This item of adornment has been concealed in a small jar in the recesses of my gym bag and I wasn't certain it was affixed correctly. Seems I stashed it away when mounting the rear-entry stairs became an ever-increasing challenge.

Not even a mouse witnessed my joy. I knew the place was open because the door was unlocked and Fleetwood Mac filled the air. (Jeff, about my age and mentality, must be at the front desk.) I removed my smile so as not to waste it and replaced it with my personally popular cool and under-control face. What a relief. I thought I'd crack at the cheeks and chin.

What shall I do? Anything I want. Well, not anything. The bench from which I once pressed 400+ reminded me of my limitations. Scanning from the center of the gym floor, my eyes encountered the sturdy squat racks that held 400+ not that long ago. No, I'll pass on those today. There, upon which my water bottle rested, was the designated lifting platform, often the support of 400+, a nifty weight to empower my back. Ah, deadlifts! I remember when.

I walked over, retrieved my water and took a slug. What shall I do? Same question, another time, same answer: Lift weights, hoist iron, toss steel, pump and burn.

I did rope tucks for the torso (can't be beat), leg extensions supersetted with leg curls and calf work (healthy and exerting, complete and compact), and Bodymaster squats (if I didn't know better, I'd think I was squatting). Four sets of the required and desired reps KOed the lower body with a neat and robust combination, just what I needed, just what I deserved.

Feeling good and yearning for a touch of upper-body stimulation, I added press-behind-necks with maximum form and focused muscle exertion combined with one-arm side lateral raises (if I didn't know better, I'd think I was in The Dungeon forty years ago). Four sets of 6–8 reps made my day.

Keep it simple, blast it but don't blow yourself away, smile and live another day.

It's a bird, it's a plane, it's the bomb squad in tight formation. They fly as one.

23

The Essential Nothingness of Weight Training

I'M DRAWN TO LOOKING OUT a narrow window aside my desk that views a steep, wooded hillside. Two men are hard at work chipping fallen branches and reducing stout limbs to firewood—worthy tasks rendering valuable fuel for the winter.

Watching makes me weary. Chainsaw buzzing, chipper grinding, arms full, backs loaded, up and down, back and forth. I'm humbled.

Muscles functioning, calories burning, hearts pumping, works accomplished. I'm envious.

Laree gathered the pile of debris the size of a turnip truck during the early autumn from a fifty-yard radius. Assiduously, painstakingly, she dragged—lifted, hoisted, heaved, pushed, pulled and tossed—the woody detritus, not as labor, but as muscle- and balance-building exercise.

"Weightlifting primarily works the body in a limited plane of motion. Balance and mobility suffer. We need to accommodate our bodies' complete structural strength and health by exercising in multiple planes of motion," she says, "and smartly performed physical labor can do the trick."

I agreed, noting that years ago I found furniture building with heavy wooden beams a most natural and beneficial addition to muscle building with heavy iron weights. I continued to offer her encouragement and masterful advice. Alas, she rejected my advanced training scheme, which included two very productive shoulder and arm movements: scrubbing and polishing my truck.

A Wiseman is not enthusiastically greeted in his own backyard. Thus, I'm off to the gym, leaving her to her multi-linear home training: stacking the firewood recently cut by her hard-working associates.

Gym Time. Over the highways, through the intersections, across the parking lot, up the staircase and through the double doors; toss the tote bag in the corner and head straight to the hunky pulley machine. *Hello, hunky pulley machine, how're your cables hanging?*

Enough of that, no time to lose, here's where the action begins, the friendly and cooperative iron confrontation.

First, the search for the perfect handle to attach to the end of the dangling cable. Happy hunting. This can take a few testy minutes as there are about thirty handles of various lengths, shapes and thicknesses snarled in a heap, along with hooks, chains and carabiner. Priceless tools of the trade.

Many a pinched finger and bloody knuckle are retrieved from the mess, only to dig out a mere look-alike contrivance, a piece of mistaken identity, a cheap imposter. Nothing less than a specific handle—the real McCoy, the genuine article, the *grippus perfectus*—will do for the neurotic lifter. Anything less and he's outta there.

Well, not exactly, but he will cuss, act up and throw stuff. Come to think of it, that's common behavior for most muscleheads east of the Mississippi.

I don't recall when muscle building became such a fussy business. For years I lifted weights wherever I found them and left them wherever and whenever I was done. Seemed to work okay at the time. Of course, I was limited to a single corroded dumbbell and a space the size of an Army footlocker. How messy can one soldier get? Besides, those associated with the Army try to be all they can be.

Nowadays I am orderly and precise. Form and focus have replaced the amount of weight used and the strength exerted as the lattermost elements require continuous updating (they fade into the shadows of time).

Pace has gained importance (steady as she goes) and exercise grooves have been slowly modified and perfected. They are precise, barely resembling the archaic oversized, far-reaching movements of my earlier training days.

Where would we be without the progress of time and the latest technology? Precision Exercise Performance (PEP) is the Advanced Training Methodology (ATM) of applying the Only Exercise That Doesn't Hurt (OETDH), or the Last Remaining Groove (LRG), or the popular This Way Or No Way Dynamic (TWONWD).

Life Made Simple (LMS). Life simplified.

I hasten to catch up with you, my devoted training partners, and march by your side with iron determination and steely deliberation. Having heaved heavy metal for more than half a century, making light of all levels of lifting, I only know how to live. Sticking to it and never giving up and staying airborne are our daily objectives.

Flying, soaring, bombing and occasional taxiing are our foremost objectives and mutual responsibilities.

I maintain all we really need to know about muscle making and strength building is wrapped up in a seed the size of a dumbbell containing a bowl of good food and an attitude of appreciation. Once planted in fertile soil, it grows by continued watering and faithful attention.

Health and might imperceptibly pierce the soil and die off if not valued and cared for. This doesn't mean we need or ought to worship the living thing, but feed it we must. Nourishment must be provided during the cloud-covered and frosty months and in the heat of the dry summer. Let's be there side by side to offer a breath of fresh air and appropriate provision.

Push that iron.

Many of us regard weight training as the most important thing in our lives. Well . . . mmm . . . not more important than, say, our family or friends or our precious and flourishing almighty dollar (ha . . . cute, very cute), but the relationship between us and them is directly related. Our workouts are up, our treasures are up; our workouts are down and we're broke, busted, not worth a dime.

Exercise sensibly and eat right are the rules of engagement. Keep it simple and make it a joy are the codes of performance.

Button up, buckle down, breathe deep and barrel ahead. The challenge now is to not let go and lose momentum.

In closing, before I fold up my wings and tuck them in my tote bag, before I deflate my hovering dirigible and stuff it in my backpack, let me assure you of this: Never do I engage in a set or rep without total involvement.

My kicking, screaming body might occasionally become snared in a net or cage, a pit or an illusion, but never do I relinquish my grasp of the iron.

It's not the workouts as much as our relationships with them. We strangely and regularly encounter an invisible pull or magnetic tug, a cosmic force or soulful union compelling us to surrender our being to the touch of iron. Be not confused, bombers. Love is expressed in infinite ways.

That's a wrap, airborne ironminds and flying muscleheads.

24

Hey, Buddy— Got a Minute?

We are weightlifters and muscle builders, strongmen and women, fitness freaks and health nuts. We train, we lift, we work out, exercise, push the iron and lift the steel. We eat right and avoid the junk food most of the time . . . or some of time.

We could do better, but we do what we do and we do what we can.

We do better when we share our little journey and when we are encouraged. Basic information in training and eating and attitude go a long way in deepening our understanding of ourselves, our workouts and the world around us. A weekly reminder that what we do is important, beneficial and admirable is priceless and uplifting. It is, in fact, the reason we meet here each week.

Take me to the iron.

Something like fifteen years ago I started this parade and you dropped in step one at a time. Let us at this time introduce you to a character, an old friend, who will share his experiences with us that we might continue to live, lift, learn and grow.

Rather, let him introduce himself. The Bat and his bud have a lot to teach us:

The booze and cigs have got to go.

I took one more drag, a deep one, before I snubbed the butt in an ashtray I lifted from the Asbury Hilton. They'll never miss it. The tray's full and my pack of Camels is empty. Story of my life. Same with the bottle: The more I drink, the less I have. Jack Daniels has never been in such a hurry with no place to go.

Cigs and booze, this has gotta stop. I miss the gym and protein and a good pump. I leaned back in my swivel and put my feet up on the desk . . . something to contemplate.

The backdoor squeaked. It never squeaks unless someone is opening it.

I killed the gooseneck and reached for the drawer where I keep my revolver. The chair creaked. It never creaks unless I reach for my revolver. I began to perspire. I never perspire unless I'm nervous. I wasn't nervous, but it was hot and the overhead fan was on the blink.

The backdoor is my secret exit leading to Y Street and known only to my friends. I didn't have any friends, except Marlene and Crazy Joe, and Marlene is a girl.

Crazy Joey Norton slipped into my office like he was playing hide 'n seek with one of his nasty poolroom creditors, the ones who break pool sticks over the heads of hustlers who don't pay their debts. I grabbed my bottle of JD and stashed it next to my pistol. Crazy was crazy and out of breath.

"Joey, are you nuts?" I said, "It's three in the morning, only cats and crooks are crawling around."

He leaned tough against the door and took a deep breath of relief. I could feel the room empty of oxygen. Craze was 6' 4", 240 and built like a bomb with Howorth's shoulders. He put his ear to the door and listened hard to still silence.

"I gave them the slip," he said.

Crazy backed away from the door and slipped into a chair in front of my desk. I didn't want to ask why, who or how many he slipped, but it seemed like a suitable inquiry. I retrieved my bottle from the gun 'n bottle drawer. After a long swig, I offered him a shot. He did not refuse my hospitality.

"Tell me," I said.

"We're okay till dawn," he said.

Here's the thing about Crazy. Crazy and I go back to the '70s when we lifted weights together at the downtown Manhattan Y. Lifters were loners in those days and the iron was an extraordinary friend: solid, bold and mighty.

That's another way of saying "honest and faithful." You got from the friendship what you put into it. It's the same today, only the tin tinkles and muscles are the fool's gold crown of false glory.

We did what you needed to do when you grew up where the world lived on top of itself. Neither Joey nor I could hurt anyone unless they absolutely insisted on hurting us. We were good at protection.

Cops for ten years, our dance with the NYPD came to an end when some stoners decided to feed junk to kids in the Y Street neighborhood. Any street was too close to home, but Y Street was where Crazy and I were born, where our gnarly youths unfolded. Some people say unraveled, but I say unfolded, carefully, by the angels above. Not everybody believes in angels.

Six punks, like a pack of rabid dogs, roamed the alleys and edges of the school grounds grabbing thirteen- and fourteen-year-olds to introduce them to dope and easy money. The dope was wrong and the squirts knew it, but money was not in abundance, at home or on the street. They knew that, too. Hard choices were everywhere.

Crazy and me, good cops with ears to the ground, got word of the devil's deeds and trapped the stinking little mob in their digs in the basement of a crumbling condemned tenement. What a treat. They yapped and snarled and tried to run, during which time we dismantled a few teeth, relieved them of their weapons—two small-caliber revolvers, knuckles and assorted knives—and burned their baggy, smelly clothes in the archaic oil furnace.

Naked and tied together as they were with old clothesline, they wouldn't get far. In the middle of the circle of boney tattooed and needle-marked bodies, we heaped their weapons and significant stash, paraphernalia and cash and IDs in a battered galvanized washbasin. Reaching the treasure trove or exit was not possible, guaranteed by the network of ropes and handy-dandy duct tape.

Crazy's muffled voice from a payphone across the street at Paco's Liquors told police of the whereabouts of the wretched creatures, violent, salivating and bound together in a huddle. It was our attempt to clean up some rubbish in less than thirty minutes without the muss and fuss of an entire police force and its attending bureaucracy. We'd seen that fuss happen over and over again.

Enough is enough, as they say in politics.

Justice sometimes comes in odd-shaped, hand-wrapped packages. There they sat in a circle, arms and legs entangled, apparently by a bunch of hooded amateurs. Their escapades were undone. They were busted, shamed and sent away enduring withdrawals during a sufficient term at Riker's.

The six creeps were not the first to receive our brand of justice. But this time Crazy and me got whacked. The precinct commander dug what we did, but not our "flagrant vigilante tactics, ya dumb-ass muscleheads."

It was one of many questionable good deeds we performed in the shadows and behind closed doors that could undo the department. We often pushed things.

We were discharged without ceremony "before heads begin to roll, you oversized mugs."

"See ya at the gym Wednesday," Marlene had said as she escorted us from the rear exit of the precinct. Her voice was hushed, her lips didn't move as she unconsciously tapped her holstered Glock. Her Captain's badge was crooked.

About the booze and cigarettes. I lied. Promise I'll never lie again. I don't smoke or drink, although I confess I was a vegetarian for a month, and Joey drinks beer with his Quiznos. I still eat vegetables . . . along with thick steaks and whole milk. Gotta be huge and ripped to fight crime.

A .357 Magnum helps.

Well, bombers . . . that is, those of you who are still with me . . . Dave here. I'll let the rascals get back to their lives, such as they are. Sounds like they could use a good feed and a dose of iron to unwrap their heads. Maybe sometime they join us again and tell us how they bruise bad guys and stay in shape at the same time.

Both are full-time projects.

25
Now and Then, Muscle and Might

WE SAT AT OPPOSITE ENDS of the long, polished mahogany conference table. I seldom enter the stiff and proper arena unless a systemic problem of considerable proportion arises. The board deemed the circumstance at hand worthy of critical discussion. I disagreed.

Leslie Rothschild, underscoring the broad range of my readership, suggested I was too frequently referencing my less-than-youthful years.

"We have young men and women seeking inspiration and motivation, Bomb Guy," said IronOnline's marketing senior, "not a battered bunch of dilapidated duffers swabbing their swollen joints with liniment."

I imagined a 100-pound dumbbell chained to this guy's leg as I tossed him off the Santa Cruz pier.

His deep-throated growling was supported by the songbird whining of Ms. Chelsea Billingsworth, CB, my chief PR strategist and travel coordinator.

"I urge you to maintain the youthful and sexy approach of bombing and blasting, DD," said the lady in the tweed pantsuit, "It's your signature."

She wouldn't know a bomb from a blast if they burst in her pants. I grinned; a fifty-pounder would be enough for Chelsea.

Bartley, assistant CFO, pleaded for me to curtail my talking-up the good old days, thus implying davedraper.com was a diminishing blast from the past.

Lilly from Draper International Products (DIP) begged me not to say "post-op" again.

"It depresses them," she warned. Lilly, the poor thing, has fibroids, polyps and herpes.

The maintenance guy, Chuck, who happened to be removing shredded documents, politely interrupted the esteemed financial advisor, Bertie Madenough, amid his urging everyone to invest briskly, asking, "How can I retain muscle mass, Big D, while I'm training to lose fat and get ripped? You've been around, like, forever. You've gotta know everything."

You can always count on the Chuckster.

As if on cue, Katie, the buffed lass from the warehouse, entered the conference room with a tray of Bomber Blend, coffee and high-protein snacks. Yum!

"Refreshments, everyone," she sang out.

Above the commotion, she asked, "Bomber, can you still make the afternoon workout with the crew at the hangar gym? Chest, shoulders and back? Please? Somebody's gotta keep us focused. Also, the Boy Scouts from Troop 50 were hoping you'd critique their training routines, and the high school cheerleaders could use a nutritional update."

I said, "Absolutely, KT. All I have to do is refill my oxygen tank, increase my morphine drip and change my diapers. Chuck will roll me over in plenty of time."

The Chuckster nodded. Meeting adjourned.

Excuse me, bomber-type rascals. I take a jab at the aging thing because it's the best defense I have to prevent it from sneaking up on me. Some of you understand my position, some of you will soon, and some of you have forgotten or are trying to forget. From time to time I poke the senseless bully in the snot-locker to let you know I know he knows we know. Ya know?

Then comes along some old-timer (eighty-five or ninety) to straighten me up and straighten me out and bust my butt with advice about aging gracefully. I love it.

Now, back to work, everyone, and no more trash about youth or age or who, when, why or where. No complaining, no doubting, no hesitating.

Can't handle it? Keep it to yourself! There's nothing more rewarding, more beneficial, more exhilarating and more fulfilling than a mean tangle with the steel, a round or two with the iron.

I was lying on the floor and my cat was lying on my chest and we were both purring. I had an extra ten minutes and wanted to rest my bones and consider the workout before me. I was fueled, yet needed to rev the engines. A little pre-workout visualizing always does the trick. You might call it psyching up.

I imagine that which I am about to encounter: the gym, the familiar faces, the background music and me (selfishly in the center of things) and the exercises that might suit my body today. What would I like to do, what do I need to do and what can I do are the three main questions with which I wrestle as I mind-stroll the gym floor.

What's gonna do it for me? What's gonna ring my bell? Will it clang or jingle? Fascinating! Maximum effort, minimum demand.

I know what you're saying. Doesn't this guy have anything better to do, like take out the trash, feed the birds, upgrade his iPod . . . text?

These brief mental-meanderings prepare me for a solid work-out. Often I encourage impromptu workouts as part of our training discovery and understanding. Enter gym, follow nose, work hard, have fun, feel and play seriously.

Imaging is one step removed from spontaneous. I stand before the weights with a low-contrast mental picture of what I'm about to do. Because it's not yet done, I can change it any time to suit any circumstance, whatever it might be. As I go, I know. I call this over-sixty-five precision.

And whatever I do, it's going to be good and it's going to be done right. That part is certain, the effect of strong visualization.

Training back in the day, there was no straying from the set routine. None! To wander was to weaken; to drift was to die. Strict training principles were necessary, mandatory. The stern approach made working out almost fearful.

Nuts to that. The last thing I need in my life these days is fear. Today, wandering and drifting under the calm supervision of wise and mature eyes and a knowing nose is the way. The yellow brick road, the golden ironway.

Now, if you were twenty or thirty or forty and had been around a tough neighborhood gym for at least a year, and didn't wear a pink tank top with your hair in braids and wanted to build big arms, this is what I'd tell you: Maybe you can, maybe you can't, it depends . . . Do you have what it takes?

Whatever, this is what I would do if I were you—in fact, this is what I did:

Triset 1

Standing barbell curl (4–5 sets × 12, 10, 8, 6, 4 reps, ascending weight)

Lying barbell triceps extension (4–5 sets × 15, 12, 10, 8, 6 reps, ascending weight)

Pulley pushdowns (4–5 sets × 12–15 reps, ascending weight)

Triset 2

Seated dumbbell alternate curl (4–5 sets × 10, 8, 6, 4 reps, ascending weight)

Overhead two-arm triceps extension with dumbbell (4–5 sets × 12–15 reps, ascending weight)

Overhead pulley pushes (4–5 sets × 12–15 reps, ascending weight)

Forearm triset

Wrist curl (4 × 12–15 reps, ascending weight)

Thumbs-up dumbbell curl (4 sets × 10, 8, 6, 4 reps, ascending weight)

Machine dips (4 sets × 12–15 reps, ascending weight)

You'd be surprised how much upper body and torso comes into play to blast your way through this mean and hungry combination. Twice a week should be sufficient. Works best when accompanied by some protein before and after the workout. Some version of this workout went on year after year, from the mid-'60s to my mid-sixties.

There are those who say this is too much. There are those who think freedom is free.

Excuse me. I've got to lie down for awhile. I'm exhausted. Be in the back of the hangar on the cot under the wing of the biplane.

26
Attitude and Altitude—
Higher and Higher

I'M A VERY BUSY PERSON and my plate is full.

Full of crumbs, that is. Perhaps if I scrape them together, there'll be a sufficient heap of stuff to get me to the gym. Each crumb is a remnant of responsibility, need, desire, discipline and obligation, with a few flecks of inspiration along the edges. What's this? Yuk, a morsel of guilt.

Trouble is, I don't have an appetite.

However, I do have excuses: The gym is thirty minutes down the road, the truck's dirty and the traffic stinks; it's cold, windy and grey outside and my favorite T-shirt's in the washer; there's a newsletter to write and my cat is curled up on my lap, purring.

I'll go to the gym tomorrow.

Crazy! There was a time fifty years ago I had nothing I'd rather do than go to the gym. Forty years ago contests were coming up . . . off to the gym. Thirty years ago I ran the juice bar in the gym. Twenty years ago I owned the gym. Fifteen years ago the gym owned me. Ten years ago I morphed into the Bomber writing tales about the gym. Boom-Zoom.

Today, "I'll go to the gym tomorrow"? I don't think so.

I've heard rumors of people who did the "I'll go tomorrow" act and haven't been seen or heard of since. Story goes they stepped too far from the pull of gravity and drifted into the worldly wastelands. Life in the world minus the tug of iron is often pointless and demoralizing, fattening and enfeebling.

I exaggerate. It's not as if postponing a workout shrivels your biceps like prunes or causes your obliques to hang down in gushy slabs over your beltline or make your butt wobble and sag. The absence of one training session does not result in the deterioration of hard-earned musculature. It's scientifically impossible.

Calm down, lighten up.

Two workouts without the iron, however, and you're in big trouble: Bloating, drooping and drooling are inevitable. Three and it's too late—delirium and bed-wetting are not uncommon. Four and you're tabloid headlines . . . cute photos. And five, they forget your name—you become a tube-fed number and are assigned a cot in Ward X.

Dave who? The what? Never heard of him.

I don't care if it's all in my mind. I miss a workout and I'm overcome with anger, guilt and irrational behavior. I'm bitter and cruel one minute and pouty and sad the next. I pull on a baggy sweatshirt only to rip it off and replace it with a size-small black tank top with "I'm Bad" slashed in red across the back.

Then, I'm in the bathroom crying for no reason.

I do not like to skip my workouts. I cannot afford to. Time is short. I only have sixty years invested in the action-packed sport, the first six or seven wasted on tag, kickball and the alphabet. Time is of the essence. Time is muscle. Time flies.

Time out for a shot of protein. Yummy, yummy, good for your tummy . . . and good for your muscles, too.

We're told when lifting the iron is no longer appealing, when we'd rather be changing a greasy truck transmission or undergoing a liver transplant, it's not the workout that's out of order, it's the attitude. Iron is iron, it's lifeless. We—you and I who live and lift—are the problems, the troubled, the weak, the lost.

Gee, thanks for the head trip. Another heavy load to carry, as if the metal wasn't enough.

Attitudes are not fashionable or transformable like colorful balloons in the white-gloved hands of a party clown—blow them up, stretch them here, twist them there and tie them all together. Squeak, squeak, squeak . . . a happy face. It is, in fact, working out that transforms the attitude.

Move that metal.

Remember, missing a training session is not an option unless you fall from a three-story window, take a bullet in the butt or are beamed up to Pluto. Not likely, nice try. The only solution to attitude-failure, training-ennui or workout letgosis is to drag yourself to the gym burdens and all, and dump them when you get there. Kerplunk! There's no load too heavy that a hearty workout won't fix, moderate or eradicate.

Push that iron.

You can work seriously on your funky attitude before you heave the weighted bars, but why bother when in ten minutes under their force, the mind is revived, riveted and recharging anyway? Attitudes are unstable wavelengths. You can think positive, imagine life is neat, suggest to your unconscious you will have a grand workout, but the fact is in the act.

Lift that steel.

I get a headache when I think positive. Besides being strenuous, it's like admitting I'm negative and need a fix. Rather, I go straight for the fix. I dash to the iron, grasp it and toss it around the gym. Thud, crash, clank.

It puts up a pretty good fight, even the light stuff, but I always win. It's certain; even if I lose, I win.

We know the inside of a gym and the underside of a loaded bar. We know there was a time—early childhood, or so it seems—when planning our training was vitally important: the order of exercises, the sets and the reps. Today we know our training so well we can go by smell. The nose knows. Too much planning puts a tickle in me ole schnozolla.

I can talk myself out of a good workout—the greatest invigorator of the body, mind and soul—by thinking too much about it. "I don't want to go to the gym," is not a casual comment I share with myself.

I'm succinct:

Go gym—plentiful rewards in powerful hands.
No gym—tremendous burdens on trembling shoulders.

Be there or be square. Or, probably, round: floppy in the wings, dumpy in the tail.

This is your Captain speaking . . . Trim your ailerons, bombers, suck in that fuselage . . . we're flying high.

27

A Day at the Beach on a Sunday Afternoon

SHALL I ENGAGE THE IRON or ignore the defiant scraps scattered across the rubber mats, amassed upon racks and poised on Olympic bars?

I want to go, but my musclehead unequivocally says, "Umm, give me a sec . . . err . . . sorta, maybe . . . sure, why not?"

But the brain says think twice, Tinhead, is this for your health and well-being, your muscle and power, your ego and amusement, or your addiction and neuroses? What drives your train wreck: responsibility, obligation, approval, insecurity, entertainment, fulfillment, fear, pleasure, pain?

Dementia?

Gee, put that way, it sounds like a thing of great consequence. No trivial matter, this relationship between iron and man. When did it become so complicated? It's just iron. You lift it or you don't.

I went to the gym Sunday early afternoon—one PM—and it was as empty as a bank vault after closing. The treasure was there, but no one to plunder it. I felt like a thief about to stuff his bag with bounty: any exercise I want, as many sets and as many reps; squats, supersets, dumbbells, benches and cables.

It's mine, all mine. I'm rich.

At that point a straggly part-time guy—he's broke and has no life—stepped from behind the front counter and requested my membership card and reminded me to sign in, "It's policy."

The dirty little . . .

He introduced himself, Billy Jay Whimple, like it was a number he was assigned when he swiped his first breath. With emphatic mockery I said, "I'm Steve Reeves."

"A pleasure, Steve," he said, assuring me it was never too late to exercise. "Have you been a member for long? I don't recall seeing you around."

I was robbed right there in what was once my very own muscle bank by little Billy Jay with jump ropes for arms.

Empty bag in hand, I dragged myself to a bench, sat and glared at the sun-filled parking lot through the airy doublewide doors. Sunday, now 1:03, and the place was packed with a crowd of three—Steve, Billy and me.

At least Steve knew who I was—The Sunny Sunday Sunshine Bomber. I should have gone to the beach.

I trained for seventy-five minutes while BJ Guns studied the TV above the front counter. I think it was a reality show. I had an oddly rewarding workout, like cold soup on a hot day.

I learn something new every time I work out. Or I uncover something old, so old, it seems like something new.

Like, check it out . . . that guy grabbed the bar above his head and is pulling himself up to his nose and down and up. Original noses, old as Muscle Beach . . . ya feel what I'm saying? I cannot remember the last time I did wide-grip noses.

This particular day I rediscovered standing barbell curls are indisputably the best exercise for building massive biceps and they, combined with overhead triceps extensions, will complete the deed for colossal arm development. Who is willing to dispute these facts, who would dare?

I felt empowered, alone and drenched in silence.

I applied my discovery with concentrated enthusiasm, intensity and might. Another pure truth unfolded: An ordinary exercise performed with focused enthusiasm, intensity and might becomes an extraordinary exercise, extravagant in yield. I was raking it in as shadows crossed the floor.

I inhaled deeply, threw my shoulders back, spread my lats and flexed my tris. Ever try that one? Looks dopey, but feels cool. Emboldened and undistracted, I pressed on, taking advantage of the calm and solitude.

In less than a rep and as suddenly as a torn rotator, a vein of unflawed certainties lay bare before me. Had I had hit the mother lode, the pot of gold at the end of the rainbow?

To demonstrate the veracity of the find, I blasted a superset of dumbbell incline curls and pulley pushdowns. The reality of the matter is this: Dumbbell incline curls define the biceps and contribute unselfishly to their density and shape.

There's more: Combining them with pushdowns etches a rugged grin on your face, unless you're a girl, whereupon it's a sassy smirk.

It doesn't stop there: Intense pushdowns add horse to horseshoe triceps, as they can be performed 100 different ways according to the practitioner's needs and desires and intentional positioning of the cable. Thus and therefore, they are multi-applicational and multi-engaging.

The practitioner (with a little imagination, this could be you) is in total charge of the action of the exercise. You're not on the other side of the handle or bar going through the motions. If you're going through the motions, you might as well go home or to the beach or wherever.

And no talking while in the middle of the set . . . this place look like a social club to you?

In charge means you control the effort, the groove and the pace, all of which take persistent practice, attention and time. Here's where most wide-eyed gymsters fail: They don't persist. They are persistless!

Flooded with knowledge and understanding and rediscovery, I topped my arm workout with a triset from heaven's storehouse. I imagined thunder broke the silence and a streak of lightning devoured the shadows. Wrist curls were followed by thumbs-up curls followed by machine dips—epic poetry in decided motion.

The combination of movements consumed the arms from the tips of the fingers to the shoulders they hung from. No new discovery, but the reminder was exhilarating. This trio wrapped up a powerful arm workout, and it wasn't as if the rest of my body was not vigorously stimulated.

A constant revisited: There was something throughout, above and beneath it all that would always be true—nothing like a silent, empty, shadowy gym to brighten the day . . . add clarity and sparkle to an ordinary, sunny, summery, Sunday afternoon.

Oops. The Jayster's standing at the backdoor jingling the gym keys like they were gongs. Closing time already? Time flies when the sun shines and the beach is mobbed.

28
Muscle Building Made Simple

It's UNTHINKABLE FOR ME to enter the iron-and-steel chamber without seizing any number of its assorted implements and flog myself till I howl. Then, typically clutching my throat with both hands, I stagger backwards into a wall and slide down to the floor in a battered heap before crawling out the back door. Very dramatic.

I mean, like, what are my options: pushy-pulley, patsy-platsey, sit on the leg extension while texting the girls or blast it? I hate decisions.

It's not punishment I seek, nor do I find pleasure in pain. Victory is my goal and I've noted the mean approach to the steel works best. In fact it's the only approach I know or have ever engaged. Enter chamber, bomb, burn and blast, exit chamber.

Clean and concise, simple and stunning. It works.

Over time, however, I discover this bullish Type A methodology has developed disadvantages: mainly swollen joints, body aches and fatigue; diminishing strength, muscle and appetite; loss of humor, friends and hair. I suspect my methodology needs re-tuning.

Here's the stinker: I have made adjustments throughout the years: exercises and exercise patterns, sets and reps, volume, duration and weight. These essentials have been finessed according to the highly accurate and scientifically sound principles of touch and guesswork, instinct and wonder developed in the iron research labs from the Dungeon off Muscle Beach to Minichello's Mid-City Gym off Times Square in Manhattan.

The only dynamic I cannot modify is the intensity factor. Kicking and screaming, I've fractioned the days in the gym, the hours of the workouts, the exercises performed and the weight on the bars. What remains is an anemic collection of sets and reps and a puny pile of metal. The least and the most I can do is shove the craven iron clump around the gym floor with all my might.

Thus, in my heart I know my input has not diminished. I'm doing no less today than I did fifty years ago: 100 percent, my very best, the maximum weight and the last rep with total intensity.

These thoughts in mind, I ask myself—the only mug who'll listen—why not alter this tactic as well?

Lighten the load, back off the last reps and move at a smoother and readier pace. Choose a weight for any given exercise that allows X reps maximum, but perform X reps minus two. Move on according to recovery, whether the same exercise or the second of a superset, and perform with similar intensity. This scheme enables more exercises, sets and reps in a shorter, less drastic period of time with less abuse to the joints and system.

I like the theory, as I sit here in my snug little nest in the woods. I think I'll dash to the gym and give the soft touch a try. I'll wear my smiley face as I skip to the front door and dance across the thick rubber mats to the dumbbell rack. No wraps, no ugly faces, no groans, no guts, no glory.

Here's a bold and inventive arrangement of exercises to engage the upper body:

> Do legs tomorrow, or walk home with a fifty-pound pack on your back. Take the short cut over the mountain, across the plains and up the five flights of stairs.
>
> Rope tucks and hanging leg raises (3 sets × 25, 3 sets × 12)
>
> Steep dumbbell incline press (4 sets × 6 reps)
> *superset with*
> Stiffarm pullover (4 × 8)
>
> Flat bench dumbbell press (4 sets × 6 reps)
> *superset with*
> Seated lat row (4 × 8)
>
> Standing barbell curl (4 sets × 6 reps)
> *superset with*
> Lying triceps extension (4 × 8)

Now this routine, awarded the Most Original at the Summer Bodybuilding Festival last year in Tuscan, Italy, can be comfortably accomplished in sixty minutes by any exercise enthusiast. However, if it is muscle and might you seek, say, of the variety one imagines when huge and ripped are suggested (seriously, what other variety is there?), then you must consider adjusting the training intensity upward.

Here's the stinker, again. There's no avoiding intensity. It's the only thing big muscles know.

"Where are my wraps?"

As the years go by and I mature and grow strong, gathering wisdom and insight and clarity, as I develop depth of character and expand my spiritual dimension, bittersweet humility steps forward and seizes its ultimate role as the shaper of my soul.

"What a dork."

Where once I was bound to childish wanderings and inconsequential deeds, I am now on the path of the timeless masters, the dust of their footsteps before me yet unsettled. I remember "huge and ripped" and "lean and shapely," trivial and absurd as if these conditions held importance. My face flushes as I recall the foolishness of my youthful pursuits; my heart aches with disappointment upon noting their meaninglessness. I sigh with frustration while summarizing their emptiness.

"What a sap."

What advantages do hugeness and rippedness of muscle offer eager seekers? What opportunities are missed in their quest? How does one stray so far from normality and rightness, and where were those whose duty it was to steer the lost aright? Ah, but only the fool looks back and regrets his behavior. We are who we are and we press on.

"You press on alone."

Here I sit and consider ways to make my next workout more memorable, more effective and more precise—discipline, perseverance, gratefulness. I'm especially buoyant after the first two or three sets when the engine is warm and the compass is set. For the next hour I'm flying solo, feeling the winds beneath my wings and reaching for the sky.

Huge and ripped are masters in disguise.

29
Gravity, Iron, Force, Time, Space (GIFTS)

Life bears the same grin on its deeply etched face. I see the expression as a smile, tentative and faint, but agreeable. Humankind, life's players, pad along like little kids, curious, playful, busy, productive and mischievous, all in hopes of finding a good thing—amusement, comfort, satisfaction, and perhaps a puddle of naughtiness or a loose thread of tomfoolery. Oh, boy!

The good stuff is so good and enduring it outweighs, overcomes and outshines the bad. A grin is the best life will offer us this day; a broad smile will surely come later. Today we must lift the iron and respect the steel and recognize our cause, our inalienable right to build muscle and might.

Only the strong smilers are worthy of its shine. The unworthy, the weak, eventually smirk or sneer or wear a mask with upturned lips. Personally, I go to the gym with a brown paper bag over my head.

No, duh, I don't bump into stuff. I poke two holes in the middle for the eyes.

Few things prevent me from going to the gym and having a satisfactory workout (an overturned tanker on the freeway containing hazardous waste, femoral bleeding, misplaced propeller). Let's face it, bomber, that's what it's all about. Iron! Gravity! Force!

Some folks think there's more to life, like, "What are we here for; what's it all mean?" By the time they come to zero conclusions, I have half my workout done, a good burn and a decent pump.

Huge and Ripped, that's my motto. Veins and Striations, that's my cry. Thick and Powerful, hear my plea. Sheik and Svelte . . . my heart's desire, I suppose, if I were a girl.

Weird there for a sec, thinking of what a girl might be thinking if I was one . . . gave me the shivers.

Lord, have mercy!

Tans are well under way; the guy in the tee shirt dropped twelve pounds, his girl in the shorts, fourteen. Gyms R Us parking lots are full at five PM, promising cleavage and abdominals by the end of the month. Warm breezes, long weekends, beaches, barbecues and beer. Things are looking up. I bet people watch less news during the summer, freeing their spirits, like long-tethered dirigibles to rise in the fresh air.

The goal of the smiley, wide-eyed gym member is no deep secret: to look good. Power is nice, but slice it, dice it or stand it on its head and the main aim of the game is the same: to look good! One might elaborate upon one's emphatic or faint gestures at a spa and health club, conveying messages of health, athleticism, inner strength and discipline, but the story is the same short story: to look good.

Maybe, when the sun's shadows shorten and the temperatures drop and fair-weather festivities fade, they'll notice health is wealth and discipline builds character—the oneness of lifting weights and the magic of hocus-pocus focus.

More power to them, but right now, looking good tops the charts.

Nothing's changed. It hasn't gotten better. The swelling of the swollen, having swelled swells on. The same folks who vowed and sought to look good a year ago are back for more . . . or less. A few are absent (having succeeded or surrendered) and more are present.

Alas, the crowd is growing bigger along with the individual.

Nothing's changed. It hasn't gotten easier. Losing bodyfat, building muscle and accentuating curves—looking good is not an easy gig. The way may be clear, but those with no will have no way.

No courage, nowhere. No discipline, nothing.

Nothing's changed. Take hold of the iron, set your mind to the steel, make the metal move and make good things happen. Muscle and might are born, strength and health come alive and the mind and spirits awaken.

While shadows are yet long and the sun pours down like molten gold, let us cast a pair of pure and precious bodyparts. Chest and back are my favorite grouping, unless we're to consider bis and tris, whereupon we just might agree those two are a handsome and accommodating couple.

Shoulders and arms, on the other hand, are a mean alliance devoted to long and deliberate torture. The truth comes out before the first reps, but the truth isn't enough. In charge of the brutal act, we, the frantic lifters, seek the essence of life; another dimension, a portal in time, a bold glimpse of the future.

We also seek bowling-ball deltoids, lightning bis 'n thunder tris. Call us crazy.

Here's one (don't ask me why, it just feels good): a powerhouse leg workout (squats, squats, squats) followed by a closet-size arm workout . . . just big enough to rack four or five pair of well-pressed close-grip benches with matching Olympic bar curls. Nothing sophisticated, basics only, moderate impression with subtle effects. Think casual and comfortable, pumps and burns only.

The last time I did a split routine—half in the AM, half in the PM—was the spring, summer and fall of 1970. The reason, as I recall, was the upcoming pro contests which involved duds like Zane, Katz, Columbu, Arnold (Schwarzenegger) and Tiger Woods, I think. Did I say duds? I meant dudes. Honest!

I was twenty-eight, going on twelve-to-life. That's what you get, if you get caught and don't have a good defense lawyer. I escaped shortly thereafter and fled LA to hide out in the vast, bewildering forests of Central California.

Funny, the things you remember without really trying. Funnier yet, the things you cannot forget with really trying.

Remember when the greatest sci-fi flick ever, *2001: A Space Odyssey*, lighted the silver screen in 1968? I stood in a crowded and excited line on glittering Hollywood Boulevard one summer evening to attend the opening of the unforgettable epic. What a trip!

The improbable 2001 came and went, though not without fracturing the world and its inhabitants. And, here we are today, a million years later, iron in hand.

We press on. We never let go. We never quit.

30

Summertime, Summertime, Sum Sum Summertime

WHO DOESN'T LOVE A VACATION? Head out the door, bags in hand and put everything behind you. No boss, no responsibilities, no chores, no alarm clock, no time clock; different faces, different places. Anything but the same-old, same-old—a bad vacation is better than no vacation at all.

Well, that's not exactly true. I remember sleeping at O'Hare Airport for two nights while union workers haggled, or sitting on the runway in San Francisco for eighteen hours (maybe it was eight) before disembarking a cancelled fight to London (engine repair), or the time I showed up in Australia for a month-long tour and my luggage didn't, ever.

And do not lose your passport in Germany, kids . . . a nightmare I never want to relive. The worst was a flat tire on the ole' Buick station wagon halfway through a dark tunnel in the rocky wilds of Utah.

Sometimes the best vacations are spent in your own backyard. Freedom to melt down with a root beer float amid the chaos-as-usual.

I'm smarter now. I don't leave the house except to go to the gym or the health food store. Truth is, I miss a workout, I go into convulsions. I eat junk food, I stop breathing. My social worker, brother, personal trainer, UPS guy and psychiatrist (separate persons) all agree I need help.

Some new-age lifters and lazy old duffers say a layoff will do me good. Now that's dull misconception. What part of "just do it, shut up and lift, no pain, no gain, one more rep and no wimps allowed" don't you understand?

Ten minutes into the wasteland of an iron-free vacation and I'm climbing the walls.

Notion: Summer vacations are pleasant pauses in our disciplined musclebuilding routines and we don't want to diminish their welcome by fretting over, say, the fear of getting fat and flabby, the guilt of slipping out of shape, or the shame of bearing the accompanying adverse side effects: stressed, irritable, nasty, pathetic, shattered and pouty. I hate pouty.

An occasional and well-planned training respite is good for all your bits, parts and pieces. An enthusiastic musclebuilder—half-crazed, iron-slinging, muscle-pounding, self-brutalizing weight lifter—is notorious for over-engaging mind and body.

What a relief it is to put the weights aside for a week and allow yourself to relax, to heal and to grow and to refresh the joy of lifting. A little time off is good for the joints and the point of view.

On the other hand, bomber with sturdy wings and turbo-control ailerons, you who are hell-bound and do not glide on the mild breezes of airhead layoffs, holidays need not be void of the uplifting disciplines and the benefits of condensed training schemes. Workouts can be on-the-spot fifteen-to-thirty-minute quasi-structured exercise injections or on-the-fly aerobic and freehand improvisations.

Here are a few thoughts to consider: Miniature workouts are better than no workouts at all. They kick butt. When under limited training conditions, smart eating—when, what, how much—is extra important. It'll save your butt. Accepting, believing and applying the aforementioned tips bring truth and effectiveness to the pair. They'll shape your butt.

That was deeper than it sounded, trust me. No, don't read it again.

The eating thing is easy: No junk, lots of water and wholesome food in sensible quantities throughout the day. It's unlikely you'll eat too much with no junk added to your menu. Sensible quantities, however, might cause the hunky to trip. "Sensible" is a word one can conveniently misshape, stretch, twist, distort and abuse. Do not eat too much of the good stuff or any of the bad. You'll be sorry, you'll feel guilty, you'll feel soft and sluggish and self-conscious, angry and defeated.

No casual grazing, no sudden stuffing, no jolly drinking. Discipline, responsibility, self-regard, honor, courage and strength—these are the qualities for which ironclad bombers are celebrated. We're battle ready. We're fighting fit. We win wars. We're bored and boring.

No more chit-chat! Your vacation is unfolding. Here's what you do: Everyone's asleep, the birds are stirring and you can hear an occasional car starting. The morning buzz is building in the air. Out of bed (quiet), start the coffee, swig some water, wash your face (quiet!), brush those teeth and get into comfortable gear. Stretch like a cat; knock out some sensible leg raises and enough situps and good mornings for warmth and momentum. Call it taxiing.

You are there, bomber; wings are catching air, landing gear is up and clear skies are ahead. You're embracing the day as you knock out some friendly and accommodating pushups (super exercise—flat out, feet up on a chair, wide-grip and close), chins from a broom across two chairs or from a rafter overhead (no way to beat this exercise performed by a dedicated blaster who knows how grip changes work different muscles) and dips between chairbacks that remind you of when you were a kid . . . not so long ago.

How many? As many sets and reps as you please, need or are able. Work and play and work, as the muscles flex and the heart finds its rhythm and the endorphins rise and your creative calorie burning lights a fire.

Be attentive: listen, feel, urge, seek; don't hurry, don't worry. Tris and bis, delts, back and pecs, we thank you for your generous participation.

Less-than-dazzling sample workout: 2 or 3 sets × max reps—eighty-percent effort—of three exercises using any body part or grip placement.

You bring the dazzle.

Tomorrow you sneak out of bed again and, after quietly washing, hydrating and stretching (What? Am I your mother?), jog a hill, run some stairs or do a bunch of sets of freehand squats for slow, thoughtful, prayerful reps. A few of these and you'll know why you're praying. God, help me!

Toe raises between sets and some hip mobility movements while leaning against a sturdy counter (I pretend the counter is my pickup truck that needs a jump-start . . . again). Push, harder, push, faster . . . thighs, calves, back, shoulders.

I hope this vacation never ends; I'm getting huge and ripped while my loving, long-suffering and sympathetic family enjoys the early morning quiet. Listen . . . I can hear them moving . . . quiet voices . . .

Hey, somebody want to help me push the truck? The sooner we get the thing started, the sooner we get on the road.

I love road trips.

Next time I'm bringing my exer-cables and TRX . . . Olympic set . . . kettlebells . . . platform.

Just kidding about the platform.

31

To Twitter or Not to Twitter—Tweet Tweet

I'M CONSIDERING TWITTERING. Some influential friends of mine (Joe the gardener, Buzz the pizza-delivery guy) say if you don't tweet, your voice is not heard. My fear is once you Twitter, there's no turning back. Thou must Twitter. Tweet or die.

Sounds like a bird thing, and not of the hawk and eagle variety, soaring and bold, but more like a canary with clipped wings perched in a cage.

Then there's Facebook: No face, no trace.

And texting . . . Give me a break. Now I should abbreviate, condense and tweak our alphabet and exclude the prolific use of adverbs and adjectives. No way, no say, Jose.

I miss my yellow legal pad and cup of well-sharpened pencils, Ticonderoga #2s. Sit, think, scribble, erase, scribble, doodle, gaze, sit.

Newsletters, like newspapers and Golden Age bodybuilders, are becoming obsolete. I'm applying for a job at the solar and wind factory down the street. I hear there are openings for dazzling blowhards like me . . . Better get in line.

I don't think so. The only thing I get in line for is an In 'n Out burger once in a while when we hit the great California highways to stretch our bones. Zoom.

What is it with me? It's Sunday, just after noon and the sun cannot empty itself fast enough on the gorgeous world outside these doors. It's warm and clear and there's a hopeful breeze in the air. "God's smiling down on us, Davie," my grandma used to say.

I'm seriously considering going to the gym to improvise a way to rig my lifting belt and a heavy-duty rubber power band to the squat rack to enable me to perform bent-over rows without overloading my testy lower lumbar region.

I can hear you saying, "Gee! Why didn't I think of that?"

So, while the surf crashes and Frisbees fly and beers are guzzled and girls meet boys and kids scream with laughter along the shores of the Pacific, I'll be causing a ruckus at the gym, clashing with steel boy-toys and raising real-boy noise.

Brats-r-us.

You'll note I'm developing my Twitteresque style and a repertoire of Twittercisms as we twatter.

Since the lami-wami (affectionate reference for laminectomy), I haven't been able to give barbell rows a go. I miss those suckers. Seated lat rows and one-arm rows do the trick, but where's the beefy bar? I also miss squats big time. Leg presses and Bodymaster squats work, but there's nothing like an Olympic bar across the back, especially with a Top Squat slapped on for control and comfort and shoulder safety.

Here's the plan, minus the exact engineering genius: I wrap a double strand of power-band around my lifting belt and, allowing a three-foot lead, attach it butt-high to the squat rack—a tether of sorts resembling a leash.

Next, buckle up for safety—click it, or ticket—and, standing upright with chest out and shoulders back (tris fully contracted and face grimacing), step forward until the tension on the power band lifting-belt contrivance feels right.

I woof once or twice, bend over and grasp the bar like I did in the good old days not that long ago, and proceed to test the action with ninety-five pounds (bar plus two 25s). Testing is a curious and entertaining practice to determine feet and body positioning, band tension and support, realistic muscle engagement, range of motion and exercise viability.

I tip, teeter and tilt when attempting barbell rows and it was quickly evident no practice was going to improve that groove. The stabilizing effect of the bands could be subtle and just enough to maintain the balance this ole bowwow needs. Might work with deadlifts, as well—no records, just exercise and health.

Life without deadlifts stinks.

What would my orthopedic surgeon, physiatrist and neurologist say? Just sayin.'

"Woof! Woof! You can do this! One more rep, Big Dawg! Woof!"

Unlikely.

Squatting presents a similar problem. Heave ho, whoops, he's going left, he's going down, no, he's going across the gym floor, sideways . . . I envision myself amid the squat rack tethered off in a web of power bands from all directions.

Life without squats sucks.

I've been putting off both these experiments for lack of energy and time and care. When I make it to the gym in one piece after scrambling down highways and bi-ways, I don't want to mess around with a possible—a trial, an attempt or a maybe. I want the most and the best for the buck, the sure thing, the real deal, without much more than a block under one end of a bench or an added length of chain to the cables. I don't have time to play, energy to spare, or the curiosity to satisfy, or wonder to please . . . except today.

Play, time, energy and wonder have collided like a big bang and now I'm going to create a new world within the silent space of the gym. I'm ready, I'm stoked, I'm hungry for the iron and itching for the steel. Stand back, I'm coming through and nothing's going to stop me.

Oh, no . . . It can't be . . . Not again, not today . . . It's a plane, it's a bird, it's a blue jay. He just flew through the open French doors and is fully loaded and highly agitated. This is a bi-annual occurrence and not a pretty one. The frightened and furious bird heads for the sky-high windows seventeen feet above and cannot be convinced there's another way out.

This unscheduled stopover requires immediate attention as emotions run high and feathers and poop are in the air and on the walls and windows. I'll use a long pole and a clothes basket hastily duct-taped to its end, gently attempting to snare the little sweetie tweety as I'm balanced on the back of the couch, before I clod off to get the hook n' ladder.

The scene continues—basket is now on my head, pole duct-taped to the wall, bird clinging to a rafter—for another screeching, feather-filled minute before I clamber up the ladder and rescue what's left of the guest. He's out the door and in another forest in less than two seconds. Bye-bye, tiny tweeter.

While the ladder's in place and the windows are smeared and I'm feeling loose as a goose, I have a brainstorm—let's clean the walls and polish the windows. I promptly and cheerfully undertake the back-breaking endeavor, and so much for a pliable Sunday of flexing and stretching at the house of iron.

Maybe tomorrow . . . I'll keep you posted . . . or not.

32

Where Do We Go From Here?

Ever get one of those wild days when you are so alive and bursting with energy you just don't know where to go or what to do? Think back.

Way back . . .

Well, Speedo, I'm having one of those days. Wife says I'm acting like a kid (she doesn't want to go for a ride in my weighted wheelbarrow), I'm being silly (quit rocking the porta-potty, now) and it's about time I grow up (get down from that flagpole). I could drop the top and take the Ferrari for a spin, or mount the Arabian and let him stretch his legs on the beach, or race the Jet Ski to Mavericks and hit a few monster waves . . . nice day for skydiving, chute's packed.

Boorring!! I need a serious outlet for this awesome and dynamic charge. I thirst for extreme exhilaration. I hunger to go where I've never gone before. I crave the cliff's edge, the mountain's peak, the sky's outer limit. I must experience life at its grandest moments.

I know what I'll do. I'll go to the gym and blast the iron, melt the steel and rip the reps. I might even (gasp) superset.

Stand back, step aside, or, as they boldly and urgently say in emergency rooms, CLEAR!

I'm outta here, taking the dirty four-wheel drive beast in case I need to climb over traffic, dividers and rails, roadside debris, fire hydrants and parked cars.

It's hot, very hot, and it's Sunday on the gold-lined coast of sunny, once-flourishing California. The gym will be empty and quiet, but for us, me and you, my imaginary friends, whooping and hollering and hoisting *metallicus objectus supremus*. I never party alone.

So, who wants to ride shotgun?

The rest of you can pile in the back—no standing, no hanging over the tailgate and no mooning the other cars. It's arm day with a brief exchange of legs and midsection.

I'll spot you, you spot me—we'll have fun. You go first. Put your weights back when you're done. Training gear only, no jeans or street shoes. No cell phones. Hands off the mirrors. Keep your voices down, no cussing. Don't clang the dumbbells, and don't drop them . . . settle them down after your set.

You wouldn't want to train with me, bombardiers. Trust me. I'm boorish, grim, sulky, negative and given to sudden outbursts of anger and the tossing of plates.

Train hard or go home, Bozo . . . squat or rot. Hey, I'm using that bench, and that's my bar. Scram!

Time for Disneyland, Looney Tunes and stability ball exercising, girls and boys. Give me the iron, but a man's gotta do what a man's gotta do, right?

When nobody was looking, I rolled out the giant purple exercise ball—the Swiss ball—and gave it a few whaps and a squeeze before alighting upon its gushy surface. Hmmm, same height as a bench, flexible and bouncy, too (duh!). This could be useful.

Secure in myself and my lifting prowess, I thought, gee, maybe this playful circular doohickey could be an assist to my . . . um . . . limited shoulder training and deltoid development. Seems those dumb 'bells don't go up with the ease they used to and the muscles don't engage as cheerily. Maybe it's something I ate, bad night's sleep, low-grade virus, allergies, moon risings, atmospheric pressure, overall mood of the nation, biological cycles, Satan.

Who knows, but the disturbance needs attention, and now. Being a now kind of guy, I'm thinking with the submissive surface of the ball beneath my back, there will be less stress on my scapulae, more muscle comfort and improved range of motion. Just what the doctor ordered. The rigid surface of the bench resists the scapulae's freedom of natural movement and significantly contributes to the shoulder damage proud bench pressers endure.

Don't you hate that?

There's another thing: Having come a long way in personal maturity—wisdom, values, understanding women—I no longer depend on how much I lift to determine or display my rugged yet humble strengths. (Get the hook!) It's the resistance I bear and how I manipulate that resistance that matters. The muscles of those whose years have accrued love to be warmed up, coaxed, urged and enticed into action.

Explosive motion is kid stuff, sudden max effort the way of the young and foolish. Real lifters lift the steel slowly but surely, with a hint of friendly persuasion. Here's where the flex of the big round bouncy purple people-eater comes into play. I choose a lighter weight from the rarely visited end of the dumbbell rack (yeah, right! Last time I wandered past the fifties, they were wearing bellbottoms), and heft it over my head as I assume a prone position on the properly inflated ball.

Whoosh . . . easy, big fella. Positioning takes practice and courage and three or four spotters till you get the hang of things. I, of course, practice alone in the dead of night and with a flashlight.

It's an image thing.

It gets better all the time. Once balance is understood, you can position yourself variably like a rag doll and engage the muscles as you please, need or are able. Lots of stabilizing muscle activity is required, lots of focus and, when you need it, just enough bounce—that hint of friendly persuasion—to affectionately force out another satisfying and productive rep.

These are the reps that count, the missing reps in those sets that were colorless, fell flat, had no tone, served little purpose, were a half-step along the way.

This is not cheating. This is finessing—hardcore finessing.

The rep I couldn't get on the strict and lifeless bench because the triceps stagnated, or the elbow yelped or the shoulder growled like a bear, I now complete with loving persistence and a bump from the flexible and giving stability ball, or, as we here at Draper Advanced Research call it, the Bubble Bomb.

33

Musclehead Kaleidoscope Mind

AHHH . . . LIFE IS GOOD.

When's the last time you sighed that sigh and said those words with peace and conviction? Gotcha there! Probably the best we can do is to recall the feeling we had after our last workout. Of course, not long after the shower, the temporary relief, a ray of sunshine faded and the storm returned—lightning and thunder.

But we're tough. We rock, we roll, we bomb and blast; we adapt and hardship becomes relative. I shudder to think where I'd be without those workouts.

Larry: "Yo! Did you look in the dumpster, beneath that heap of cardboard in the alley, under the 2nd Street overpass . . . ? He's an ornery fella when he doesn't get his fix. Check the ER or the county lockup."

Moe: "Found him! He's in the junkyard sprawled across a V-8 engine block doing presses with twisted truck axles in his greasy grasp. The nearness to iron evidently lightens the load and soothes the pain. And by the look on his face, it brings ecstasy and great satisfaction."

Curly: "Hey, can I work in? We can superset axle presses with bent-over driveshaft rows."

Something you might have noticed: I've suffered, among other things, from inter-transphasial discordance since my birth in 1942. Once I was a child and I thought like a child. I became an adult and I thought as a child. Now I'm beyond adulthood and I think like a child. Did I miss something, anything, along the way?

Gee, I hope not. I can't face a redux.

The very first thing I remember as a kid was waking up one morning at the crack of dawn with a dumbbell in my hand. You think that's weird? I was supersetting concentration curls with triceps extensions. Superior pump for a child!

"Tell them," said a tiny inner voice again and again. My mom wiped pablum from my face and the rest is history.

It's like this, kids: time and patience, experience and common sense, trial and error, daring and audacity . . . cleverness and foolishness, curiosity and discovery, energy and industry. These are the sources of the knowledge I present to happy wandering ironminded gypsies.

If I'd had to go school for it, I wouldn't have gotten it.

I'm not opposed to school and reading, 'ritin and 'rithmatic. Those enable me to count my sets and reps and regularly share with you using a keyboard, but I prefer action to analyzing, doing to didactics, working to wondering and rack rattling to rote researching.

Tips and hints from fellow muscle-makers and consistent observation also contribute to my frayed-backpack education.

Look, listen and learn; play, practice and perform; grab, grapple and grow and push, pull and press.

Moving more metal makes many muscles and much might.

I'm particularly aware of my sketchy knowledge of exercise-relativity and muscle mobility when stopping occasionally to read some of the principles informed and practiced instructors offer. Invariably, I realize, "Oh, that's how it's done," or, "That's why," or, "I never thought of that."

Silence falls; I hunch over my keyboard seething with envy and wrestling with my dummy-complex. Embarrassing! This is my backdrop as I proceed to concoct my next secret muscle- and strength-building blast for the *IronOnline* newsletter: Training in a closet wearing polyester with the lights out and the water dripping.

I've gotta come up with something more original, something deep, mysterious—prophetic, maybe. Time for me to re-create myself, re-invent the wheel or discover the truth.

The secret is there is a secret. The basics are a rip. Perseverance leads to destruction. Discipline is for losers.

I'm off to the gym to save myself from imploding. I don't care what I do; I'll figure it out when I get there. Getting there is the battle; it is also the triumph. The workout is the war; it is also the peace. Knowing when to fight is enlightenment; knowing how is discovery. Fighting is courage, performance and play; fighting is winning by not losing.

You've come this far, warriors, here's the bodybuilding revelation of the week—you might want to jot this down.

Curious thing: I never think of my workouts as wars or battles or fights. Those activities and actions concern drugs, crimes, gangs and terrorism. They are a struggle, that is certain, and a challenge of course, though I don't like the lattermost terminology because it is so contemporary intellectual—PC for relentless, brutal, blood-thirsty combat.

Yes, I know; I'm stalling. I have no revelation this week.

I go to the gym as always with everything I have—on my back, in my hand and on my mind and within my soul. And there I unload it.

I go from exercise to exercise in a sensible, quasi-spontaneous order according to an amenable plan. I perform the sets I need and must, and repetitions I should or can. I approach each movement with probing certainty and from it I squeeze all it has to offer. This might be a lot, a little or nothing. It will be hard; it's usually painful and might cause injury.

None of what I do is unintentional, though it may be impulsive or accidental. And not a single rep of it is done while talking or daydreaming. I might want to be done or be somewhere else, but I grip the weights and there am I. Distractions are filtered and discarded, few escaping the hefty built-in B-72 security system.

No enemy stands before me. My workouts are not battles, though often I face surrender; fights they are not, but wounds I occasionally incur. Wars, not they, but upon their completion, victory I claim.

"He who lifts weights regularly and eats right and is good to his neighbor is a noble, wise and sinewy companion."

Tarzan to Jane, *Tarzan and the Apes*, MGM Pictures, circa 1949.

34
Sights and Sounds Free of Charge

Three hours ago I glubbed an ordinary yet spectacular Bomber Blend concoction, grabbed my lucky gym bag and blasted off my remote launching pad toward the gym. In less than twenty minutes I was barging about benches and racks, setting up my gear for my first incredible series of multi-sets. Without pause I was immersed in an authentic muscle-building workout.

The sets were flying, exercises were strewn across the floor and a pump emerged beneath my sweaty t-shirt; within the depths of my muscles a searing burn smoldered.

There were no jesters, jokers or jerks. I was not hurting or busted, bored, fatigued or flustered. The exercise choices were mucho perfecto mundo, senior, as they say in the south of France.

Zip . . . "Huh?" . . . Zap . . . "What the . . . ?"

Free of charge—the building's electricity stopped, went off, shut down halfway through the workout, providing sweet silence and sufficient natural light from the glass entryways and skylights to distinguish a barbell from a broom, a dumbbell from a donut.

Swell . . . heaven and hell.

A few disappointing moans came from wheezing treadmillers in the cardio area as their whirring travels to nowhere hopelessly ended. That's life in the fast lane.

Don't you just love the iron? It is so absolutely independent. A hapless tree had fallen across a luckless electrical line in the innocent park across the quiet street, and the rockin' barbells and rollin' dumbbells did not skip a beat, a clink or a clank. The racks stood tall, the benches held their ground and the pulleys twirled on like the wheels of time.

We're good. Who needs electricity when the dynamics of iron and might are in our hands? Lifters of metal bars and steel plates are radiant; they provide their own energy and generate unique electricity. Lightning strikes in the field of steel; thunder can be heard in the distance if you listen.

It's a very different story, Skyrider, when light turns to dark and noise fades to silence and clarity slips to vague. Distance vanishes, boundaries contract, edges sharpen, distractions diminish, your focus sharpens, your heartbeat intensifies and you become you. The abrupt alteration, the sudden reduction of sights and sounds and sureness baffles the system.

Curiously, the short in the circuit is short-lived when you're in the middle of a meaningful workout. I noted an audible click of an internal switch and a perceptible zing in my central nervous system the instant light and sound vacated my senses. I was drawn to the weights—connected, magnetized—as if they were an extension of me.

I grabbed a pair of dumbbells and felt the rough knurl of the handles and the brazen heft of the iron. They were no longer thirty-five-pounders—black, circular behandled steel. They were tension and resistance within my muscles and bones, invisible and indefinable objects not separate from me.

I heard every sound without listening: the scruff of my grasping hands against the bars, the anxious scraping of plates released from the rack, the groan in my shoulders as they grappled the familiar load; heavy breathing, a swallow, a snort and the ruffling thrust of iron moving against fabric and air and struggling sinews. Steel benches squeak and creak, unsolicited comments when no other sounds can be heard.

To the composer, the sound of an orchestra in the pit tuning up before a great concert.

There are hoots and howls and growls and yowls and hisses and snarls and expletives accompanying the metal as it rises from down to up and down again. I knew it wasn't quiet but forgot how noisy the action of pressing a weight can be. Metal against metal is clamorous, but man against metal is cacophonous. There's a difference, you know. Who'd of thunk it until the electric went out?

Without electricity, an ironhead has extra time to think.

This is not the thinking of the sort that solves problems (the coefficient of 1,234 minus the square root of NYC), or answers perplexing questions (The Nobel Peace Prize? Why?), but the mind work beneath the skin, geared to scrutinize and investigate and assess and wonder.

Not a rep goes unnoticed when electricity stops dancing through the wires and flooding the mind with light, sight and sound. On the contrary, each rep assumes increased dimension, more curves and intersections, expanded coloration and contrasts and deeper nature and character. They, the actions, are no longer simply black and white, heavy and light.

And the unfolding elaboration doesn't make them confusing. It makes them fascinating and alive . . . exciting and spontaneous.

Of course, you've pondered similar experiences yourself, the primary motivation of your continued training engagement. Yup, for sure!

I also dig the shredded muscle mass and brute strength my bouts with the weights produce: small yet worthwhile fringe benefits, fun added attractions, mentionable exercise byproducts. These alone are great temptations to cart the stout metal contrivances from point A to point B, again and again.

Kid stuff—big guns, deeply carved pecs, Herculean shoulders—but admittedly alluring.

Did I hear someone say, "Hey, Instant Replay: You forgot to mention patience and perseverance, respect and responsibility. You don't want a bunch of bombers to leave here half-winged and partially propelled. They might miss their targets and flip their flaps and alienate their ailerons. And what about health and fitness, Son of Jersey?"

Yeah, yeah . . . always a bat in the belfry: May the wind beneath your wings, like whimsical electricity, vanish into the thin, still air.

Do this—you've got an hour. It won't build any muscle, unless you train hard and consistently and believe it will. With any luck, the generator will run out of fuel.

Midsection—core workout to include high hip bridges, leg raises off a bench or hanging leg raises (five to ten minutes). Cycle, jog or walk on off days (fifteen to twenty minutes).

Day 1. Chest, lats, shoulders, legs (tris, grip)

Bench press (2, 3 or 4 sets × 6 to 12 reps)

Straight-arm pullover (2, 3 or 4 sets × 8 to 12 reps)

45- or 60-degree dumbbell incline press (2, 3 or 4 sets × 6 to 12 reps)

Side-arm lateral raise (2, 3 or 4 sets × 6 to 10 reps)

Walking lunges with light dumbbells (2, 3 or 4 sets × 6 to 12 reps)

Day 2. Biceps, triceps, legs (grip, shoulders, back, chest)

Standing barbell curl (2, 3 or 4 sets × 6 to 10 reps)

Dumbbell alternate curl (2, 3 or 4 sets × 6 to 10 reps)

Dips (2, 3 or 4 sets × 6 to 12 reps)

Lying or overhead triceps extension (2, 3 or 4 sets × 8 to 12 reps)

Dumbbell squats and calf raises (2, 3 or 4 sets × 6 to 12 reps)

Day 3. Shoulders, back, legs (bis and tris and grip)

Front press (2, 3 or 4 sets × 6 to 12 reps)

Bent-over lateral raise (2, 3 or 4 sets × 6 to 12 reps)

Wide-grip chins (2, 3 or 4 sets × 6 to 12 reps)

One-arm dumbbell row (2, 3 or 4 sets × 6 to 12 reps)

Farmer walks, uphill if possible (2 sets × 25 yards)

One set is for beginners, two sets are for girls and old men, three are for guys and dolls, four sets for the serious and Chiquita Gorilla, and five sets are for maniacs, lost causes and nincompoops like you and me.

Every other day with two days off between the threesome is authentic and legal and presentable.

Smile and soar silently when you have the chance.

35
Pressing On

"How do you do it, DD?" my colleagues ask. "How do you continue to expand your operations in a bleak and hostile business climate?"

They're stunned. I understand.

It's a tough slog being the creative force and CEO of several major corporations—Draper Long Johns, Socks and Jocks Inc., Bombs Away Diaper Service and Dave 'R' Us Smarty Party Clowns, yet I remain closely connected with my people through eco-friendly email.

"But that's not all, gentlemen. That's not enough."

I close my solar-powered greenmails with the casual expression "press on" and often, taking my chances, I add "Godspeed." It's my genuine yet unobtrusive attempt to identify with and relate to my gracious recipients. "Press on" covers things. It is all we can do. Some days it's a shove, other days it's push and then there are the days we thrust, heave and toss . . . even pull.

Yeah, now you've got it. We press on, brothers and sisters, with muscle and might and good cheer.

We're a motley crew, yet working out is deeply rooted in our being. It's what we do so everything else we do, we do better . . . and feel better about it.

And there it begins.

The gym is much more than a place housing the tools of our training activities. It's an assembly line, a forge, a refuge, an emergency room and a ballroom; the place downtown or under our house where we build the body, mind and soul; where we play, we suffer and rejoice.

We press on.

The weight lifting tools, the bars, dumbbells and plates—the iron—are far beyond the heavy forms of resistance they present to our muscles. They are protagonists and antagonists that push and pull, and clumsy toys too big for children's hands. They are the source, the center, the heart of the grand challenge with which we struggle, and without which we fail.

And the subject of our training is not limited to baseball bis and horseshoe tris.

Seriously. Like, did we forget stealth-wing lats and cannon-ball delts? The weights and the weightroom present a library of universal teaching and development. Corners of the mind and levels of the soul are stimulated and strengthened. Skills, gifts and talents are revealed and released. And ugly is disposed of like mold, dust and webs.

The weights might not make you a doctor, carpenter, pilot or nurse, but they will make you a better one.

And no matter how basic and simple our training is, it's quite complex. Complex doesn't make it complicated, bombers, as long as we press on. Stop pressing on and we have complicated. Trust me; you don't want to go there. Pressing on might not save us, but it prevents us from falling into the pit. And the pit is a very bad place.

How to proceed from here, we wonder, on mornings when the sun is already setting in the west?

Follow the trail, blaze a new path or sit on a stump in the shade and muse. The stump thing works for a while, until the sun goes down or the dark clouds move in or you get ants in your pants. And following the trail is a fair choice, moving along swiftly and comfortably by the well-trodden lead of those before you.

We press on, water bottle in hand, until one day the trail narrows, grows thin and fades, or thickens and becomes a tangle. Where are we? Not the end, but not a clear passage for the lethargic and uninspired.

The rest of the way is left to the trailblazers. That's us, Dick and Jane, Bubba and Babs. Bombers are also trailblazers. You might note authentic bombers have been referred to as explorers, pioneers, inventors, brave souls, Vikings, chieftains, disciplined soldiers, cuddly heroines, shepherds, animal lovers, fairly smart, or at least, not dumb, poverty stricken and just plain cool.

I'm off to the gym in about two hours, enough time left to knock out a few words to faithful and robust sky-riders from here to the moon (the communication always provides energy and encouragement) and to gather my implements, attitude and plans for some rough trailblazing.

My subconscious is already conspiring with my conscious (an awesome duo) to pull off the deed.

Implements—basic fuel and gear—are habitual, simple and easy, but absolutely essential to a productive and uplifting blazing session. You know: protein shake, lifting belt, iPod, Blackberry, laptop, charts, Steve Reeves posters, Hercules ring with secret compartment, clips from *Rocky*, powdered methedrine (just joking about the meth).

Attitude is arguably of greater value, but it's far more elusive and less tangible. Standing amid a thick forest equipped with energy and tools and no will, rhyme or reason to press on will take you in tight, frustrating circles and lead you to a stump upon which you might nervously perch. This can give the weak among us the twitters and reduce us to tweets.

The plans unfold like pages of an unwritten novel, an exciting chapter long overdue. I sit silently and reduce myself to this, the moment of my existence. It's amazing how, when I control my being so totally that my heartbeat and breath and neuron impulse merge mysteriously like . . .

Oh, dog poop!

I spilled my stinkin' coffee all over my desk and keyboard and it splashed on the screen in frigging streaks. Major poop, man! It's not my fault. The coffee cup was in the wrong place.

Just get me to the gym and cut me loose. Lead me to the iron and stand back. Take me to the squat rack. You want a trail . . . I'll give you a trail . . . How about a highway from here to Tallahassee. Four lanes and a bridge?

Once you tap into a little adrenalin (engendered by emotion, fright, anger or emergency), the system comes alive with spontaneity and strength. The mind retreats and the instincts kick in like wild horses.

Expression is creative and immediate.

Step aside. Gotta keep moving, or as we say in the trade, press on.

36

Open Door, Enter Gym, Lift Hard, Exit Gym, Close Door

"Together we raise our hands to the sky and await the next dumbbell to drop. Heavy may it be, but not so heavy for us to retreat. Our backs may bend and our arms cry out, but our spirits shall greet the load with valor and daring. No thing is so great to defeat our center, our soul."

~ Dramatic prose expressed by Hercules to Yoli from his chariot in *Hercules Unchained*, Steve Reeves, circa 1956.

HERC'S MESSAGE: We are in this good fight together, warriors. Neither alone nor afraid, we stand united. As bombers fly in tight formation, we charioteers charge uniformly across the field. Watch my back, I'll watch yours.

I entered the gym this afternoon and the floor was empty. I was alone, all by myself, most singular and unaccompanied. Where was the "we" and the "us" as declared in the stirring aforementioned language? And who was this guy Hercules anyway?

Just another oaf with a horse, a woman and a cart . . . shave the beard, big fella, and work on yer calves!!

Warning, crew: I'm gonna blast my arms. Bim, bam, boom. When I said I was going to blast my arms forty years ago, half of Joe Gold's gym members scattered out the back door and the other half—Zabo, Zane, Katz, Columbu, Arnold—cowered behind the counter.

The cinderblock walls rocked, dumbbells rattled and barbells rolled. Thunder roared, lightning flashed. The workout was a heavy metal concert.

Just kidding . . . nothing bothered Zabo.

Nowadays, I say anything about blasting and some guy leaning on the squat rack yawns and the duffer staring at the corner scratches his butt.

One cannot blast arms without the inclusion of standing barbell curls, overhead triceps extensions and reasonable and authentic grunting. Proper grunting is important. If the grunting is false, exaggerated or otherwise concocted, biceps will not grow and triceps have been known to shrink. Excessive groaning of the fake variety is highly discouraged.

Furthermore, any and all moaning whatsoever is intolerable. No moaning. None! Growling, however, works under certain . . .

Sorry, went off on a small tangent. I do that a lot lately.

I've always trained arms directly once a week, biceps and triceps together. Hardly rated as blasting sessions (blasting today would cause rips and tears, crumbling and demolition), the workouts were tough, paced and focused. Risks—heavy tugging, quivering presses—are no longer welcomed or entertained, though merely entering the gym feels risky on some occasions.

I follow this pattern with the remaining muscle groups—once a week devoted to a direct bout, while the remaining workouts stimulate, more or less, the whole body's system of muscles.

This methodology—love that word, "methodology," sounds so intelligent—enables me to train the entire structure, sorta, like ("sorta, like" . . . not so intelligent) twice a week. Just right for a gritty man-child with well-earned shreds in his training gear.

Here's a thought: Once time has been invested and the muscle has been established and a few years have mounted with distinction, intense training isn't useful and can be counterproductive. The muscles refuse to grow larger, insertions are less flexible and more prone to injury, and recuperation slows.

Another thing, "intense" might not exactly be in a less-than-youthful trainee's personality and plans and schemes. Endurance wanes, madness fades, so they say, and incentives droop.

Sounds like scare tactics to me.

So, what did I do on that particular arm-blasting day, which did not qualify for true blasting, but was certainly sufficient for sound muscle work and not necessarily restricted to biceps and triceps?

Well, I'll tell ya. Pull up a bench.

No, no, no—not that bench. I'm using it.

I did four sets of standing and kneeling rope tucks for the core and other associated muscle parts. If you do rope tucks with pizzazz and finesse and creativity and gusto, you can walk away from the pulleys as a well-trained (blasted) tinhead. I'm just saying they're dynamite.

I proceeded to execute five sets of wrist curls with an Oly bar. The wrists have known a lot of curling, twisting and turning, and I treat them with care and respect. The reps are slow and thoughtful and momentum builds. Once part of a triple-set, I now reserve wrist curls for single-set training to avoid torqueing and overload.

Live, learn, accept, smile. *Never Let Go.*

Have you read that book? You should!

Drum roll . . . I then leaned a bench on a milk crate and did lying dumbbell curls for a long stretch and total biceps concentration. I chose this exercise because it's simple, effective and not exhausting. Conserve wisely thy energy, lads 'n lasses.

Four sets of six and eight reps were supersetted with pulley pushdowns, 12–15 reps. Neat, clean, deliberate, tasty . . . intense enough, though the wrapped right elbow growled conspicuously, as I grunted inconspicuously. We're a team.

What do you mean, "I don't have a milk crate"?

I love standing thumbs-up dumbbell curls, starting with devoted isolation and moving into bold thrusting, as the weight and reps and tiring and burning and pumping muscles demand. Great for forearms, bis, shoulders and back stuff.

Like popcorn and a movie, this hunky movement goes well with dips. Yeah, I know: What happened to the standing barbell curls and overhead triceps extensions? I'm saving those for my next arm workout, when I'm sure to have more energy and my elbows won't be sore. You see, that's the way the training goes these days, with changing tides, abilities, wants, needs and cans.

You pleasantly mix what you want to do with what you need to do with what you can do.

The workout was a blast, though I didn't blast it. Actually, bombers, I did blast it.

Just the charge was smaller. Ordinary dynamite, none of that C-4 stuff from TV.

The only thing greater than supple and vigorous youth is advancing age well-received, embraced and adored. I mean, like what's the option? You can run, but you can't hide. Come to think of it, you can't run.

When the time comes, I intend to age in full view of my youthful peers.

I say that now, but twenty to thirty years from now I'll be training in a closet.

37

Don't Just Stand There, Go to the Gym

I SIT BEFORE MY COMPUTER deliriously unloading thoughts and images racing through my mind with a force so great my head throbs and emits a low-grade heat. Not only is my brain on fire, but my fingers sizzle across the keyboard as they work furiously, almost desperately, to match my mental output.

The racket is deafening. I should be wearing earplugs and shin guards, but instead I'm in my sweaty wife-beater, boxers and socks.

Two fingers, the index of both the left and right hands, tap like tiny dancers with pants on fire. I'm knocking out about twenty words a minute, many of which are two syllables and are spelled correctly. Occasionally, an arthritic pinky gets in the way and deletes a whole paragraph of unparalleled, never-to-be-recalled stream of consciousness.

Brilliant, spontaneous thoughts inscribed across a gleaming screen, clarifying moments in time scrolling down a miraculous glass page, illuminating threads of gold laced on an unfathomable technological fabric, erased as if they never were . . . lost in time and space, dark and light, at the flick of a lagging appendage.

My behavior upon such daunting occasions is observed by no one. Hysterical, beaten, but not broken, I move on.

You have just witnessed a small slice of one harrowing day at the Draper Laboratory and Training Center in Central California.

There are times, believe it or not, when I don't have a whole lot to chat about, new, old or make believe, aka made up from a fake hint of memory. Balderdash, you scoff, the subject matter is limitless: bis, tris, supersets, the list goes on . . . Vitamin A, B, C, D, E . . .

And then, of course, the challengers among you point out that I haven't revealed all the secrets buried in the sands of Muscle Beach or the crumbling walls of The Dungeon or the racks and benches of Joe Gold's original Venice gym.

Many have I exposed, but not the last of them. The superior and wonderful secrets, those pertaining to long life and extended muscular achievement—those I've kept to myself.

Hey, it's my choice. I don't have to tell you everything.

Don't whine. Bodybuilders are like little kids. Fact is, the secret is there are no secrets. Stop brooding.

I loathe brooding, as I loathe leprosy, animal poachers and politicians, convulsions and hemorrhoids, wobbly dumbbells, bent barbells and plate-dragging pulleys. The negatives of life deplete existing muscle stores and prevent new muscle from developing.

Note: The first sign of negativity in my world and I go to the gym.

Commit to memory: The onslaught of pessimism—the woes, the foes, the lows, the nos and Joe Schmoes—are best fought off with rippin' barbells, rockin' dumbbells and rollin' pulleys.

Pulleys are particularly cool because they have a handle for absolutely every mood and occasion, and because they don't have the immediate look of "heavy," like a barbell or a dumbbell, especially if the weight stack is adjusted to match one's pipsqueak estimation.

It's not the weight one handles, it's the action and focus and attitude we apply. Well-oiled pulleys work best: no inefficient, distracting plate dragging.

Got the blues? Go to the gym. Girl left you? Go to the gym . . . unless that's why she left you—too much time at the gym with the iron lady.

Boyfriend left you? Go to the gym . . . unless you don't want to see him—because that's where he probably went . . .

Go anyway.

The gym, where the iron is stacked and the steel is piled and where it builds muscle and might. Yeah, sure it does. You can hoist and scrutinize for months and never be convinced. But that's what they say and you believe them.

In fact, every once in a while, lo and behold, you could swear you detect a bump or a vein or a snugness around the sleeves. And those barbells . . . they're not as heavy as they were just last month. Not often, but often enough, you have these vague, fleeting, yet, hopeful feelings.

That's all it takes . . . a hint.

You have a favorite mirror, too, the one above the forty-five-pound dumbbells and especially in the afternoon light. "Not bad, Dude. Check out the tris when I throw the rascals a subtle flex. The front-on shot is best with a little twist in the hips and the right leg forward. Gotta be cool so you don't look like a dip ship checking out your reflection. Embarrassing. Keep it to a quick glance as you pretend to adjust the plates on the bar."

Careful how you walk. Don't swagger, spread your lats and all that kid stuff. You don't want to appear stiff, stuffed, self-centered and silly.

However, never, ever casually saunter past a length of mirror, relax your gut and check out your reflection at the same time. Ill-timed glances can be devastating, the image indelible and the damage long-lasting. Be alert always.

I've spent a lot of time in a gym. Not all that time was I physically in a gym, but in the gym within my mind. I have created, over the years, a huge training area in what feels like the Central Cortex of my brain. Bars and plates everywhere, beastly platforms, hefty benches, dark corners, well-lit floors, lots of air and a couple of friends.

When in doubt, when I need stimulation, when joy and laughter are limp and need refreshment, if ever a pump is deflated or a burn grown cold, I enter the mental hall and grasp a bar loaded with memories from a rack full of recollections and play. Or I lie down on a bench, stare at the ceiling and count the sets and the reps of the days gone by.

Gadzooks, Peabody, it's two PM and I've missed my Sunday training time slot. Too much frivolous poking at the keyboard and not enough time in preparation for my workout. Oh, no! Ah, geez! Oh, crap!

Guilt, doubt, failure, defeat, misery—woe is me, a victim of my own irresponsibility and carelessness. I have only one recourse: Go to the gym and toss myself at the mercy of the iron.

Never say never, unless you say, "Never Quit!"

38

A Toll-Free Bridge,
Workout to Workout

It's Monday, the sun's hiding behind a thick cloud cover, the wind is still and the hillsides are silent. No chainsaw, no barking dog, no bird calls, no stirring neighbors. I feel fine, not nursing any wounds or gasping for relief. It's a good day to count blessings, thank God and pray for more (because I'm greedy).

I have no plans to go anywhere, which suits me just fine. What to do, what to do? The choices are divine: eat, take a stroll, stretch, work the foam roller, practice my bird calls, compute, couch, TiVo, to bed early, arise early and do it all again.

Scary. I'm tempted to remove the above sally of listless notions so they don't enter my mental pores via osmosis of the subconscious mind. Furthermore, I believe it's a sin for spiritual folks and atheists and androids to reflect on such notions, with the exception of, maybe, Islamic terrorists. I'll check with the Administration and get back to you on that one.

Tomorrow, Tuesday, in the middle of the day, I go to the gym to rough house and cause trouble. Rumbling pickup, speeding traffic, changing lanes like cards in high-stakes poker: pulleys, plates, benches, dumbbells and bars—clank, clank, thud, hiss, moan, groan.

The elbow sounds like a chainsaw, the shoulder barks like a dog and the back calls out with the cry of a night bird. The gym is alive with the sound of music.

The lifter who foregoes workouts is a loser. Workouts comprise any combination of deliberate thrusts with iron-bound barbells, dumbbells, cable handles and machines. A major portion of one's might and energy must be applied with maximum focus and imagination when engaging the various thrusts.

That might and energy might be limited by injury or age or any such ghastly intrusions is to be courageously accepted and wisely accounted for. Desiring to go beyond limitations is natural to a disciplined and determined ironhead, but it can be unhealthy.

Danger ahead. Proceed with caution.

Note: A person is not a natural and authentic ironhead if that person is not disciplined and determined. This person is only a lightweight, a wannabe.

Sorry. Get a life. Join the circus. Get a job. Get a loan.

I say these things because (I may have mentioned this before) I'm not as strong as I used to be. At first I thought it was something I ate. Then I blamed my depression on the 9/11 attacks. Then I was certain it was the 2008 election and Chicago (silly late-night TV joke). Now I think it's wear and tear and the mounting years.

Who'd a thunk it? Live and learn.

When my dad was sixty-seven years old, he had another twenty-five good years ahead of him. That's like a lifetime. By the time

I was twenty-five years old, I was the dad of a six-year-old cutie, was Mr. America and Mr. Universe and Harry somebody in *Don't Make Waves*, and was by then an old friend of Zabo. Just think of the pump and burn I can get in the next twenty-five.

It all depends on the last workout and continues with the next. I can't wait until tomorrow to carry on the journey. In the meantime, I sit at my computer and tell you about my last workout as if you might be interested.

It started like all the rest: enter the gym, review the surroundings, untangle and retrieve my wraps from the stinky little gym bag, then head to the pulleys for a round of rope tucks. One of the best sets of the workout, excluding the last set, is that first set of rope tucks.

It reminds me of an animal when stretching after a lovely nap: The paws reach out in their turn, the body gets low and elongates like a loose coil and he shakes briefly and uncontrollably, starting at the nose and ending at the tail . . . or, maybe it's the other way around. The creature then sits up, licks his chops and looks around in total innocence and refreshment—almost a smile. I'm convinced this is an animal's survival instinct, an inborn technique to extend its health and well-being.

Those first reps of the first set are determining: Their sensitive execution determine our abilities and desires, aches and pains and strength and weakness. The manner—the attention and appreciation and excitement—with which we perform the reps and set indicate our training determination; the success of the reps and set performed determines the success of the subsequent sets, and the entire workout.

I let the first set take me where I'm going, knowing the closer I get to it, the more I embrace it and surrender to it, the more I will enjoy it, respond to it and learn and grow from it.

Gee, you'd think it was the stairway to heaven.

Now the second set is where and when it all takes place. Readiness observed, it's with the second set that the hormones are reminded they have an important part in the process and need to be ready for the third set, the hot set that overloads the involved tissues and prepares the muscular system for—you know what I'm going to say—magnificent hypertrophy.

Momentum builds with the completion of the third set, readying the mind and body for the synchronicity of the fourth set, which global-warming scientists assure us furthers the capacity for dynamic muscular development, including thick veins and deep cuts. The fifth and sixth set, no matter what exercises they might be, jar the reluctant muscular system into powerful forward motion.

Ka-thunk!

Hold on tight. Drink water, rest adequately between sets, yet focus tightly on the course ahead. Not that you would stray or relax your intensity, but the internal electrical structure dare not be compromised when it is at a heightened state. It's a law of physics and it's out of our control. Be strong and courageous.

Zoom, zoom, zoom.

The exercises fall into place as if we knew what they were beforehand, but this is an illusion. This is only experienced by 3-D ironheads of the disciplined, determined and dynamic nature and by anyone fifty to 100 years old.

The remaining sets seem like a dream until you wake up on Thursday morning, stretch, drink your protein shake and read the *IronOnline* newsletter. Then you know they were real.

I have no idea what I'm talking about. I think I have a fever. Maybe it was something I ate . . . a long time ago.

Miss your bus and you arrive late.

Miss your workout and your day collapses, the world ends, your shorts start on fire, withdrawals begin . . . and then the hallucinations.

You don't want to go there, bombers. Trust me.

All aboard . . . Next stop, Paradise.

39

Pushing and Pulling in Concert

THIS IS A GOOD DAY, in case you hadn't noticed. Soon it will be spring, a time to leap into the air and throw our hands skyward as we shout with delirious delight. Our bodies automatically shift into the muscle-growth cycle, which is accompanied by the fat-loss period, the energy-expansion phase and the power-enhancement rotation.

Of course, to take advantage of this natural succession of multiple dynamics, all we need to do is blast it, eat right and embrace life with overflowing enthusiasm.

I'm ready. Are you?

Cynics!

I just returned from the gym after a very fine workout. I used to call them "great" or "ferocious" workouts; now "very fine" is just right and will do nicely. See what happens to exclamations of glee and excitement after you hang a quick turn at a certain remote corner, the corner with the lamppost flickering at night, the same lamppost you tell all your secrets to? You settle for words like "fine" and "nicely."

"Fine" and "nicely"—along with their equally expressive counterparts, "good" and "swell"—translate muscle-wise into "somewhat spontaneous," "well-executed," "balanced and orderly," "effortful" and "productive" and "gratifying" . . . and "humbling."

On second thought, iron rockers, "great" still applies.

Not to be redundant or to bore you—far be it from me, your bim bam boom bomber, to be redundant or boring—but I suspect you're wondering, *What exactly did this very fine workout consist of?* Good. Wonder is a very fine feature.

There's that very fine thing again.

Plodding along, it's not what exercises we select—the basics for sure—but how they're treated . . . with enormous respect and total attention, smartly placed and precisely paced, affectionately persuaded, yet aggressively executed. An exercise and its practice is not a thing to be scheduled and done, an action after which you move on.

It is to be greeted, experienced, encouraged and developed, alive and lived and applauded.

Yeah, I know. What happened to storm the gym, slap the dumbbells silly, pounce on the squat rack, bend the barbells and toss the forty-five-pound plates like Frisbees? Well, once I was a child and did childish things, now I am an adult and do very fine things . . . and anything else I dare or am able to do.

Sure miss being a kid.

Not having been in the gym for a week due to a cold the size of Texas, anything I did would be monumental. My fat and skinny body was eager to sniff around the dumbbell rack, like a mutt cruising hydrants and park benches anytime, anywhere.

Self-assurance sure takes a hit when the weights are absent from eating, sleeping, living and breathing.

I'd rather be naked in Grand Central Station.

It wasn't long before I found a pair of familiar pint-sized rascals and tossed them overhead as I plopped onto a comfy forty-five-degree incline bench. Warm up with high reps, seek the perfect groove and go for broke . . . without breaking or compromising or being childish. I am an adult.

If you can tolerate a layoff, it sure feels good to knock out the very first set upon your return. Four more sets with precise direction and form, gradually increasing weight and decreasing reps added one hefty pound of pure gold to my revenue of confidence.

Pushing dumbbells from an incline adds character and voice to the shoulders, pecs and triceps. If I'm in a rush, three sets would be enough (bronze), four would be just right (silver), but I wasn't in a rush. Five, thank you (gold).

Rushing a workout is for children.

Time to pull, where the seated lat row is meant for pulling and building and making a weak person strong and able, sweeping and tingly from head to toe. I dare say it is great and very fine.

But it all depends upon how it is done. Full range of motion, vibrant extension and contraction, accurate and controlled thrust, measured release and meticulous yet growling reps between six and twelve. The reps come down as the weight goes up and the spirits climb.

I did five sets.

Since I wasn't supersetting, between sets I leaned against a racked barbell and pushed heartily, as if I was at the rear end of a stalled pickup truck in a nasty neighborhood and I was desperate to get the darn thing started. The sun was going down fast. Great for the legs and the core and for staying busy.

Casting creativity aside and focusing on what needed to be done and what I wanted to do, I did five sets of flys on a fifteen-degree incline. Done correctly, the pecs and serratus and bis and associated muscles scream like fans at a rock concert. Done wrong and the insertions squeal like pigs in danger of being roasted.

Note: Done correctly means you don't just grab the dumbbells and flail around on the bench like a crab. You direct the pectorals muscles to move the iron by upper-level focus, concentration and feel.

Fifteen sets, each a minor production, plus a half-dozen frightening pickup-truck jump starts, and I was closing in on my enough-is-enough, red zone for dysfunctional, ever-rehabbing, post-Texas-size-cold-suffering adult children.

A symphonic superset was in order, a small reward for swell behavior.

At the gym there was a 1990 custom-made Excalibur piece, a handsome charcoal black pulley device for working the pecs if we sit facing machine-outward, or the rear delts and upper back if facing forward. Got that? I face forward and bomb—yes, bomb—the back good.

From there I slip over to the dipping unit and I dip . . . I dip good. Lean forward, lean back, arch or hunch the back, think tris or pecs or back or shoulders. Ride 'em cowboy . . . four supersets of ten to fifteen reps. We're making sweet music, pulling and pushing in concert.

Some of you are saying, "That's it!"

That's what I used to say, when I was a kid.

40

Be Here Now, Then and Always

A THIRD OF THE YEAR has moseyed (dashed) across the skies, trudged (darted) a winding path about the deserts and prairies, pushed (zipped) through the forest and underbrush and stolen (ripped) its way amid grim city alleys and towering buildings.

You were there, I was there, and here we are now. Time plods (races) on.

I'm not at its rear with a whip in hand, a yelp in my mouth and a spring in my step to hurry time along. I'd stand before the unstoppable force if I had to, if it would do any good, but it won't. As this is the case, I, to save face, accept my due space and agreeably join the race at its immutable pace.

I'm an ace. The stress and energy I save is timeless.

You thought I misspelled "ace," didn't you, inserting a C and an E where a pair of Ss belong?

I remember thirty years ago when my partners and I completed our first World Gym, paint still drying on the walls and a pile of mats yet to be positioned, and we decided to grab a workout while waiting for the first wave of enthusiastic cash members to mob the place. A pair of hefty dumbbells in her hands, Laree perched on the bench I was planning to use. I don't think so! I blurted emphatically, articulately and songfully, "No, no, no, no. I'm using that . . . I'm supersetting."

The attitude was palpable: "Scram, girl" was in my tone.

Laree had been on her own since she was fifteen; spent four years in the Air Force, during which time she monitored suspicious military aircraft, was a powerlifter and was hired by firms across the country to detect fraud long before she met Mister New Jerseypants.

"Oh, yeah. I'll show you no, no, no, no," she said, and pulled out a Glock, Smith and Wesson intercontinental ballistic missile and mowed me down right where I stood. Well, not exactly, but it was in her tone. I'll never forget it.

Lessons: Be nice to your wife; there are things a man cannot live down; there are things a woman will not forget; rage has no bounds; and humility follows a fool's folly.

It's like I always say, team: We live, we lift, we suffer, we rejoice, we learn, we grow.

Time to lift.

I would no longer share a workout with someone as I would share my Lamborghini or my Legos. Over the years I've become selfish with my toys and playtime. I like to do what I want to do, when I want to do it and I need to be first, last and always.

Of course, with those parameters I don't have a lot of bombers lining up to be training partners anyway.

Nevertheless, I manage alone and highly endorse it. It's just me, the lone rider, the free spirit, the top dog—pilot, copilot and bombardier. I mess up, nobody knows.

Fact is, there is no messing up when chucking the weights unless you injure yourself, and even injuries prove to be valuable. Mistakes teach, and a good lifter depends on them. These are the true personal trainers.

I must admit I had the best training partners back in the day, the day being those days I spent in The Dungeon, '63 through '66. All the other days were just days.

One at a time, line 'em up, something like a year with each: Dick Sweet, Fritz Sills and Rick Josephson. We put away press behind necks and side-arm lateral raises like they were gumdrops. I still do, only they're jawbreakers and seem to act similarly on the shoulders.

I miss those guys. Fritz left us young and early, Dick vanished into the shadows of LA, and Rick, after timeless solitude in a cave in Maui, is a monk who reconnected with me recently to say hi.

My training with Frank and Arnold and the Joe Gold originals was touch 'n go, our nearby, alongside presence enough to power us on, inspire, teach and encourage. That's all it takes when energy and vibrations are strong and contagious.

I'm back there as I write and my mind is looking around. I see all there is to see, barbells and Olympic bars and sturdy dumbbells from five to 150 and Joe Gold's handmade pulley systems and benches and racks.

If a body could be built into something magnificent, it could be built there. Determination and guts were at the door, blood, sweat and tears distributed abundantly across the gym floor.

No, we never cried, but we did work till we bled. Gee, that was more than fifty years ago, when gas was thirty-two cents a gallon.

Another thing I notice as I mentally roam about Joe's hunky equipment and the colossal, ill-fitted wooden constructs of the Muscle Beach Dungeon: The workouts that worked then are the ones that work now. Reassuring. Nothing's changed—the same routines, sets and reps, movements and schemes, exertion and attention, only the weights have changed to protect the innocent.

Fritz and I did seated lat rows and wide-grip pulldowns with frayed, twisted cables across oversized pulleys bolted to the ceiling. Fritz was the closest thing to Steve Reeves other than Steve Reeves, down to the square pecs and diamond-shaped calves and tall good looks.

Sweet and I managed steep-incline dumbbell presses with 125-pounders for commendable reps. The guy reminded me of a panther on the prowl and introduced me to wide-grip chins, authentic focus and supersets with rhythm and song and dance.

Rick was a skinny teenager; I saw him grow two inches taller and gain forty pounds in the year we blasted it from six to eight every morning. Last seen, 6' 4" and 230.

My partners and I did things like standing barbell curls, lying triceps extensions, bent-over barbell rows, front presses and squats and deadlifts. We focused, we spoke just enough, we encouraged one another from the soul, we exerted with all our might, we had ferocious fun and we never quit.

I wish I had a training partner.

The Lamborghini is jet black and made in Taiwan of cheap molded pig iron. The doors actually open and there's a teensy scale engine under the hood. It's sooo cool.

41

The Home Is Where the Iron Is

THE GYM I TRAIN AT is a muscle builder's dream gym, just right in every way. The only drawback is it's down the hill, up the coast, through three towns, around the fishhook, across a dozen intersections and into the industrial district.

Spare me, Hercules!

This gym rat nibbling at the keyboard is considering the pros and cons of training at home: convenience and certainty are the most attractive features—limited equipment and space, the least. Attitude and spirit while training alone, and the sameness of the day-to-day fight are additional wonders and concerns.

After all the years at neighborhood gyms, though carefully choosing isolated hours, I might need the presence of someone, anyone, during my solitary iron exertions—a shifting silhouette in the periphery, an occasional clank, a grunt, a nod.

Hello . . . anybody there?

Perhaps the moments of intense effort will become so alone, the fight will become wholly and utterly mine, undiluted and unadulterated by the presence of a random figure across the gym floor. The silence will be more penetrating, the isolation more complete, the sensations more acute.

Desirable, manageable or impossible? A little familiarity, a few rounds of practice, a fair measure of compromise, a flash of imagination and I bet I can develop the training steel and fervor to carry me forward.

Questions: What equipment do I need in my limited space (we're talking bench and dumbbells), where is this limited space located, what do my workouts look like (a wet goat) and will they be satisfactory (is half-empty considered satisfactory)?

Gee, no pulleys. This is tragic, catastrophic, a calamity of epic proportions, as they say on CNN; no rope tucks, pulldowns, seated lat rows, cable crossovers, tri-extensions; no joy, no fun, no rhythm, no rhyme. No good. Can I survive dangling by the end of a TRX, though it's not wrapped tightly around my neck? See how my thinking has deteriorated? No cables? Shoot me! I refuse to eat.

Breaking News: Bomber on a Bummer

Dumbbell exercises to choose from:

- Biceps—curls, seated, standing, alternate, together, various inclines, preacher

No problems in the golf-ball biceps department. There are more movements than a bomber can shake his booty at, which is an exceptional thing this day and age.

And I don't need a bar, thanks . . . haven't had a drink in decades.

- Triceps—overhead extensions, lying extensions, kick-backs, dips

Those old, threadbare horseshoes will get all the action they can handle and from plenty of angles. I notice the tris thin out as time collects dust, the elbows thicken and they both squeal like pigs when provoked. Dare I pursue strength, health and function before certain pain and unlikely mass? Sanity over insanity? This would be novel: timely, fashionable . . . quaint.

I miss those pulleys already.

- Shoulders—standing, seated, incline and flat presses, clean and press, lateral raises, dips

There's nothing missing here to stimulate, propel or preserve the cannonball delts, unless I ponder the larger-than-a-breadbox Smith Press. The bar, guided or free, is a powerful tool, but as necessary as a pile-driver for granny in the old folks home. Seriously—in my yet-to-be considered, written or published book of *Draper's Fact and Fiction*—I put forth the notion that dumb-bells exceed barbells in all conceivable ways: natural shoulder action, safety of performance, freedom from injury, total muscle and strength development and the joy of motion and, last but not least, plain cuddliness.

Besides, the time and effort wasted in loading and unloading bars can be invested in dumbbell nuance and finesse, snuggling and stroking.

- Chest—flat and incline presses and flys, dips, pushups

I miss bench presses like I miss boating off the coast of Somalia or backpacking in Yemen. Though provocative, they're not absolutely necessary, healthy, safe or productive. The heck with them, I say. Pass the short, stubby utensils and let me rrrrip [rave, rage, rock and roll in peace].

- Back and lats—rows, deadlifts, pullovers, pullups

Problems of the barn-door-width variety! A simple overhead chinning bar is the best I can do, which would be handy if I could chin. Alas, a threadbare biceps from the bygone, happy days prevents me from risking the movement, a sure tear should I hang 'n tug repetitively.

Lying stiff-bodied on the floor beneath a low horizontal bar and performing a focused chest-to-bar movement will serve me well, along with one- and two-handed row and deadlift variations. Improvise, retool, re-create. Obvious limitations and no record-setting, but the way is clear. Never look back, never let go.

- Legs—DB squats, sissy squats, lunges, hills, stairs

No more full squats, blessing or curse? I'm way ahead of my time in this frolicsome escapade, my ticker and get-alongs having been cleverly modified to foster growth in my character department.

Now you know from whence my courage and honor cometh— stoic suffering and humble self-sacrifice. Did I mention charm? Vim? Swagger?

I assume the muscles, having sought and endured hard and heavy workloads and having developed muscle mass to accommodate those loads, have also reserved enough pluck and memory for the hefty burdens ahead.

Prod before launching rockets. I shall replicate any leg motion I can with zeal and bearable distress, sending seriously affectionate signals to those muscles gone drowsy. Wakey-wakey, Mister Legs. Rise and shine, thigh-guys.

Squats can be cruel, according to my swollen, stiff and achy back, butt and knees.

- Core and midsection—hanging leg raise, incline leg raise, good-mornings . . .

There are enough freehand exercises to do the trick. Let's face it, Bud, six-packs are for kids. I shall miss the rope tucks and the variety of motions and muscle-recruitments I can accomplish. But I'm a mature person, an adult, a grownup, a responsible dude . . .

I'll hang a pulley and cable from the four by eight support beams in front of the TV in the living room . . . also a good place for my bench and assortment of dumbbells. Next to the pulleys there's a perfect place for the chinning bar . . . hmm . . . a small platform in front of the fireplace . . . move the stereo equipment aside and bolt the dipping bars to the studs behind the sheet rock . . . take down the portrait of Obama, Pelosi & Reid and replace it with my favorite mirror, the one that makes me look huge and menacing . . . I can squeeze the squat rack next to . . .

Hey, is this couch absolutely necessary?

42

360 Days to Get the Year Right

I REMEMBER A RECENT WORKOUT, a seventy-five-minute knockdown, drag-out affair. Upon its completion I staggered to my car not knowing if I had won or lost. No sooner did I regain my breath when someone rapped on the window and demanded I get out of their vehicle or they'd call the police. Startled, angered and ultimately embarrassed, I escaped through the trunk, concluding I had lost.

This was not the training moderation I promised in my annual resolution. I had chosen three well-proven axioms, cleverly strung them together and added my name for emphasis, thus devising a surefire New Year pledge: Slow down, take it easy 'n steady as she goes, Draper.

Subtle, yet spunky.

I advise myself regularly, expecting I'll learn something as I continue my journey, but seldom do I heed my own instruction.

I insist upon accompanying myself to the gym with a big stick, a cow prod or a Taser. It gets worse: I'm so impressed by the presence of those implements of persuasion, I've not once been required to wield them against myself.

I cannot resist pausing to evaluate the psychology of this accommodating response: Is this cowardice or submission, intelligence or discipline? I suspect it's some admirable adaptation of courage and strength, wisdom and inner spirituality.

Whatever . . . the point is this: Excessive demand, workload and expectation are distressing and counterproductive. Should I continue engaging maximum force, the day will come when confronting the weights will be absolutely objectionable and detrimental.

Consider the following scenario of a hyper-workoutism: You're racing to the House of Iron on Laverne Avenue for a typical onslaught and you cannot face it anymore, so you pull a U-turn at Slocum Boulevard and your gym bag flies out the window hitting an elderly man in a electric wheelchair, knocking him into the path of an oncoming van (which, incidentally, he miraculously survives without a scratch) that was smuggling strangers, guns and drugs from the border town of Chappahapez, where stupid terrorists wrapped in blankets are discovered hiding in a camel shed behind the Marry-Us-Now-Por-Favor Chapel. Just when things couldn't get worse, Eric Holder arrives with Janet Reno to determine the authenticity of the marriage certificates obtained from the Department of Justice, and Animal Rights . . .

You see where I'm going with this? Slow down. Take it easy. Steady as she goes. What's the rush?

I received three suggestions from curious, desperate and ever-searching diehards about some classic training MOs for the aged, injured or otherwise impeded: the 100-rep system, the fifteen-exercise peripheral heart action (PHA) and the slow-rep methodology.

The light-weight, super-high-rep system (one set of 100 reps of one exercise per body part) I equate to pinching the muscles with tweezers until you're burning with pain and your mind is numb. Does it work? Who has the patience, the discipline, the continuity to find out?

And with computers and calculators and widgets these days, does, can or will anyone count that high?

It sounds like self-imposed iron-boarding, and none of us have secrets so important to hide. I'll pass. Let's raise the weight, lower the reps and increase the sets to two or three or four. Maybe five. Reality training for all ages, breeds and sects.

Multiple-set training is fun and effective (they call me Kid Superset, or at least they used to . . . I think), but having fifteen exercises at one's disposal is a bit of a reach. This extended methodology was researched by notable champs for about ten minutes during the '70s when bell bottoms were the craze. I'm good for five complementary exercises in a row for four sequences of medium reps, and let's revisit the plan from time to time for the pleasure and value of it.

Give it a whirl. Repeat after me: Slow down. Take it easy. Steady as she goes. What's the rush?

We're working on it.

I'm an advocate of focused, creative, groove-meticulous repetitions ranging from six to twelve and fifteen. Four sets have become standard issue, sometimes five when I feel zippy, and a total of six movements will wrap it up. Gee, sounds like a confession . . .

But slow reps of the two-to-three-count contraction and two-to-three-count extension are more than I can bear. This measured tempo might enable hurting lifters to proceed with caution, but as a preferred muscle-building method, it is to me intolerable. Safety first, hypertrophy tomorrow or next week.

One, one-thousand. Pumping! Two, one-thousand. Burning! Three, one-thousand. Scream! Brief, miserable pause and down. Barf! One, one-thousand. Pass me the rifle. Two, one-thousand. The shells, please. Three, one-thousand.

I jest, sorta. The gentleman who kindly recommended the slow-rep methodology is not alone and hoped I'd relate the advantages of the style to his fellow bombers. I'm sure it's beneficial. Try it . . . or not.

I think it's a personality thing, like driving on the freeway; I've got to be in the fast lane, even if I'm in no rush, even if I'm in stalled traffic, even if I'm a passenger on a bus. Let's go, coming through.

I'm not frustrated.

How's it go again? Oh, yeah! Slow down. Take it easy. Steady as she goes.

43

Like I Said Before, We Press On

It was Monday morning and I was slouched at my desk poking with my fork at an open can of sardine filets. Been a long time since these little guys splashed around in the ocean, I thought. I gave myself a D for posture, sat up and arched my back into a tight contraction. Feels good to straighten, stretch and contract.

Sardines are good for you, did you know that? Omega-3 oil, high in protein, no carbs, smelly and not too appetizing. I like the crunchy little bones. Oops! Slouching again, another D. What time is it, anyway?

Time for another cup of coffee.

I wonder if coffee and sardines are a bad mix. I know they're not a good mix, like tuna and water, but are they bad? You know, like, do they produce enzyme malfunctions or corrupt hormonal activity when they're combined? Is the protein neutralized by the caffeine or do the omega-3s turn rancid and become triglycerides?

Coffee and Danish pastry go well together. I love Danish pastry. I haven't had a piece of Danish since I was a kid living at home . . . sixteen, maybe. I wonder if it tastes the same. Huh, nearly sixty years with no Danish.

Still raining. Going on three weeks. It's been raining for so long that I'm getting into it. The world gets small. The darkness and the haze limit the distance you can see and the blue sky is gone, cloaked in grey and brooding clouds. You go out only when you must, to run errands, go to work, the gym, church—wherever—and you mostly look down, or from the underside of an umbrella if you're with your wife or girlfriend.

Guys don't use umbrellas, unless they're business guys, which I am not. No wingtips and knee-high socks, though I do have a couple of ties and a jacket . . . somewhere.

The indoors is where it's at. The crackling, flickering hearth is the center of attraction with me feeding the fire according to its appetite. It's warm, comfortable, alluring, hopeful and alive. Homemade soups and stews nourish the body, heal the wounds and soothe the spirit. Shelter takes on new meaning and I'm grateful to be living, breathing, working and protected.

The gym, always a refuge, becomes a special place away from my digs. It's good to mingle, hear my voice among other voices and bear the struggle of unkind and peculiar weather with like creatures—friends, indeed. Between sets I go to the gym's open back door to peer at the rain and inhale the fresh, wet air. Very nice.

I don't gaze too long because I don't want to lose my rhythm or body warmth or pump or concentration or favorite bench. The rain's nice, but not that nice.

Fewer people make it to the gym when the wet weather moves in. Traffic slows down, wet clothing, hair and feet are uncomfortable, and, like I said, the world becomes small.

And inconvenient. The gym seems far away—into a hooded slicker, out the front door, beyond the gloom, through the downpour, puddles and mud and across the flooded intersections. Cars are slipping and sliding, and who can see out the windshield in weather like this? It's confusing and messy. Wipers and heaters and defrosters work overtime. The carwash is empty. So are the swings, barbeque pits, street corners, park benches and jogging paths.

A little lonely, you can feel it. Just you and yourself.

Ah! But in the gym there's a good group: serious, dedicated, appreciative; industrious, willing and able. They're getting their money's worth, investing in their health, wasting no time and increasing their personal wealth. They're working out. This is entertainment at its best—beneficial, exclusive and confidential.

Nothing like a little active privacy and treasure hunting on a rainy day, that's what I always say. It may or may not cross their minds, but somewhere in their consciousness they know they are where they belong, safe and sound and dry and pumped, and it's teeming outside. The black afternoon sky is emptying itself and they're doing chins and bent-over rows.

The power could go out, lightning could strike or the forceful wind could blow off the roof, yet here we are, the intrepid few.

I'm into my workout. How much I lift isn't as important as the very fact that I'm lifting in the powerful and secure confines of the darn-near-sacred gym. I move the iron with a different effort that arises from a palette of multiple strengths, desires and needs. Desire is the predominant factor affecting the shape and outcome of the action before me.

The music and clang and shuffling bodies don't compete with the hush that prevails. The symptoms of the weather have become almost endearing and penetrate the edges of our minds and souls. We need the rain, the water that gives life.

I find a corner of the gym and practice side-arm lateral raises. This once-favorite shoulder movement had been relegated to the exercise junkyard after a dumb accident disconnected my right infraspinatus, an important rotator cuff support mechanism. Since that fateful day forty years ago, my shoulders, the poor mutts, have had to eat scraps and work hard for their run on the beach.

Today, prompted by a calm thoughtfulness and nostalgia resulting from the confinement of inclement weather, I decide to revisit the long-lost friend. I'm in the mood for discovery, or re-discovery, as the case may be.

Just to assume the starting position—slightly crouched with the dumbbells held fixed and ready before me—and exert the outward and upward action with that particular shoulder contraction at the peak would be enough, no matter how light the resistance. I start with five pounds and exact the movement. All these years later and I feel a chill of rebirth.

I know that groove, like an old song when I was happy and growing up with my buds. How does it go again? I go to the tens, brace my body and retrace the groove. At ten reps I'm burning and pumping and singing in the rain. Draper's smiling.

I grab the fifteen-pounders like they were my third and final attempt at setting a new world record: tense, deliberate, prepared for the high risk, yet confident with hope and faith and need. I can do it. With extraordinary focus, rep upon rep I fight my way to another stunning ten reps. The muscle activity is real, the pump and burn are not imaginary and I devour the encouragement.

The telltale twang on the last reps don't scare me, but give me kind warning. Be smart, bomber known for making crash landings in dangerous territory. Go slowly. Build up and support the area surrounding the absent spinatus muscle to permit further action, heavier weight, tighter contraction, greater overload and to enable the delts to assume the proportions and consistency of watermelons . . . um . . . make that cantaloupes.

Grapefruits?

Two more sets with the fifteens and we'll sneak up on the reluctant exercise over the next months. I'll need to fashion a new groove.

I'm singing and dancing in the rain.

There are four of us standing at the back door, none of us fighting to get out first. The rain is inviting, but wet nonetheless. We agree the miserable weather conditions are good for the dry landscape and our spoiled-rotten nature. We're done here today, thank God, and better prepared for tomorrow.

Not one is taller than the other, race and gender don't matter and any one of us would carry the other if he or she asked. We're in this together.

See ya later . . . stay dry . . . don't slip on the stairs.

44

The Bench Press
Revisited

I TOOK A SENTIMENTAL JOURNEY on a recent Sunday. It was warm, the skies were blue and the gym was empty at four PM. A guy and a gal were hunched over smoothies at the juice bar, watching grown women kicking a soccer ball across a field on TV. I thought, *Don't they have anything better to do?*

I retrieved my wraps, grips and water from my mangy gym bag and tossed it in the corner. I was in no rush. Rushing is a thing of the past. I used to rush when I had time, and time quickly passed me by. Now, as if I knew better, I struggle to reclaim time by urgently slowing down.

I sat where I seldom sit, at the end of a bench press with my back to the rack. Once upon a time, boys and girls, a great big Olympic bar amassed with forty-fives stretched across those sturdy uprights awaiting my sudden and powerful clutch, responding to my down-up directions like an eager student to a master, an obedient child to a parent, a broken captive to a captor.

Now, I plop there because I'm stiff and sore, worn out and daydreaming.

Quiet and alone, I heard music drifting from the speakers. Wait . . . that's the Drifters drifting . . . "There goes my baby, moving on down the line . . ."

1959: I was seventeen, bright-eyed and bushy-tailed, sitting at the end of a chrome-legged bench with gold-flecked red vinyl upholstery in a Vic Tanny's Gym in Jersey City. The Drifters were the sounds, and in the rack was a stiff, one-inch chrome bar strewn with twenty-pound chrome plates with chrome collars on the ends . . . just to be sure.

The whole catastrophe weighed 395 pounds. I added up the weight ten different ways, but could not make it total 400. Rats! Too dumb to be afraid, I clearly remember pressing that bar with record-setting wonder, strain and pain. No one resembling a spotter hung out in the fluorescent-lit, mirror-lined, shiny health club featuring those revolutionary electric rollers and belt massagers.

Whoa . . . Listen . . . Brenda Lee is singing "I'm Sorry." My favorite.

Spring of 1960. I had a bar at the end of my bed in a dismal yet airy room I rented from the Scambati's in Secaucus—perfect for curling and pressing and rowing and pullovers. The floor was slanted by time and creaked fiercely with each rep. I hated the collars and the wrench and the bloody knuckles, but loved the pump and the burn and the notion that I lifted iron in solitude.

I decry the bench press for its terror on the shoulders and its imperfect development of the chest, but let's face it, plate-heads: It's the original, our very first heavy-metal love affair.

I racked the three-inch Apollon's Axle and stuck a plate on the ends to be sociable. Ever-so-slowly and with focus, precision and mature fear, I plodded through six sets, the last four of which were supersetted with wide-grip pulldowns.

Now, Danny and the Juniors, "At the Hop."

I was a junior in high school and my arms were fifteen and a half, sometimes three quarters . . . "Let's go to the hop, oh, baby . . ."

It had been a long time since I assumed that familiar position at the end of the bench and recalled the clanging plates and impossible tonnage, the hesitation and anticipation, the doubt and certainty, the dream and drama, the chalk and gripping, the pause and deep breath, the absolute glory . . . the devastating defeat.

Momma said there'd be days like this, there'd be days like this, my momma said.

I'll never forget the Shirelles and how they made me tingle all over. I'll bet girls like strong muscles. Life, though taking shape in a hurry, was new, undiscovered, an adventure full of hope. Barrels of laughs were yet untapped and furrows of worry had not yet plowed their way across my brow.

Yes, sisters and brothers, it was oldies weekend at the gym. I finished my workout with one-arm lateral raises, wrist curls and hanging leg raises. The drive home was dreamy.

Two days later my right shoulder was in a cast, in traction, swollen, aching and the color of tar mixed with road kill; the pain level was between 9.5 and 9.9 on the chart measuring deplorable and despicable things. Nobody listens to me. I'm telling you, girls and boys, the bench is murder on the delts.

I'm okay today, day four, because I'm tough and durable; I eat road kill occasionally and drink Bomber Blend all the time.

Besides, I lied about the cast and traction and excruciating pain and roadkill.

Did you know Fats Domino was a strongman? That he pushed his grand piano across the stage with his gut muscles as he sang "I found my thrill on Blueberry Hill"?

Wait. Women soccer players are seriously, totally awesome athletes: courageous, dynamic, inspiring and gracious. I'd say "lovely" and "cute," too, but that might be a little sensitive.

We rock on . . . El Bombo.

45
Can I Go Now?

IT'S FIFTY DEGREES and gloomy in the middle of the day in the middle of summer in the middle of coastal California. I'm wearing long johns under my tank top.

I'm not complaining, but then, when have you ever heard me complain? If I can't say something positive and uplifting, no matter what the circumstances—divided country, lousy economy, joblessness, corruption, terrorism, warring nations—I just keep my stinking mouth shut.

Inspiration is my thing—inspiration, encouragement and love. You don't like it, step off a cliff.

So, there I am minding my own business, sitting on the steps to the back door of gym in the grim sunlessness of the fading summer when some old dude about my age drags his sorry butt over to me and says, "I need help."

Right away I'm thinking, lay him down gently, loosen his collar, check his pulse and air waves, maybe administer CPR, if I can remember how that one goes and call 911 fast (ring, watch, check his wallet for cash).

"My condition is not critical," he assures me, "Just a word or two of advice will do."

He goes on to tell me he's a new member of the gym and totally new to exercise. "All those bars and iron plates and benches and pulleys. Really?"

He wonders what I'd do if I were him.

Immediately, I picture a recliner, TiVo, warm milk, e-z chew high-fiber biscuits and low stress. And, then, I recall he specifically asked what I'd do if I was him, man to man, duffer to duffer, relic to relic, geezer to geezer.

It touches my heart. I'm an old softie.

After I explain hypertrophy, anatomy, physiology, training psychology, nutrition and the powers of protein powder and tuna and water, I secretly devise three routines he can execute, rotate, alternate or combine over the next few months.

He tries to escape on two occasions. Once, offering a lame apology (*Sorry . . . gotta go*), and a second time, threatening to call the police, but while he's nodding off, I apply a head-lock and step-over toe-hold to demonstrate my elder-fellow nimbleness and enthusiasm.

Having regained his attention, trust and confidence, I present my trio of workouts. They are short and sweet, simple but tough, basic yet challenging; plain, nevertheless interesting, unadorned and attractive.

He agrees emphatically, eying the duct tape.

Each routine engages the body completely, head to toe, inside to outside. They utilize an assortment of hefty equipment designed for straightforward development of strength and health, to be handled with one's preferred degree of effort and level of understanding.

You betcha.

I suggest he ride the stationary bike for five to fifteen minutes, or until he falls off or needs to scream, whichever comes first. I sympathize, a complicated choice and not for the mathematically challenged. Good warmup, good cardio, good leg work, good grief. I scream after twenty seconds . . . actually, it's more like a howl.

Smiles (duct-taped to the squat rack) nodded . . . a good listener after all.

Routine One

1. Kneeling rope tuck (1 set × 20 reps)
2. Bent-leg dumbbell deadlift, up into shrug and relax (2 × 10 reps)
3. Flat-bench dumbbell press (2 × 10 reps)
4. Seated lat row (2 × 10 reps)
5. Barbell curl (2 × 10 reps)
6. Pulley pushdown (2 × 10 reps)

Routine Two

1. Bent-leg leg raise (2 sets × 10 reps)
2. Full squat while minimally holding onto rack for balance (2 × 10 reps)
3. Heel-raise off block (2 × 20 reps)
4. Very light dumbbell flies (2 × 10 reps)
5. Straight-arm dumbbell pullover (2 × 10 reps)
6. Thumbs-up curl (2 × 10 reps)

Routine Three

1. Kneeling rope tucks—heavier weight (2 × 15 reps)
2. Incline dumbbell press (2 × 10 reps)
3. Sidearm lateral raise (2 × 10 reps)
4. Wide grip pulldown (2 × 10 reps)
5. Dumbbell curl (2 × 10 reps)
6. Dips—machine-assisted (2 × 10 reps)

Each routine, though not sophisticated or grandly engineered, is a standalone. Combined with one or both, as you please, they become serious musclebuilding efforts. And performed with consistency, intensity and enhancement, they will bring you joy, wealth and recognition . . . or make a monkey out of you. Trust me.

They never fail, most of the time.

They are reasonable versions of the routines I do today: enhanced, mixed, thoughtful and grateful.

46

Here Today, Gone Tomorrow, Never Forgotten

Do you ever wonder what you were thinking or doing ten years ago? Me neither; I have trouble remembering this morning.

But think about it. If you were ten, your curious, accidental and chaotic teens have entirely come and gone. Who am I and where am I going are yet unsolved, though you don't know that.

If you were twenty years old, the bright-eyed twenties are suddenly gone and you wish you could have a do-over. Thirty is, like, mature . . . adult, serious, all grown up. Ick!

Say you were thirty. You are, OMG, forty, four zero, and there's no turning back. You tried. Time has deceived you. Life is set in stone. You blinked and you missed. Bye-bye, all gone.

Are those wrinkles, is that fat? Where's my hair, my past, my future?

You noticed when you were forty, and now you're fifty. Gee, half a decade! Able to look outside yourself these days, you note you're not alone. Big number, you saw it coming and it's not so bad on the morale.

The forties started with desperation and flailing, rejuvenating and restoring, and halfway through you grew weary and grew up. "It is what it is," you say to each other, "Get over it, get on with it. Never quit, never let go."

Here another person is sixty, going on seventy, and life is in the rearview mirror immediately before him. Let's take a short journey from here to there to see where he's going and make sure he doesn't get lost . . . or didn't get lost . . . or whatever.

Ten years ago, when we were kids—

Barring accident and illness, if you've been active and eaten in moderation since your high school days, you're probably not in bad shape. You are also in the top twenty percent of mainstream society. Nice job.

If you regularly lift weights and eat smartly, you are probably in very good shape—the top five percent. Congratulations, brothers and sisters, you are safe and on your way to consistent improvement in your health and physical condition. Bravo. That's what happens when you train hard, eat right and stay hopeful.

The only category left is the big one, which includes those who are unenlightened, undisciplined, misguided, lethargic, time-poor, unable or unwilling . . . the remaining seventy percent. This big group needs big help, big time, now.

Our group primarily comprises hardy trainees between thirty and fifty years old: athletes, white-collar and blue-collar folks, moms and dads, powerlifters, bodybuilders, Joe-Bob and Mary-Jane, life-loving characters all. What does time hold in store for us?

What can we expect to compromise and when? What should we do now in preparation for later? What to eat, how to train, how much, how often? What about supplements and special foods? What's the word on skin tone, muscle density, strength and endurance?

Those are the sort of the questions we've asked for years at every stage of our training, and now they take on a different hue and bear a bolder question mark.

Kicking rusty cans . . . I'll offer my answers and points of view based on experience and observation and intuitive logic. I'm not gifted and I'm happily imperfect. Do not inscribe my words with a sharp instrument across your pectoral muscles. My training background, influences, motives and body chemistry do not match yours, yet I represent some point of reference—a marker of comparison—with which you can identify and adjust accordingly and from which you might gain insight.

Consider: I'm a guy who's been under the iron for about sixty years, has not always led a wholesome life to amplify my longevity and internal health, has worn parts, tingling nerves and joints that complain and the usual allergies, hormonal inconsistencies and neuroses that face any compulsive, over-trained, highly stressed and otherwise arguably well-adjusted earthling.

The good news is I love to work out more than ever. I've basically accomplished the physical mounds we set before us: decent muscle shape and size, reasonably low bodyfat, sufficient strength, energy and endurance, with an ever-growing understanding of training. Therefore, trust in my training and enjoyment of its benefits are for me almost a daily experience. This doesn't make it a walk in the park; it enables me to blast it.

The simple point: Thus far, I've discovered weight training works well and it gets better. Stick with it.

Injury and illness befall the most careful, stable and healthy individuals. Common sense develops with our attentive training, and internal and external resistance improves with the rigors of exercise and proper eating. We're stronger, more coordinated and better balanced, more flexible and resilient, smarter and wiser.

Subsequently we tend to care for ourselves better, break less easily and restore more quickly. Nice return for the investment, no?

The injuries that come with years of impact, overuse and misuse can be dealt with because they must. There is no choice (note the attitude of perseverance that accompanies disciplined exercise). The painful shoulder, immobilizing lower back, stinging biceps insertion and hammered knee can be depressing and threaten to put us out of commission, and sometimes they do. Apply the ice, ingest the anti-inflammatory and give the injury its due rest.

But I encourage you like-minded, determined trainees of all ages to work around injuries and maintain whatever percentage of training intensity you can. Diligently investigate the damage, scrutinize the pain, understand the limitations and apply minor, lightweight movements that match the capacity of the problem area. Pain can be your guide.

Warm-up movements are precious and allow us to proceed with safety, confidence and familiarity; they provide blood support, warmth, alleviation of pain, awareness of mechanical tracking and estimation of exercise potential. They refine our focus and prune our patience and exact our form. When you're fifty going on 100, who wants to let go and become idle and weak, fat and skinny? Get to the gym, exercise and thank God. You'll heal faster and live longer and be happier.

We are more injury prone as we get older, and repair is slower. However, we get smarter and wiser (that's worth repeating). With each passing year I become more attentive—perceptive—not wanting to endure the pain, frustration and limitation of yet another injury, possibly one that is chronic and unfixable.

And rather than intolerant, I am a graduate student of injuries, fascinated by what they have taught me and respectful of their power. By necessity and performance preference, I am a more patient and focused lifter and am hopeful that the improving awareness, workout style and attitude permit me—and you, my co-worker—more productive years in the iron and steel toolbox.

Or is that a toy box?

47
Ain't It Funny?

THE TIME HAS COME to open the door and walk through. Youth for some of you isn't exactly ancient history, but it and the dust around it has settled in the past. Nod and toss a mock salute. What youth didn't do for you, you must do now: Pick up the pieces and put them together.

That's why today you stand beyond the door and on the gym floor. Say goodbye to the child, but be sure to take the kid with you.

The people who, over the years and by accident or design, built a foundation of muscle, fed themselves decently and treated their bodies fairly are rare and far ahead of their neighbors. They can step into a training program and proceed without the turmoil of emotions and toil of mind necessary to center themselves and aspire.

Those sterling characters who started their robust fitness ventures years ago and have persevered are aware of the precarious twists in the road ahead. They are even more rare and accomplished and will not be thrown off course.

The few who gather in a tight circle around the piles of iron and steel, belt and wraps dangling from their strong grips, access the hairpin curve that edges the heights of the mountain they've climbed; they lead where no one has led before. Tilted heads studying, narrowed eyes focusing and knitted brows concentrating, they improvise the next uncertain move. Stoic grins crowd their faces.

There's a smart way for each of us to go, depending on fitness level, experience, constitution, health, means and available time. Here are some non-technical generalizations about aging based on my limited observations:

- Needless to say, the timeless teens and the twenty-some fly high, far and fast. They are not, however, invincible; they strain and they break, they overtrain and complain. Age . . . it begins.

- The terrific thirty-some grow, muscularize, further perfect shape and tone while they gather and apply wisdom. Injuries and plateaus are responsible for the latter. Risk taking, heavy weights and mean persistence do the job, yet take their toll on the hardcore. Growing up and growing older . . . it continues.

- Forty-some, frivolous and frantic, provides a stretch of positive growth for the trainee who didn't ignore the responsibility to fitness for a regretful length of time—the longer out of the loop, the bigger the penalty. The slightly abused or negligent pick up where they left off after dutifully and painfully reestablishing their parameters. Strength, muscle size and definition can be achieved by the tough, perceptive and determined, given time, and time moves on.

- The overused over-forty can do wonders to restore health and well-being, control bodyweight, improve energy, strengthen the back and flatten the stomach. Self-esteem is added to the bargain. There's no time or effort to waste . . . ever again.

- The early fifties rock on as you suspiciously glance over your shoulder. A ding here and a ding there become more frequent and last a little longer and cause more concern. Human nature, I guess. To push or not to push, that is the question. We hesitate briefly, yet we don't stall and we don't fall apart. Caution is coolish . . . fear is foolish. We're hanging in there, mister and sister, as we head for sixty. Very becoming.

- The sixties! Oh, my. Sixty is not fifty-something. It's larger, it's more. It's older. It's old. Grandma and grandpa were in their sixties. They played cards, ate too much and went to bed early.

- Those precious ten years between sixty and seventy have gone by and not by accident and not without my observation, consternation and aggravation, nor my humility, futility and senility. Did I mention yelling, kicking and screaming? I squeezed each year, month and day tightly as if I could prevent their advance. Alas . . . ain't it funny how time slips away . . .

Be aware. It seems the curiosity and care I integrated and the wisdom I gathered during the latter half of the fifties gave me a head start on the big six-oh. During the first 1,200 days of those unpredictable years (after sixty-some weirdoes selfishly, slavishly

251

count time by the day), I was on an ascent that I hoped was not a rare and isolated phase. I was stronger, healthier and fitter than I was five years prior.

Stand back, coming through! On Memorial Day in the spring of '06 I squatted 430 and deadlifted 460. No big deal and I ain't braggin' (I had a great spotter), but it was an indication of my reasonably sound condition.

Hmmm . . . How long can I keep this up?

That was sometime in my mid-sixties, just before the notorious "other shoe" dropped . . . long before I realized I had worn holes in my socks.

Nowadays, with the dazed seventies making a humble appearance front and center, I'm an awestruck front-row spectator applauding the preposterous acts to come.

I'm hoping the show has a long run, there's a feature film to follow with sequels and, eventually, a continuing TV series.

48
Trash Disposal Technician

I REMEMBER THE FIRST DAY I lifted weights like it was just sixty years ago.

The mad pursuit emerged from an active kid who loved to climb trees and jump from their heights. I had a favorite limb from which I chinned, on a favorite tree I called the Monkey Tree. It was my original and personal gym that served me and me alone for years.

There were two chairs in the cellar by the coal bin that I placed back to back. I performed thousands, maybe millions of dips between those old splintered chairs when I wasn't chinning on the Monkey Tree.

Handstand pushups came later when strength and balance were at my command.

Then the weights rolled onto the scene: the bar, the plates, the collars, the wrench, the clanging, the improvised exercises and the gravity and the pain. I loved the idea of lifting weights—the height of manhood to a twelve-year-old—but they weren't as much fun or as free as the Monkey Tree or even the dirty old rickety chairs. I soon hated the dinky wrench and the smashed fingers caught between the cold and noisy plates and the downright uncontrollable heaviness of the mute metal.

Sheesh. I'm still just a little kid.

I pushed and pulled and from the corner of my eye wondered if anyone cared. No one noticed. Not once did a brother or parent say, "How cool" or "Let me try." It was like I was invisible.

I was lucky, really. They didn't laugh, nor did they tell me to stop that banging and clanging and get those miserable things out of the house. The nasty devices, when not in use, were rolled under my bed, which was next to the beds of my two older brothers. Tight quarters and tight muscles for a little squirt.

Nineteen and just married, three nights a week I drove three exits on the N.J. Turnpike to the Elizabeth Y's closet-size weight-room. That went over big. I soon took a second job on weekends (precious daughter on the way) at the Jersey City Vic Tanny's Gym. That went over big.

Before a year was over, I moved to California to train at Muscle Beach. My young family (Penny, seventeen—Jamie Lee, nine months) soon followed. That went over big.

In each period after the novelty wore off, the work became Work with a capital double-U, "U" for Ugh. Early mornings or after work, long sessions, pain, sweat, compromise, sacrifice and hard work are the components of commitment.

"Why" I know now, but didn't then. The twenty-stair descent to the floor of the Muscle Beach gym, The Dungeon, held apprehension every morning for three years. I trained six days a week and never missed a beat. Each workout was to exceed the last. The pressure was self-imposed and mounted day after day.

The titles came and went. The reps, the sets came and went. The days and nights came and went. The '60s came and went.

Between '70 and '80 I hoisted the steel no less than four days a week. Whatever else I neglected during that notorious decade, working out was not one of them. Iron and protein in sufficiency accompanied me wherever I dared to go. Nothing fancy: curls and presses, tuna and water and a hunk of beef. Did I mention the alcohol? No? Good. I won't. It's barely a memory nearly forty years old.

In September of '89, along with the California earthquake there erupted a World Gym well within the rumbling epicenter. We breathed life into the dual stone-and-steel enterprises, assuring their verve to this day.

Now, all these years later, I'm a simple yet loyal member of the shrines, good for two or three staggering workouts a week. Stand back, coming through!

I do what I have to do, must do, need to do, can do, am able to do, want to do and don't want to do, and not what someone tells me to do. Come to think of it, no one tells me what to do. I just do it.

"Take out the garbage!"

"Yes, dear."

I still don't know what to be when I grow up.

Perhaps I'll become a garbage man.

Be all you can be.

49
Animal Rights for Muscleheads

It's Sunday morning and I'm planning my work-out for later in the day. I like Sundays; the roads are traffic-free, the gym is light in attendance and I entertain the casual yet fictitious notion I don't have to submit to the cruelty of the relentless iron master this fine day. I choose to.

Let's see: bis and tris? No. Chest and back? No. Thunder thighs and rippling abs? Certainly not. It's all so exciting, I don't know where to begin. Should I focus on the almighty pump and burn, or seek rhythmic fulfillment in precise set and rep performance? Neither. Should I seek looming bulk and power or swift, chiseled definition? Both. At once, simultaneously, together and at the same time?

Yes! Maybe!

"I don't know what to do," he said fretfully, as he gouged at his eyes and yanked clumps of hair from his head. I shall discover what to do, as always, when I skip gaily across the enchanted gym floor amid the beguiling assortment of bars and benches, pulleys and cables.

. . . tic-toc-tic-toc . . . Time flies . . . I'm back.

I had a superior workout: tight, balanced, bold. The legs do little more than transport me from bench to rack and back, but from the waist up I cause a small riot. The iron experience is never casual. I regularly offer myself the legitimate option to train slowly over an extended period of time, allowing comfortable pauses between wholesome sets of modest reps.

"Let's face it, Bomber of the B-70+ variety," I say to myself as I mount the stairs to the perpetual pleasure palace, "the craft's a bit shabby, the fuel's low, the runway's short, the load's heavy and the time's light: revive, restore and rejoice—stimulate, satisfy and smile. What's the rush? Where are you going? Take it easy."

Then I grasp the cold, knurled bar festooned with decorative black plates of alluring iron and something snaps inside my head. My countenance contorts, my eyes widen, my lips quiver, my muscles contract and my body lurches as if charged by electricity.

Restore? Stimulate? My inner voice snarls like a tormented pit-bull.

Seriously, really, not exactly and I don't think so. Intensity rules! A light weight in hand may be right and fitting, but slow and easy I cannot grasp.

I mean, I'm mean.

Alas, power is gone and strength has left the structure. Energy I seek with spyglass and searchlight, only to uncover lingering fragments. Endurance, once savory and abundant, has vanished entirely with the foul north wind.

Yet, know-how and finesse remain deeply etched in my forehead; determination and persistence I retain in generous stores; faith and hope, my gracious eternal gifts, go wherever I go. Absent these treasures I am no one, nothing, a void, a shadow in the dark. An oaf, a booger, a poop.

Sooner or later, amid kicking and screaming, we must give up the heavy weights. Heavy weights are those weights we can no longer lift and when we do anyway (any way we can), we break, burst, bust and burn.

"When the time comes, I'm ready," said the slightly sagging warrior with the receding grey hairline wearing a tight tank-top and bright red Keds in a voice of magnified ignorance and tones of overflowing arrogance. "That's life."

"That's life?"

A bit wordy, Rip Dip, but poorly said. However, saying a thing doesn't mean we know it, and knowing a thing doesn't mean we accept it. A child says it, a grownup knows it and a mature person accepts it.

None are enough. A bomber embraces it.

Accepting is for the rational. Those who lift weights feverishly are not rational. Their pursued, practiced and highly developed character qualities—patience, determination, perseverance, passion, commitment—are tempered, hardened, into insistence and stubbornness . . . analness. Their ability to overcome and pummel senseless immovable metal objects into submission fills them with a false sense of inevitability and invulnerability.

Along comes buster bad boy injury and his whacky, wicked associates: pain, incapacity, soreness, limited range of motion, throbbing, wraps, curses, ointments, aches, woe is me, lay-offs, sleepless nights, misery, Doctor Who, lousy mood, tenderness, bad attitude, weird exercise grooves, moan and groan.

We must turn our back on them, the stumbling band of fools, without submitting, without surrendering, never quitting, never letting go.

An absurd word from the loose goose is candy for the dandy gander.

"Seek and discover muscle exertion in light weight, intensity of performance in passionate focus, serious pump and burn in amplified set 'n rep application. It's all there at your command, not at the demand of punishing, oversized barbell and dumbbell extravaganzas constructed for young gorillas. They'll make monkeys of us every time, after all." —*The Loose Goose*

50
Me and the Mob

SELDOM DO I DRAG MYSELF to the gym unwill-
ingly. It's not often I stand before the barbells and dumbbells with
drooping shoulders and hesitation. And though I don't feel like
Superman, never do I question why I'm about to fatigue myself
and inflict hard work and pain upon my body. That's all behind
me and has been for a long, long time. Today, I roll out the ole
Harley, run a cloth over the chrome, crack the pipes and let 'er rip.

This all began years ago.

I remember when I was a kid; no problem, the weights were
playthings. You push, pull, toss, lift and grunt. Great fun. Clank,
rattle; where's my wrench? As a teen, lifting was like a sport to
play; you win, you lose, the days came and went and skipping a
workout was no big deal. Let's see, should I lift weights or play
stickball at the park?

One day—who remembers when; it's all a haze—I noticed
guilt had taken up residence in my ever-present shadow, a nagging,
smirking wise guy—a jerk, really—that made me irritable when I

missed a workout, miserable if I was delinquent a week. Training became important, a thing I had to do, and the fun was leaking away. Most anything became more desirable than the weights: studying Latin, changing the oil or cleaning the garage.

Thank heaven there was no TV. I pressed on.

Then some raggedy habit took form and the walk to the weightroom became regular, and labored and cheerless. It's lonely on this bench, under this bar and counting sets and reps. How many do I have to do today? The number was a pain in my head and completing the prescribed task before me was a dull feat. Twenty (ugh), nineteen more (aay), eighteen (oof), seventeen (urp).

"Will the workout ever end?" was my approach. The color around me was gray. This must be done—press on.

It wasn't long before anticipation, the kind with a sour puss, started hanging around with guilt. Put these two thugs together and we have tension, nervous tension. Now it's not only hard work and lonely under the bar, it's tiresome and exhausting thinking about it, all day, at work, at lunch, on the road and in the sack. By the time I got to the gym, I'd been there, I'd done that. Not another rep! I'm beat.

Swell, but that's not enough. Besides feeling guilty for missing a workout I haven't missed and badgered by a workout I haven't hit, I'm feeling disappointed with the progress I haven't made. A mob is gathering in my shadow and I'm just a skinny kid. We have Guilty Gus, Big Al Anticipation and the notorious Duke of Disappointment conspiring in the dark.

Step aside, mutts, I'm using that squat rack.

Duty calls when you're still and listen to your soul. Taking the three pot-bellied bums down became my mission and I knew it—the first sign of instinct, survival of the fittest, which plays no minor role in the muscle-builder's life. Instinct rules.

In this life you win, you lose or you crawl. It's not that I wanted to win, but I cannot lose and I will not crawl.

Elementary, really, and I worked by elimination. I gathered from their focus on me that what I was focused on was very important and very good because they're so bad. Despite, or because of, the combined efforts of the gloomy threesome, I pressed on.

I discovered devotion and intensity.

Strangely, my shadow grew larger with my body and the three wise guys grew smaller. In time I replaced guilt with discipline, a stern but agreeable character. Negative anticipation submitted to positive preparation and psyching up, a pair of confident spirits with lofty goals.

And disappointment, sour and ungrateful, left one fine day without a word.

Like mistakes, the scoundrels taught tough lessons. Their departure was an unconscious relief, dirty snow and slippery ice slowly melting in the spring.

The walk to the gym became hurried, not soon enough, and excitement accompanied my footsteps. Miles were behind me and miles were ahead and somehow I knew the way.

You never know the way unless you walk it and climb it, get lost, lose ground, grow cold and hungry, and insist on walking again. Nobody can tell you, exactly, what, how and why; they can only offer their hopeful presence, wise suggestions and solid encouragement—gold ore and uncut diamonds.

My word, what's the big deal? It's only lifting weights; it's exercise and good food. It's not life, liberty and the pursuit of happiness.

Or is it?

51

Me and the Mob, the Grand Conclusion

It's springtime in America. The sun appears more frequently and hangs out longer. If you sit still and look close, you can see the forest grow; brown's down and green is everywhere, the birds are frisky and the squirrels are plump.

Yet I look out the window and the world's not smiling. Something's wrong. For the first time in my life I sense someone is trying to tell me what to do, whether or not it's right, whether or not I like it.

Get ye behind me, Alphonse.

There's an occasional burst of nervous hilarity, a few tentative laughs and a handful of polite chuckles. You can count a fistful of smug grins and copious smirks of sarcasm disguised as humor, but authentic smiles are rare. Content, fulfilled, safe 'n secure, good ole feeling good—these are missing, hiding out, undercover, conspicuously absent.

These are the days when the gym serves double duty, when gravity gives generously, and when the iron is half as heavy and twice as light. Merely address the weighted gear with gratitude and intent, and before you can count to ten, you're building muscle and eradicating stress—the dynamic duo.

A cascade of cooperative twin benefits are enjoyed with moderate engagement: You develop strength and relieve anxiety, increase fitness and diminish frustration, grasp steel and release tension, add power and lighten the load, pick up good stuff and let go of bad stuff.

That's a smile.

Soon I stepped back and realized its indispensable worth, when I resumed doing it for its pure adventure and immediate reward, when I trusted its permanence and investment, when training was no longer an obligation but a wise choice, a desirable means to eliminate barriers and overcome obstacles and to express myself without screaming periodically throughout the day.

And it's no big ego trip for a vigorous lifter to enjoy physical strength, endurance, reasonable confidence and a body that doesn't resemble a pear balanced precariously on a pair of toothpicks. There's no more ego here than a long list of letters after one's name on a letterhead, a tattoo in the right place, a yellow Carrera in the driveway, a $1,000 suit or a shaved head.

It took some time, pressed together with considerable doubt, curiosity, pain and sacrifice to make the discovery, but it's worth it. To settle into your training with certainty is like sitting back in an easy chair, comfortable and relaxed. Just don't fall asleep on me, bombers, we have work to do—fueling up, checking the landing gear and clearing the runway.

Of course, the choir agrees, and loves to be reminded. How about you, whose T-shirts are getting snug and triceps are forming horseshoes?

Those who are relatively new (though proudly invested) and struggle to maintain their training focus and zeal can reduce the less-than-delightful learning and growing curve by accepting the precepts put forth on the well-shared pages of *IronOnline*. Trust, press on toward your sensible goal and put in your time with renewed enthusiasm, because it's happening and it happens no other way.

Consider how far you've come and imagine—visualize with certainty—where you want to go. The only thing that stands in your way is time and doubt. Time will pass, but doubt must be removed.

What you need to correct or alter in menu or exercise arrangement, attitude or workout intensity, you will surely attend along the way. Today's questions are tomorrow's answers. Mistakes and injuries are the instructors.

Be strong, nourish your sense of humor, stay alert, be positive and hopeful, drink your protein shakes, be nice to your neighbor, squat (of course), and don't ruin your shoulders with heavy bench pressing. As far as it is possible, allow no unsightly gaps to develop in your eating scheme or your training thrust; gaps have a way of growing out of control and they are unbearable. Beware.

That we are aware of what we must do places us well above the rest. That we practice what we must puts us on top.

Let's taxi down the runway and take off one by one in fine form till we fill the skies with roaring and fill our hearts with fire.

52

Seven Sons of Samson

Day by day information bombards us from every direction. Thousands of bits of odd-shaped thoughts, facts, figures and ideas randomly collide in our reposed minds. A fair portion of this mental detritus is sought by us to educate and guide; much too much, however, is aimed at the cortex by an alien to sell, persuade, condition and tame. It's a jungle out there and we need a machete, a strong arm and a sharp eye to cut through the overgrowth and make clear a path.

Nutrition and physiology, anatomy and kinesiology are fascinating subjects, the favorite pursuit of many professionals and hungry-to-learn fitness enthusiasts. These fields are vast, stretch like the plains of Africa and are often intertwined and unexplored. How can we not be drawn to the mystery and allure? Yet, the calculation and regulation of the mass of information available and the reliability of such information as being pertinent to our real fitness quest is absurd and a real hindrance.

My creed goes something like this: Keep it simple, stick to the basics, train consistently with enthusiasm and intensity, use logic, be creative and intuitive, be confident in your applications, be happy and deal with your misery. Be real. Stop fussing.

There are absolutely no secrets. Nothing's new. Collect the necessary information and get to work.

The clutter of intelligence, the waste of words describing a simple thing, the superior heaps of decaying mental rubbish surrounding the notion of exercise and sensible eating is maddening. Why, there are people who have read so much they think they actually know something.

The learning's not in the reading, it's in the doing.

Here we are on the web, of all places, to add multitudinously to an already out-of-control catastrophe. Smart cookies we are . . . getting smarter. There's no better place to grow a discerning mind and gain sound footing than in the gleaning fields of wild information.

A process undertaken single-handedly can be dangerous. With no one to juggle the suggestions and directions and possibilities tossed our way, a predictable tangle will result, time lost in goofy workouts, hazardous dieting, backwards nutrition, absurd training notions from lost souls. One must learn to glean and sample, confer and intuit, risk yet listen to logic and wisdom.

Alas, where and under what conditions does one find an atmosphere to practice such liberties? How does one discover understanding?

Please, indulge me, dear friends. Often, I refer to bombers as the central subject and theme of my jabbering. This may appear as inner-circle conversation, another world, but we're alive and dimensional, offering cartloads of precious and common raw material to be refined as in a smelting pot. It is in the comfortable confines of our cyber workplace that logic and common sense surface, conferences convene and seminars spontaneously appear. Old stuff and new stuff are examined, experienced and compared, the diets, the exercises, the strategies, the gear, the gismos, the heroes, the myths.

A bar in hand is worth two in the rack.

There are times when I observe the activity from my stealth-bomber mode, and it looks like a baseball game with thirteen players and four balls on the field, two at bat and everybody pitching. "Victims of information overload, idle fools, they are," I used to think. And then it began to happen. A curious maturity emerged as the cyber participants carefully, thoughtfully applied themselves to the truth . . . because it was there, somewhere, and nothing else would do. It never does. Bags and bundles of processed data and facts were dumped out of the perimeter.

"Who needs it?"

It served its purpose, made us think, showed us left from right, caused us to flounder and re-right ourselves, separated the workers from the clowns, created some heat amidst the personalities that, in turn, created a rare unity.

He who lifts last lifts hardest.

The information is as endless as space and time, but we know better. You lift it up if it's before you, rotate it in your strong hand and if it fits, you keep it. Otherwise, go back to your squats, deadlifts or whatever else you were doing and get an extra rep.

53
Guns, Girls and Lies

I DUNNO ABOUT FACEBOOK. I've lived in a small cabin in the woods for so long, entering the social media feels like when I stepped into the Big City with its tall buildings and flashing neon lights, voiceless people in crowds and honking bumper-to-bumper cars. Then there were the alleys and garbage trucks and sirens. I got lost the very first day.

I thought and looked and looked and thought, and just before I pulled my hair out (no snickering), I stumbled across a gritty gym on the corner of First and Main. What a relief!

Down a flight of dimly lit, whitewashed stairs was a broad, column-studded room about fifty by fifty. There was sufficient light to find the iron, but not enough to sting the peepers. A classy young doll slinked behind the front counter. She gave me the eye.

"Where ya from, big guy? You wanna hit the weights?"

I scanned the layout, heavy on the bars and benches and light on the lifters and talkers. That's all I needed to know.

"How much to settle my nerves?" I asked.

"Ten bucks for the day," she said. "You break it, you own it."

She was sharp and neat as a stiletto.

"They call me La, like the tone, do, ra, mi," her muscles flexed as she poured me a powerful protein drink with one egg and a banana. I drank it greedily and felt the pump coming on.

"Locker room's in the back. What did you say your name was, again?"

"I didn't."

I dropped a C-note on the counter and grabbed a black City t-shirt from the stack of XLs on a shelf.

"Keep the change."

Locker room was clean: two-stall shower with soap, no peep holes, no graffiti; a lock for valuables (I had none) and a trash can for garbage, half full. A pay phone hung in the corner by a bin of dirty towels. I had dirt, but nobody to call.

Nothing to prove and only my soul to satisfy, I exited the room and walked directly to the interesting end of the dumbbell rack. I grabbed a pair, settled on the incline and knocked out a dozen reps.

The last rep wasn't easy; it never is, but I did it anyway. Tough, clean and mean, it's the last rep that counts. The others are just along for the ride.

A kid in a tank top with chunky arms was polishing the mirrors with newspaper and Windex. He'd be huge and ripped one day. He was paying his dues. Windex on, Windex off.

I liked to move as long as I could move and fill in the time between sets of one blast with sets of another. The pulleys squeaked and wobbled as I tugged, a perfect deep-breathing stretch to accommodate and relieve the pitiless dumbbell compressions.

Three guys the size of grizzlies hovered around a gnawed benchpress. Plates clung to the weary bar and clanged harshly in rebellion. Chalk dust, sleeveless sweatshirts, "Stay tight," hips bumping stacked wheels to assure tightness, tense laughter, "You can do this, man"—a warrior sat, stiff, silent and staring, deep breaths, hands, bar, grasp and grip, on three and lift.

Lightning and Thunder.

Returning to the incline, I stopped and leaned on a waist-high immovable object and commenced to push as if hoping to jumpstart a stalled truck: lean and push, thighs and calves contract, go, go, go, on the toes, hard reps, slow reps, faster, harder for a minute followed by ten freehand squats and jumps. A little aerobic and a little leg action and I was on the way.

The girl at the counter, Fa, La or whatever, had one of those pint-size, handheld computers which, unless she gave the thing a rest, was about to explode. How much can one person read, type, think, say, communicate?

Which reminds me: Facebook.

Quickly, I averted my mind and, while seeking a bent bar for a curls 'n triceps extensions superset (I call it the Gun Loader), I pondered how long those ponderous pandas would last under the wrath of the benchpress. You see, I love animals and I hate to see them caught in a nasty trap. We were suckers for the bait—bigger, stronger, faster, huge and ripped.

Think I'll wander over to the den of horrors and offer the boneheads some advice: Heavy benches wreck shoulders. Yeah. That'll go over big.

Look sharp, Bomb. Dollface is heading this way . . . and she's bringing that slick, trick tablet thingy with her. I'll put on my don't-bother-me-I'm-lifting mug. She'll spin on her heels and head south fast.

"Dave, you promised to chat on Facebook."

How's she know my label? I don't promise, and I don't chat! Facebook?

"Yes, dear. Whatever you say, dear."

54
Sanctuary for Social Misfits

I CAN SIT AND STARE into the corner, free of thought, imagination, emotion and responsibility— just me and nothing, no one and no place, no what and no why. Silence is golden, solitude is priceless, simplicity is lovable, freedom is precious, effortlessness is kindly and uselessness is fragrant.

Actually, uselessness stinks like doggy doo. Think I'll head for the gym and create some chaos . . . out of absolutely nothing.

Of course, if you're savvy, you know I've been consumed with Twitter and Facebook. Yeah, you can't keep the old dog from learning new tricks and contributing to the cutting edge of the slick, agile and gutsy social media.

For you exotic dull-eyed laggards, here's a peek at my latest Facebook entry: Eat better, train harder, be tougher, think surer, whine lesser and rest morer.

Elegant! Inspirational! Poetic!

While you adored, studied, absorbed and memorized my submission, I journeyed to the place where muscles are made and power is built, character is developed and spirits are deepened: the famous, fabulous and fantastic fortifying ferrous fortress, less commonly known as The Gym.

I cruised in, grabbed me some iron and commenced tossing it around. Seriously, doesn't that sound so much better than "Dizzy and gasping, I staggered in and flopped onto the nearest bench?"

There comes a time when a guy's got to add a little color to his language.

Sixty minutes twice a week is my new limit, no more, no less. I tried more and realized less. Enough iron action maintains, retains and sustains. Too much wears, tears and interferes.

Be wise. The last thing I want to do is wear myself out.

Let me guess. You wonder the same things. When am I adding to my health, quality of life and years on the winning scoreboard? When am I over-amping the heart, inundating the organs and wearing out the joints?

And about this thing called ego: when does it grow up and become an adult?

An adult? The last thing I want to do is become an adult.

This weights-sets-and-reps thing becomes tricky as time goes by. And this is the trick: feeling, focusing and savoring the fabulous ferrous fortunes, the weight, sets and reps we share day after day, even if (especially if) twice a week does the trick. Tricks are for kids.

Be happy. The last thing I want to do is tricks . . . and more tricks.

My secret MO:

> 10 sets Smith steep front press (12, 10, 9, 8, 7–6, 5, 4, 4, 4 reps), 5 final sets supersetted with pulldowns to front and rear

> 3 sets standing thumbs-up dumbbell curls (6–8 reps), superset with 3 sets of machine dips

> Tight, tough, tidy . . . gone, outta here.

> The sound of plates clanking on the gym floor is music to the ears.

55
Plenty Enough

Now THAT I'M AN OLD GUY, a whistle hangs around my neck on a chain, a beeper is fitted to a sporty wristband and at night while wandering the streets I wear blinking red reflector sneakers.

Furthermore, I'm going to the gym and you can't stop me. My bag's packed, I'm amply fueled, the truck's warming up in the driveway. I've outlined a dynamite routine, sketched precise directions (in large print) to the front door of the weightroom and prepared a chest full of food that does not require chewing. If I leave now, I should be there before the weekend.

I rendezvous with the iron twice a week. I can't do any more and that's all it takes. You see, as hard as I've tried, even with my reluctant heart, I cannot enter the gym to work out without applying myself intensely. Aware of my heart's mitigated willingness, I gauge myself deliberately. Every exercise is evaluated, every set scrutinized and each rep studied and revised in motion according to need and ability and desire.

In other words, I don't zip in, knock out the sets and reps and zip out.

"Oh, I think I'll squat and bench press simultaneously . . . no, no, no, I'll deadlift, cheat curl and perform Turkish get-ups with an engine block . . . or, I can juggle three forty-five-pound plates while eating an Olympic bar."

I enjoy my current training regimen, the engagement of precise focus and tailored form in its execution, and the effectualness of the product. En route to the playpen my workout unfolds. Energy, pain, enthusiasm, well-being, mood, life's heaviness and lightness are tossed in the brain's blender. There they swirl as I assess what I've done most recently, which muscles are presently in need of action and which should wait and rest. Too much concerns me as much as too little.

See what happens? When you can no longer lift with credibility, you describe what little you can do in complicated and convoluted ways, using multisyllabic words possibly not in the dictionary. You make it so much more than it really is. Hey, it works.

There's no race afoot. Supersets are still favored; the intermingling of two compatible exercises one after another is friendly, pleasurable, agreeable and sweetly codependent family (training is very personal). Time between sets in my training is committed to restoring my not-so-matter-of-fact oxygen debt.

Gasp . . . *Pay up or it's curtains, wise guy.*

Still, a steady pace with no wasted space is heavy on my mind. I'm down to twenty sets in one hour. Each exercise is critical. If any one movement by itself is exhausting to my puny, pickled pump, I single-set it. Every workout is different, as I want to include all the valuable exercises I'm able to perform throughout the month for muscle effect, health and strength and for interest and enjoyment.

One big, large and grand thing: The heaviness of the weight I use is not big, large or grand. It's appropriate to my struggle and strain—a rather minor factor in my twice-weekly bouts. If I cared how much weight I handled in my workouts, I'd be depressed as well as childish. Enough is enough.

Here's what I did Sunday, a most noble tribute to my 200-pound structure, Effort Level (EL)=9.2:

Rope tucks and stiff-arm pullovers . . . 3 sets × 40 reps and 3 × 12, 10, 8 reps

Smith incline press and pulldown . . . 5 × 6–10 reps and 5 × 6–12 reps

Bent-over laterals . . . 4 × 10–12 reps

Not much in numbers, but plenty in effort and application. Not much for a growing child, but plenty for a grown kid. Caveat: We must eat right, stay busy, laugh more and growl less.

The sun shines brightly on happy ironheads.

56
Bust a Slump

KICKING AND SCREAMING, I recently pulled on my size-seventy costume. At first the thing was uncomfortable and, I thought, very long and humiliating . . . certainly not my style. It was baggy in the bottom, tight around the waist and tugged under the arms.

Alas, like most things we were forced to wear growing up, I'm getting used to it. I expect after good use, I'll spring for a smart and dashing size seventy-plus before I know it. No rush, mind you, as I intend to take good care of this particular creation now that it fits.

It's easy to grumble, I'm sure you agree: weather to wars, taxes to traffic, jobs to jerks. And that's the inconsequential stuff. Dig a little deeper and we get to the core issues: weights are too heavy, biceps are too small, can't find my abs, got no definition and getting old sucks.

Hey, Bub! Quit griping. Such is life—grow up, get a job, it is what it is, you do what you can with what you've got, roll with the punches; go with the flow, what will be will be, deal with it. God's will be done. Smile, be happy. Be original.

Little-known, well-concealed, heavily disguised and deeply hidden secret: I take grumbling to the gym and search for relief somewhere between the adjustable bench and the dumbbell rack. Tell no one, say nothing. Barbells and pulleys, even kettlebells, have been known to afford comfort as well.

And, it's not always in the immediate iron actions, but within the haven of time between actions. There are reports from the rugged past, the Muscle Beach and Dungeon days, stating the sheer nearness to the still steel serves to soothe scarred souls.

Now, if you really have problems, you could break out the Slumpbusters, those nasty yet lovable exercise combinations I conceived and revealed to you, my worthy comrades, so many years ago. Like the wheel, flint and the bow, they're not complicated; they are simple and marvelously effective. The pain, pump and burn derived from any one of the fifteen combinations, robustly executed, will distract you from the nags you confront.

Slumpbusters are notorious for breaking training plateaus and developing solid and powerful muscles. These incidental byproducts or side effects may or may not be consequential to you, but I feel compelled to mention them . . . never know who's reading my pointless nonsense. They are extraordinarily satisfying too, swell time-killers, and give one the very cool appearance that he knows what he's doing.

Another little-known secret: June, July and August, three dan-dan-dandy months of the year, are immediately before us. Savor them, day by day, month by month, moment by moment. These are the times that free the souls of bombers, boys and girls and kids. Let's not gather in the fall and ask, like typical dopey idiot fool nincompoops, what happened to the summer, here one day and gone the next.

Here's a trick that doesn't work: Stick a post-it note on the end of your nose that says, "Today is the first day of the rest of your life." For one, it's not a very clever ditty; two, the note is so close to your eyes you can't read it and three, after two or three days it falls off anyway.

Better yet, make a conscious effort to notice who you are, where and why. Look and see, touch and feel, engage your surroundings, talk and listen, wonder and discover. One of the best venues for the practice of this charge is the gym.

Think about it: A man or woman who hoists iron knows who he or she is (tough), where they are when they bench press (the bench) and why (pecs and power). There's the guy at the front counter, a prime opportunity for conversation (*Hey, man!*). There are pictures of muscle guys on the walls (Steve, Reg, Zabo) and mirrors with one's pumped reflection to be observed (cool horseshoe triceps) and the inimitable sounds (slam, bam, thud, clink).

Try this trick: Instead of counting sets and reps, pretend they're months and days of the week—June, July, August—Monday, Tuesday, Wednesday. This provides relativity to passing time and appreciation for the inevitable forward motion, the unavoidable continuum, the irresistible life-happening experience.

As I've grown older or, more appropriately, have evolved, I've chosen organic names for each exercise I perform. The methodology contributes to natural life extension. Dumbbell presses are bears in thick trees, and low incline curls are rushing river waters. Catchy, huh? Seated lat rows are winds across the wild prairies and rope tucks, my favorite, are lions among the antelope. Deep squats are the full moon on a clear night.

Be there then, be here now and be wherever tomorrow.

By the time September rolls around you will be so relieved—cool evenings, bench presses, 5 sets × 8 reps, outta here.

57

White Noise, Echoing Silence of Iron

I WATCH ENOUGH SPORTS to be thrilled, entertained and inspired, but not so much to be burdened, conflicted and dulled. In stunning moments we witness power, surprise and wonder, broken hearts, graceful defeats and ecstatic victories.

Gulp, glub, burp. I'm stuffed, time for a nap.

Naps are nice, especially for mutts who inscribe B-70+ in the columns labeled "age" on forms in waiting rooms at clinics where blood tests are done weekly. There are some dynamic codgers and fogies pushing seventy-five and eighty, but they're typically 130 pounds of walk 'n talk and no iron.

"Ya wanna push the iron, ya gotta pay the price," said the gnarly duffer loading the bar. Lately, I've been considering the price. The costs rise with age (pain, swelling, limited-to-no range of motion, fatigue) and the earnings diminish . . . train, or go ca-razy.

Gee, life's a bowl of cherries . . . and then there's tuna 'n water.

"Sorry, I think he's grumpy. Mama said there'll be days like this; there'll be days like this, mama said. Just hum along and pretend not to notice . . . mama said, mama said, hey, hey . . . Shirelles, '61. Oh, my!"

Here's my approach when contemplating the gym and a workout on a cranky day: Just get there, walk in and check the vibe; do anything resembling an exercise and see how it goes. If it's not good, go home—there's another day; if it is good, stay and play.

This attitude is not for the young lifter, whoever that is. Let's just say the tactic only works for veteran lifters, whoever they are. You'll know when you're a veteran lifter. We smell, see, stand, shift and sound singularly.

Getting to the gym can be the hardest, yet the smartest part. The drive can offer relief while stirring purpose, energy and desire. Use the time wisely. Eat a banana, slug some Bomber Blend and visit God.

Entering is not exactly easy. At least you're moving, a good sign. You're free, wise, intuitive and tough. You'll know if you should be there by the first clank and groan of others and a carefully arranged, glancing reflection of yourself in your favorite mirror, if there is such a thing. Focus. Be strong.

Doing something, anything, for a short period of time is better than nothing for a long period of time. The first few sets tell you everything: hope or despair, courage or weakness, soreness or readiness, engagement or retreat, arms 'n legs or chest, back 'n shoulders.

Not good? Seriously? Too bad. You tried. Go home, there's another day. More rest and repair, more time away to heal and deal. Don't worry, be happy. Life is a gift.

Good? I love that word, that sensation, that assessment. Smile, stay and play.

One or two natural steps forward and let your God-given instincts take over. Vets can do that, though they seldom do. "Trust yourself" is not the mantra of the suspicious, susceptible, serial musclehead. It's healthy and reliable, delightful and empowering, but how will you ever know without trying it?

Tip: Go. Let go, and go.

Engage and rage and move like a Caterpillar (the machine, not the fuzzy bug), but only for forty-five minutes. Any more would be too much, any less will have been less.

Rope tucks supersetted with seated lat rows.

One-arm dumbbell rows supersetted with stiff-arm pullovers.

Wrist curls supped with pushdowns.

Why? Why not!

Drive carefully. Potheads ahole. I mean potholes ahead.

58

There's No Turning Back, This Is Serious Business

WEIGHT TRAINING IS A double-edged sword. Swish! Swoosh!

I intentionally skipped a workout last week due to severe FBMS (Fatigue of Body, Mind and Soul). The following day I suffered the ABS (Acute Blues), a case so intense I questioned the wisdom of the standard CDF (Complete Day-Off Fix). Perhaps, the CDF tactic is too extreme for us bombus radicalus.

By nightfall I was a senseless mess. I stood at the northwest corner of the deck with outstretched arms repeatedly shouting to the skies, NANU (Never Again Not Us).

What a relief to clearly express myself to the clouds moving swiftly across the darkening skies. NANU NANU! NANU NANU!

Give it a go, gorillas. I trained the following morning like a half-crazed chimpanzee.

When the energy is low and the fatigue is high and the exclusion of a workout is not an option, slip into the gym and do a handful of simple movements to soothe the soul yet arouse the beast. Truth, discovery and invention dwell dormant in plain, uncomplicated and soul-soothing movements. Trust me.

Hey, look . . . there goes one of them furry whatchmacallits . . .

Low-incline curls work nicely because you're reclining (comfy) and the biceps are easily isolated, whereas when performing standing curls you are standing (ooph) and the torso strains big-time to stabilize the action. This is muscle- and power-building, yes, but most demanding, not the goal of this fine soul-soothing day.

Pulley pushdowns work well for the triceps because you're leaning into the handles (ahh, lean on me) and merely extending the arms and involving the less-than-monumental triceps only, if that's your pleasure, which it is.

We're seeking a friendly, muscle-stimulating, nerve-calming, soul-soothing, time-saving workout. Biceps and triceps, back and forth, like the pendulum of a grandfather clock, and you have a rhythmic 'n fulfilling superset ticking away. Take your time, what's the rush? Add seated wrist curls with a handy barbell and you demonstrate breathless creativity and timeless devotion.

Tick, tock, tick . . .

Often, after a few non-threatening, nearly friendly tri-sets, I'm slightly charged. Actually, once I'm past the front door, I feel a tiny tingle in my tail. Step aside, Clyde.

Avoid all unnecessary complications when the shoddy body says no but your strained brain says yes: bending over, squatting down, setting up equipment, moving heavy weights and traveling long distances between gear when multi-setting. Concise, condensed, contained yet constantly connected.

Another thing I notice when I'm out of juice: Pulling is easier than pushing. I can always hang in there.

Pulldowns with agreeably light weights and minus heavy tow-truck tugging are quite pleasant. You're "hanging on" to a handily hung knurled bar and it's becoming your choice. Go for the burn and go for the pump when you can't go for anything else, like, say, titles, records, medals, ribbons, fame and recognition, loud applause or cold beers with the buds.

The wide-grip pulldown behind the neck, an exercise of varied dynamics, fits right in with the prevailing light-weight, low-motivation, little-vigor stats. Barn-door lats are not the target; rather, knotty upper-back and rear deltoid development become the focus. Key elements are light weight, concentration and form; wide-grip, fully extended overhead starting position, smooth 'n continual exertion to the rear, low-neck mark, a tight contraction at the bottom and the thoughtful return.

Direct the bar with defined and disciplined effort. Do not thrust your head forward to avoid contact with the descending bar. I like pulldowns combined with machine dips. Dips are pushing, yes, but you're on top, gratefully assisted and in control of muscle engagement.

If I get this far, halfway up the other side of the hill, I knock off some rope tucks and seated lat pull-ins for several rounds. Duh!! Why I didn't I think of this torso favorite in the very beginning? I think I'm losing it, lads and lassies.

Growing up and getting old are very hard to do. They're a rosy combination, I tell ya; a surefire superset, an unbeatable pair, a dynamic duo, ever-exciting twin motivators . . . dual delights . . . double dippers with syrup on top.

59
The Last Lifter Standing

LET'S FACE IT, training is a drag. There's the absurd pre-workout ritual that includes sufficient rest, clean sweats, carbing up, a gym bag full of raggedy gear, the portable protein shake and a bottle of water; the psych, the time, the travel, the pain, the exhaustion and the grief; the dreadful first rep, the impossible last rep and the delirious repetitions between. Home and shower, eat and ache, moan and groan.

That was fun. Let's do it again.

Not that I'm counting, but I've spent 86.0743 percent of my life attached to cold, clanging, motion-resistant iron. And what have I got to show for it? A pair of inflamed elbows that don't straighten, swollen knees that don't bend, stooped shoulders that don't rotate and the aberration of counting endless reps while driving, shopping, brushing my teeth and dozing.

Should I skip a workout, this is what I have to contend with: For the first few hours I'm relieved.

"Swell idea, deserving and dedicated Bomber," I say, "rest, repair, grow and be happy."

Before long, my fingers, like spies, secretly probe my waistline, gauging the depth and density of overlapping tissue. My shoulders shrug repeatedly and arch backward in search of diminishing muscle mass. My eyes glance reluctantly in the direction of my forearms, checking wrist-hand thickness and vascularity, whatever that is.

Oh! And there I am, accidentally reflected in the Wal-Mart window—a startled deer caught in headlights—front, side and rear.

There's the moodiness, the general discomfort, the anxiety and alternating diffidence and aggression, silence and complaining. Within three days I'm reduced to a drool wandering the neighborhood, not eating, washing, sleeping, changing my diaper or verbally communicating.

It's not worth the effort, tin heads; I'm going to the gym if it kills me.

But wait! I love the house of steel. It's where life begins—the concrete walls, the towering ceiling, the cages and racks, the bars and plates; the stern and the severe, the lucky and the brave, the grateful and empowered and empowering.

I'll start off with something whimsical, something poetic, something almost magical. Low-incline curls (light weight, max exertion within 8–10 reps, evolving focus and form) adeptly shifting into incline presses, similar modus operandi. Smiles come from all directions within my gratified structure. Sit up, Bomb, and knock out non-exhausting yet triceps-embellishing one-arm triceps extensions for 10–12 worthy reps.

Sit, smile, sip . . . repeat again, again and again.

I've always liked wrist curls and dips, back and forth until I don't like them anymore . . . usually four rhythmic supersets do the deed. I dip deliberately and thoughtfully, varying body position or lean or contraction or range of motion to maximize muscle engagement and squeeze the most out of the reps—now I use a machine instead of bars, but the feeling is nearly the same. Full finger-roll wrist curls across the knees are big-grin scream-ers, 4 × 12–20 reperoos.

You can do some gut work if you want, rope tucks and leg raises.

The Iron Rocks—The Iron Knows—The Iron Works—The Iron Is.

Well, not exactly.

60
It's a Funny Thing

THE WATSONVILLE GOLD'S GYM is a comfortably bleak concrete chamber with enough irresistible tonnage to satisfy Samson and Delilah. On the inside wall, high above the floor in large bold print, is the sprawling declaration, GOLD'S GYM—SINCE 1965.

The 1965 reference is Joe's Gold's original gym in Venice, the cinderblock building he built by hand, housing some of the greatest oversized machines he also built by hand in his garage a mile away. The perfect gym we all dream about, look for and can no longer find.

It's gone. It's become, well, this, a grandchild in fancy pants all these years later. The new models do nicely, for a proper, well-heeled, bare-bearded lad. The substantial room containing the iron is one corner of a 25,000-square-foot affair, the entirety of which I have never experienced. For all I know (or want to know), all that exists is this oversized rectangle, the john and the parking space immediately outside the door.

I watched the original Venice gym go up, and watched Joe form and weld the iconic equipment in his cutoffs and flip flops. Before the dust settled and the plumbing was complete, I joined. Joe called me his first member. I wasn't, I don't think, but I was one of the first. Zabo, the bronzed muscular old dude (forty-two at the time) who dug the foundations, beat me to it.

I remember one morning sitting with a handful of stout dumbbells perched on my lap awaiting the sudden thrust into position for the launch of some delirious inclines. I was conspicuously alone, the floor was bright with sunshine, full-size mirrors lined the walls (I in them, dare I look). Unimpressed cars zipped by the open front door and the endless ocean, a block away, heaved upon the shore.

I had no idea I was in heaven.

At twenty-three with a Jersey accent, a sweet and frightened sixteen-year-old spouse, a darling daughter, a furnished apartment, a nickel and a dime and an obscure brain, I thought about nothing and no one, nowhere and no how. Duh, anybody using this bench?

I spoke in clinks and clanks, emitted clunks and was working on thuds.

It was my first workout removed from the downstairs, dark, rusty, splintery, mirror-less and sort of frightening Muscle Beach Dungeon. I suspect had The Dungeon on Fourth and Broadway in Santa Monica not closed due to building demolition, I would be training there today.

Holy Moly, we've had something like a dozen presidents and a half-dozen wars since then.

Did I mention the original Gold's Gym Venice crumbled, like the Roman Coliseum, and here I am today, 350 miles north?

Mostly guys in their twenties populate Gold's weightroom floor. They look at me clinging to a bench and wonder for a split second who the heck the old guy is with the pulsating vein. They're a good group, solid, tough and hard-working; no wise guys or loud mouths. Just disgustingly young.

I slip in when the action is light. That's not true; I don't slip into anything, except an occasional coma. I park as close as I can to the front door, gather my gear, wits and breath and, carefully aiming my body toward my destination, lean forward and hope for the best. It works every time. Once I gain access and am amid the equipment, I'm safe to go, each chunky machine a support as I blast my way through a workout.

Oh, yeah . . . blasting is another thing that's faintly controversial.

I improvise as I go, as you know, keeping the distance between the supersetted equipment to a minimum. Improvisation is the foremost facility I've accrued, lesson I've learned, skill I've acquired, treasure I've heaped after the years of iron intervention.

What to do, when and how much, I'm certain; the why still gives me pause. "Because it's there" is sometimes the best answer to the lattermost curiosity. It all has to do with shoulders, chest and back, bis and tris, the legs below my waist and the brain lodged between my ears and the heart vaguely in the vicinity.

Let's see; where do I start, how do I proceed, are we done yet?

When in doubt, press, squat and deadlift.

Doubtless Sunday:
Incline curls and press superset (4 × 8 reps and 15–20 reps)
Wrist curl and dip superset (4 × 10–12 and 15 reps)
Single-arm cable crossover (4 × 15 reps)
Single-arm dumbbell sidearm lateral raise (3 × 8 reps)
Light weights, lots of force and focus, fortitude and fatigue (phooey).

61

Simplicity Made Simple: Push, Pull, Grunt, Grin

THE FOLLOWING EMAIL sorta summarizes the characteristics, nature and interest of most readers (give or take age, gender and hat size).

> *Hi, Dave . . . I've just turned sixty-five, officially an old man, fit but not muscle-bound. Not overweight. Lots of aches and pains.*
>
> *What would you recommend as far as exercises, sets, reps, weight? All the reading on the web confuses me more and more. I have dumbbells, a bar and a bench. Thanks, JW*

Clear, concise, determined—that's us. It's the next-to-last sentence that underlines my nothing-new notion: "All the reading on the web confuses me more and more."

There's nothing new, folks, just the same good, old-fashioned exercises and foods, guts and n-qs (never-quits). Remember, we're not talking about the well-oiled heavy-caliber, high-velocity, automatic-action bodybuilder on stage under the lights. We're talking about us, you and me.

Simplicity—simple goals and simple applications—is superior: health, feeling good, living long, fulfilling iron action, improving-maintaining muscle tone and strength, energy and attitude (or, let's say, certainly not retreating into old age like a hapless bystander). This can and ought to be fun—sets and reps, thuds and clanks.

Besides, as we know, sound discipline, a little sacrifice and smartly regulated, essential pain are good for the body, mind and soul . . . not to mention those horseshoe triceps and barndoor lats.

Let's assume JW is a physical working guy—not digging ditches, oh-my-back, but on the go, pushing and pulling, managing and heaving stuff because he can, needs to, wants to, always has and that's the way it is. Retirement is up to him, but he's not up to retirement.

This is what I'd do if I were him.

There's nothing like active walking to condition the legs and engage the cardio and fat-burning qualities of the body. Walk fifteen minutes, three times a week, hills and stairs welcome. Dust off your barbell, dumbbells and bench and square off your workout area. Don't make it a major project, but make it a friendly, agreeable and efficient place to be. You're scheduled to be there three days a week for forty-five to sixty minutes, cheerfully performing the basics with eighty-percent input.

This you know: There are no tricks, there are no pressures and there are no deadlines. There is simply working out with intent, feel and focus—sets and reps and poundage to guide you, not to threaten you; hardy work that agrees with your five senses and joints and incentives. Like Einstein said, or was it Zane, a good workout has rhythm and flow and balance and just enough force.

Excessive force breaks the body, the mind, the joy and the spirit.

Three days a week with the iron and another three days on the hoof. We're looking at three terrific hours neatly spread throughout the seven-day period. There are some folks who spend that much time surfing the internet every day before noon.

Okay, let's get to it. There's no time for fancy stuff—it all has to do with pushing and pulling, extending and contracting, any three alternate days a week with the walks on off-days.

Monday

Dumbbell press (3 sets × 8–10 reps)
Dumbbell stiff-arm pullover (3 sets × 8–10 reps)
Barbell curl (3 sets × 8–10 reps)
Lying triceps extension with barbell (3 sets × 10–12 reps)

Wednesday

Lateral raise (3 sets × 6–8 reps)
One-arm dumbbell row (3 sets × 8 reps)
Light deadlift (3 sets × 8 reps)

Friday

Light-weight, bent-leg good-mornings for gut, lower back and warm-up (3 sets × 12–15 reps)
Dumbbell press (3–4 sets × 8–10 reps)
Dumbbell stiff-arm pullover (3–4 sets × 8–10 reps)
Barbell curl (3 sets × 8–10 reps)
Overhead triceps extension with barbell (3 sets × 10–12 reps)

The design of the workout is to hit enough of everything in a functional, push-pull symmetry and to keep it interesting without a lot of time-consuming plate juggling. It's a friendly training plan an absent lifter can apply to re-familiarize himself with the iron and himself, and one a solid musclehead can grasp tightly and make serious things happen.

Too much? Lower the sets or only do two workouts a week.

Rule one: Easy does it.

Rule two: Easy does it.

Rule three: Lift and learn.

Rule four: Focus and form.

Rule five: Be strong and courageous.

Rule six: Be grateful.

Stick with it for four or five weeks with close attention when in action. Don't dwell on working out; that's exhausting. Apply effort and pace according to your acumen, desires, instincts and inner chronometer.

Leave your ego at the door. The dog can join you, the cat by all means, but not the ego. He's trouble.

You don't need an injury and you don't need painkillers. No disappointment and discouragement allowed.

Soreness is not unusual. Tough! Grin 'n bear it.

The workouts change when needed. We can talk again in a month after you're tuned up and tuned in. Of course, this information and encouragement is worth little without smart eating and resting.

So drink a protein shake and get plenty of Zs . . .

62

Let's Do More,
Let's Do It Again

"I'M A HEALTHY fifteen-, twenty-, thirty-year-old and want to lift weights to build strong and functional and nifty muscles. What should I do in the next thirty days?"

Nifty muscles?

Welcome, young man, young lady, and congratulations on your commendable endeavor. Smile with delight. You're at the beginning of an instructive and rewarding adventure. Endure and you will learn and grow in ways you never expected.

First of all, inquisitive young person, you need the tools to do the job. Back in my day, the tools were rocks and timbers. But today, in the age of the iPhone, a set of weights or a kettlebell will do nicely—a membership to a local gym could prove to be handy as well.

I'm going to make the giant assumption you know the elemental barbell and dumbbell movements for the various muscle groups.

Since the creation and subsequent evolution of Joe Gold's gym in the mid-sixties, curls, presses and deadlifts, biceps, triceps and shoulders have become inherent in mankind's understanding.

What's not clear is the discipline, perseverance and humility to apply, pursue and achieve.

Man, have I got clichés for you: *Just do it; Never quit; Lift and shut up; Press on, Be strong and courageous; No one said it was easy; Only the strong survive; One more rep.*

Is it time for lunch yet?

If I were you, I'd start the weights clanking with the performance of the standing barbell curl. It feels indescribably fantastic to wrap your hands around the bar in the perfect position. You do have a perfect position, don't you? Mine is hip-width, palms forward.

I see more young lifters curling from a sort of bent-forward position, hands too close for comfort, while doing a half-curl as if that was all there is. What's that all about? They use enough thrust to launch a rocket.

Building muscle is a battle, but it's not a war.

I have a sneaky suspicion they won't be around to claim victory and enjoy peace—building a pair of complete, healthy and powerful biceps.

I prefer the following sequence: Grasp the bar, stand upright, allow the bar to hang fully, inhale and tip the body forward to accommodate the resistance upon commencing the curl, bring the bar toward the chin to complete the motion, and, exhaling slowly, return the bar with controlled might to the original start position. That is one dandy barbell curl. Let's do more, let's do it again.

And do you really think the biceps are the only muscles involved in this dynamic muscle-building movement? Next time, note the engagement and flexing of the legs, buttocks, lower and upper back and abdominal muscles. Jackpot! You've struck it rich.

I like eight or ten reps to suit the biceps, a relatively small and frequently engaged muscle. Ten to twelve reps are agreeable. Sensible, calculated thrusting to coax the curl is useful. Nasty thrusting is nasty. Two sets for today—apply mild strain, Jane; don't be mean, Gene.

Next? Ready for it? Dips between a pair of improvised parallel bars, two sets of twelve reps.

Dips, assisted with your feet on a stabilizer if needed, are a valuable exercise. Get to know them well: Upright position for triceps, back and delts; lean forward for more pec and deeper muscle activity.

Every exercise, every movement, every action should be done with precision and exactness in mind. The focus and thoughtfulness, care and control, even if you're a sloppy mess, are present in your mind and assist you in your overall development. Trust me.

Trusting me is like trusting a seeing-eye dog with a monocle and walking stick. Woof.

One day you might want to do the two exercises back and forth, like the pendulum on a clock or the swing of the wrecking ball on a demolition crane. Let's call it supersetting, or SuperSetting when referencing the latter metaphor. Saves time, gets the work done, provides rhythm.

There was a time when I was attempting to grow up, when barbell curls and dips were the only exercises I did—back and forth for the afternoon after I did my homework and before I shot hoops. Today I think you need a license to shoot hoops. I sure do miss the good old days.

About feeding those hungry muscles: What do you think of sardines?

My secret mission is to remind you of the need, the good and the delight in smart exercise, healthy eating and productive thinking.

63
Rejoice and Be Glad

WE METAL-HUGGERS KNOW HOW to have a good time. Just pile the weights on the bar and commence pressing and squatting. Some light-hearted folks prefer dancing the night away or a classy show at the Starlight Lounge, but not us. Clunk, thud and no dessert, thanks.

"Let's go to the lake and fish or hit the greens and golf."

I don't think so. Slam, bam and a can of tuna, ma'am.

I am so thankful my early years were possessed with lifting weights, getting hunky, eating chickens and digging underground forts in the dried sludge dredged from the bottom of the Hackensack River and deposited in the vacant property across the road from my house in Secaucus, where the pig farms thrived sixty years ago.

Seriously, where would I be today?

And, oh, the memories . . . let me tell ya . . . I could go on for twelve to fifteen seconds! Did I tell you about the time Jimmy and I grabbed a bus, the Number 2, and went to NYC to buy firecrackers and eat at the Horn & Hardart Coin-operated Automat on Forty-Second and Broadway? We were ten, our clenched fists held hard-earned coins from our newspaper routes. We wore hand-me-down jeans with holes in the knees.

Additional highlights of the good times: The Slinky, Silly Putty and the Frisbee were invented.

Today, lookalike designer jeans go for $129 plus tax (frayed holes machine-made in China, very cool), and there are no news-paper home-deliveries. Kids have iPhones and junior credit cards (hey, there's an idea!), overdrawn allowances and Big Mac tummies.

Those were the good old days when men were men and women were women, iron was iron and rust was rust—a nickel was a nickel and frayed holes were child's play.

In the '50s every bodybuilder in the world could fit on sunny California's Muscle Beach, with plenty of room to strut. He had seventeen-inch arms, abs, a tan and a girl in a bikini. She did handstands and cartwheels. He did curls and presses.

In the '70s the bodybuilder stood upright, multiplied and grew large in size. He became they; they became beasts. The world noticed.

Nothing stopped them; ladies joined them; they filled the valleys, the hillsides and lands north and south. Ripped became popular, veiny and chiseled. Guys and gals paired up and enter-tained audiences with their grace and magnificence on stage under the lights surrounded by music. And, oh, the tans.

Big muscles became big business, the good and the creepy. A good gym became as popular as a good restaurant. Soon they became as common as a common restaurant. Health and fitness thrived. One could, in fact, get in shape and stay in shape shaking a stick at the new gyms, muscle magazines, health food stores, supplements and supplement companies, gear and toys, gizmos and gadgets dedicated to muscles.

Balls, rollers, grippers, bands . . .

I, with help from wild and crazy friends, built and owned a couple of really cool gyms from '89 to '04. Gym ownership and gym management are like a big, never-ending, joyous, get-rich vacation: squats, deadlifts, presses; opening and closing, selling and instructing, cleaning and repairing.

By the mid-'90s the ever-growing professional bodybuilder took on new dimensions. The weightlifting activity lost any likeness to a sport and the consummate champion lost any resemblance to a man or woman. Though I'm not an adoring admirer, I appreciate the top contenders as I do heavy artillery or Cat Bulldozers. Very impressive, indeed. Five-ten, 320 pounds, ripped 'n veiny, muscle upon muscle. Holy moly, Ravioli.

The guys make gains so fast they wonder what hit them. Who am I? Humility is absent, pride not calculated. Appreciation is misunderstood, value and worth unknown. Like being born rich and spoiled with the frayed holes carefully prepared, placed and tended.

Maybe it's because I'm older than dirt. That's enough to put a little snark in your jolly ole viewpoint.

Today, musclemen are like leaves on a tree—many, and they come and go with spring and autumn. There are mail-order body-builders and bodybuilders online, and every other male lead in a current TV series is a Hollywood bodybuilder. What was once odd is now almost ordinary (out-of-shape is still ordinary). What was once a result of aspiration and dedication, patience and very hard work is now available with a whiff of sacrifice and a notion of devotion.

Where there once were barbells and dumbbells and protein, now there are ingredients x thru z. An hour a day, five days a week will do the trick. Last count, there were enough bodybuilders to start a medium-sized nation of extra-large people.

64
Airborne

I've never been a student . . . that is, one who studies. School from grade one was a ladder I had to climb to get out of the hole I was in. It seemed like a very deep hole with a steep ladder of many rungs. I tried filling the cavernous space with water and floating to the top, but that failed. I did learn how to swim.

As time went by, the subterranean dearth of knowledge became a barbwire wall to be scaled. Gee, that's a very tall wall. Tunneling the barrier didn't work, and before I was ten I broke a wrist trying to leap the towering confine. I did learn how to dig, leap and fall, and I learned a thing or two about futility, patience and perseverance.

Growing up is hard to do.

My brothers were older, and from my viewpoint much better at the task. Their second-hand toys didn't help, so I got me some used weights from a neighbor. Ever since that day I ceased trying to grow up. Growing big and growing strong took its place. Now a bomber, I cruise the steel-blue skies, a somewhat sinewy child not planning to land anytime soon.

Have Iron, Will Travel.

But first let's pause. Take a moment. Dare to look yourself in the mirror without judgment, ridicule or unseemly pride. Now, take a deep breath and ask yourself, who am I, what am I doing here and what exactly do I want from my training experience?

Can you do that, bombers? It's difficult, isn't it, more difficult than you expected?

Me? I cannot do that. It doesn't even enter my mind. Why bother? For the past decades, as soon as I enter the gym, I've got to grab some iron and go. The last thing I need to do is think about stuff like who I am.

Who cares? Does it make a difference?

Lift now. Lift hard. Lift good.

Incidentally, I'm here for fun and to build muscle 'n might, health and character, improve sports performance (Slap Jack, Go Fish) and survival abilities, to kill time and overcome insecurities (neither of which I personally have), beat myself up badly, pay off guilt and keep evil away. That's it, folks.

Here's a challenge for the lifter who knows a muscle burn from an injury, a pump from an inflammation, one-more-rep from the last rep: The next time you cruise the gym (the gym on the corner or the barbell in your basement), allow yourself to go on auto-pilot for an hour . . . okay, thirty minutes. It's necessary.

Rule and order are good; routines are great. But we must let go occasionally to know who and where we are. Detach and discover; let go and learn.

You're meeting yourself in action, the only way to know the truth. The questions you ask answer themselves.

Here I am. There are the tools of resistance. Go.

But, but, but . . . I, I, I . . . duh . . .

Hint: Do some ab and torso work to warm up. Have I ever mentioned rope tucks or hanging leg raises? These get me going every time and give me time to appraise my body and assess my needs, possibilities and desires.

The first set opens the door and in I go like I own the joint.

Say today is supposed to be back and shoulders, but I notice they feel worn and achy. Hmmm. The bis and tris scheduled for Friday feel like they could use a tender-loving kick in the butt today, some trisets like old man Draperwitz brags about given half a chance.

Why's he always underscoring the advantages of supersetting? Because they're a blast and they work.

Best supersets when I was a kid (anytime between 1963 and 2006):

- PBN (press behind neck) and seated side-arm lateral raise
- Deadlift and dumbbell pullover
- Dumbbell inclines and seated lat row
- Standing barbell curl and lying triceps extension
- One-arm dumbbell row, left, then right (sort of a superset)
- Full squat and dumbbell pullover
- Seated dumbbell incline curl and overhead triceps extension
- Front press and bent-over lateral raise
- Leg extension, leg curl

Everything was four or five sets × 12, 10, 8, 6 reps . . . max effort without passing out or wiggling like a fool. Focus is intense, form purposeful, pace moderate, unfailing and steady, and lessons learned countless, constant and continual.

Not much has changed, except everything.

65
Too Distracted to Have a Purpose

GOING THROUGH LIFE without a specific purpose is okay. You get by. You don't go anywhere, but the days pass. There's television with the Super Bowl, pro wrestling, reality shows, infomercials, dramas, sitcoms, news and video games. We have food and drink, real and man-made, fast and home-delivered. There are drugs and alcohol. Our wandering attention is captured by the endless dilemmas presented by the news media, the hopes offered by advertisers and the general threat of daily living in a post-9/11 world.

Purpose? Who needs, considers or has time for purpose?

Purpose is often interchangeable with goals and motivations and is a cousin to reason and incentive.

We are choked with entertainment and distractions and goofiness. I'll just slap on my earphones and listen to some sounds on my satellite radio while I check out my iPhone. *Terminator IX* is playing at the Coliseum of Theaters and I can purchase tickets with my credit card over my cell phone.

Several dynamics are at work obstructing purpose, the main driving force in a productive and aspiring individual, community and society.

- In today's delirious world a person can be too distracted to have a purpose.

- He is rendered shallow by the senseless frivolity surrounding him and fails to consider the need for purpose.

- She recognizes the value of purpose, realizes the commitment, dedication and hard work it necessitates, but chooses ample distractions to avoid its responsibilities.

- The importance of purpose is clear; it is hastily installed, yet as hard as we try, we can't sustain its requirements. The lure and clutter of amusements are too demanding and overpowering.

Purpose never had a chance.

Life without a purpose is like a hand without a thumb; you can scratch, point, tap, count up to four, but you can't get a grip on anything. You can grasp, but you can't hold on.

Folks without purpose fall asleep at the wheel, get off at the wrong station and put their pants on backward. They get by, they make it through the day, they might even have family and friends and a good paying job, but beneath the first layer of skin there's Styrofoam.

Styrofoam is a modern invention that efficiently replaces real substance. Cheap, lightweight, a great filler, it insulates and withstands hot and cold—a perfect substitute for purpose where purpose does not exist. Styrofoam is everywhere today. I suspect I myself have pockets of Styrofoam.

Occasionally I notice I'm zipping along, yet moving neither forward nor back. I look down and lo and behold, my pants are on backward. I hate that. Not the Captain of the Bomb Squad . . . without a compass, adrift in thin air, altitude unknown, zipper to the rear and targetless.

Mayday . . . mayday.

No panic, been there. It's just a warning, like the blink on the dashboard that indicates a seatbelt is a nuisance, a painfully welcome and familiar signal to arouse and remind us to watch where we're going and what we're doing and why—huge and ripped or lean and mean—if we want to get there.

When purpose wanes, when motivation recedes, when a goal is not in sight, I become restless, sluggish and stale. I, as you, am unlike my video-game, fast-food counterpart, and the condition soon becomes evident and quickly unacceptable.

Steps must be taken to overcome the stall in my forward movement, my flight, and I look toward my training to amend the minor disaster. I have observed that my personal life and my training are inextricably entwined and fixing one gives health to the other.

And the closer I look, the more I'm convinced it's my training that determines the desirable flow of my life—events, moods, energy and spirit.

Training without purpose is like shopping at the supermarket without a list, an appetite or any memory of what's in the refrigerator or on the shelves at home. You wander the aisles and finally come home with a twenty-five-pound bag of Doggie-Chow.

So what you don't have a dog. It was on sale.

You know why you go to the gym and eat right. The list's as long as your arm, yet you sometimes forget. Life's like that. It rolls along with ups and downs, through hot and cold, and moves in mysterious cycles. We're eager and joyful and hitting the mark day after day, and then the mark eludes us—we become irritable, withdrawn and careless.

Speak for yourself, Draper.

We wonder why we bother. We punch at the air and kick inanimate objects and hiss. Swell. Now we're soft and puffy and the weights feel like they're bolted to the floor. No more veins, pump's gone . . . Good-bye, cruel world.

But wait: Don't flush away months of training and sacrifice in one push of the handle. We must continually feed the fire within. The flickering embers grow cold if we don't review the reasons for our efforts, relive our successes and revive our goals and remember we're special.

- Regular review takes place in the subconscious—preparation.

- Reliving our achievements is occasionally done when we feel generous and slightly numb—encouragement.

- Revival of goals must be done at appropriate intervals with intention, humility and high hopes, as often as it takes for them to become certain and real—reinforcement.

- Remember, we know people who don't have goals, never heard of them or made them and forgot them—dead man walking.

Your goals, your level of motivation (concentration of incentives, clarity and depth of reasons), your decided purpose—all of this determines your training efficiency and effectiveness and joy.

Think "why" before you lift, and then lift hard.

66
Sliding into Summer

OK! IT'S SUMMER AND you're not prepared. You meant to be. You even started in April, but overnight it turned into July. Your plan to get in shape got sidetracked, upended and then completely scrapped. Don't despair. They can land a scooter on Mars, you can lose five pounds of fat in a month and gain a pound or two of muscle besides.

Here's a simple program.

Set the above as your goal. It's reasonable. It's as close as mid-August. It's the best thing you can do for yourself this year, and always. Remember, an unexercised, unfit body is in decline. Young, lean muscle when unattended fades, and fat grows in the most disagreeable places.

There's more. An interesting dilemma takes place behind the scenes—body chemistry gets out of shape as well. Our fragile fat-burning enzymes fail to do the job in converting fat into energy calories, and we become sluggish, hypoglycemic and rely on carbs for short-lasting lifts.

Moody? Carbs not used as energy in a deconditioned system stores as more fat. Yikes.

Well-exercised muscle, on the other hand, is alive, responsible for quick action and physical power. It moves us around, effectively . . . gracefully. Mighty muscle accounts for ninety percent of metabolism, burning fat calories all the time, even when we sleep.

Very handy—looks good too.

This strategy is to remind, to encourage, to arouse some honest guilt and, like the Constitution and the Ten Commandments, should be in effect at all times, not altered to fit an agenda.

Adios, junko foodo. Starting with breakfast, eat three to five equally spaced meals each day, more or less depending on lifestyle, current weight, goals and metabolism. Pump up the protein (animal, egg, whey, fish are the best sources—sorry, it's true), withdraw high glycemic carbs and dump the trans fats. Drink miraculous water by the barrel, and as you do, silently be thankful—you are being restored.

Misplace your lopsided scale and rigid calculator for a month: the stopwatch, the LEDs, RPMs, compass, earphones, the entire precise mess. The task ahead is better done by feel, by instinct, by flow rather than by brains and science. Given the proper programming, you are by far the best computer ever created.

Blast the gym three times a week for an hour of weights, hit the streets three times a week for an uphill mile, and hit the edge of your bed each morning for ten minutes of joint mobility and leg raises.

Why the long puss? Is that whining, mister? Tears don't cut it, girl!

The wills are weak; the disciplines are dusty.

And that looks like a thin coat of tarnish on the breastplate of courage . . . signs of over-hibernation, comfort-zone blues and procrastination.

67

Bent-Over Rows, Powerful Mass Builder

OKAY, PEOPLE. SETTLE DOWN. Let me have your attention, please. Put your baseball cards away; we've got a lot to do. Work in physics is defined by the equation [w=fs]: force put through distance and is measured in foot pounds. Here's your assignment: calculate the number of foot pounds you perform in your next back workout and mail in the results for group comparison.

For example, the bent-over row: Multiply the weight used, 100 pounds, times the distance traveled, two feet, times the number of reps performed, ten reps. In this case we have work equals $100 \times 2 \times 10$, or 2,000 foot pounds (one ton). Multiply this result by the number of sets performed (five) and we have 10,000 foot pounds, or five tons.

Very good. So much for physics and math.

Now moving on to our study of psychology, I want you to write in fifty words or fewer why anyone in a right mind would lift this much weight—year after year. Are we strange? Do you think it's a good idea we go on like this, unsupervised?

Are we—excuse the psychobabble—all in denial?

And, speaking of the aforementioned bent-over rows, let me say they are the best of the powerful back-builders. Wide-grip chins are up there in importance for lat width, pulldowns to the front are significant for muscularity and V shape, seated lat rows are standard for full back shaping, never to be omitted.

But barbell rows are king.

Thing is, they're the toughest, meanest and most demanding upper-body movement. Bent-over rows are a comprehensive exercise like squats, deadlifts and standing military presses. They work large and specific muscles (the full back), yet engage the whole system in their execution—fingers to toes. Therefore, systemic, whole-body growth is accomplished, along with deep fatigue and an accentuated need for recovery.

Rows are a power exercise and are most effective when performed with heavy weight. The movement is basic, although it takes practice and conditioning over months to allow you to safely perform with the body thrusts that recruit the muscle mass.

The bent-over torso acts as a lever under the resistance of the bar. The lower back, the spinal vertebrae, supported by the erectors, provide the fulcrum and bear an extraordinary load.

We should all, young and old, toughen our lower backs with hyperextensions and lightweight deadlifts throughout our weekly training. This will also prepare us for the wear of everyday living, athletics and these heavier lifting endeavors.

To protect my lower back, I assume a relatively close standing position, bend over with my ribcage somewhat supported by my thighs, back is flat, eyes focused somewhere ten feet before me to correctly position my head.

I grab the bar in an overgrip some six inches from the collars of an Olympic bar. I settle in with major focus on grip and body position as I deep breathe three or four times in preparation.

Then I tightly pull the bar to the mid-chest or thereabouts and deliberately lower to the starting position, just short of tapping the floor. Then, it's up again with muscle power, down again with focus on the negative.

A warmup of light weight, 12–15 reps to locate the groove, align muscles and attachments, raise the blood flow and area temperature is always wise and welcome.

Now you're ready to continue with a smart four sets of 8–10 reps. When you're able, a 12-10-8-6-rep system is always agreeable and productive.

Depending on your level of development, you could include rows two times per week as an exercise for reps, perhaps less if you blast it. Practice this consistently for months, not just occasionally.

One-arm dumbbell rows are a great alternative to keep heavy action going, yet give the low back a rest between heavy barbell rowing sessions.

Vary your grip from wide to close to discover the change in muscle action: The closer the grip, the tighter, more central the back involvement. The wider grip means broad muscle action, more freedom, plus rear delt attention.

There's a big load on grip, forearm and biceps. Quads, hams and glutes get pumping as you get into heavy pulling. Sometimes stiff-arm pullovers with a bent bar fit well into a scheme as superset transitions.

You want the long sweep of the lower lat, thick rhomboids and rugged erectors? Reverse your grip on the bar about shoulder wide. Bend at the waist, fully extend the bar to the floor and slightly forward. Now, pull the bar just past the knees and tightly to the waist, arching the back with each contraction to emphasize the muscle action.

Better yet, use a bent bar for wrist comfort and superior contractions. Start light, practice the motion, locate your muscles and work up. You'll sleep tonight and groan tomorrow.

Nurse, we're ready for our medication now.

68
The Dungeon, 1963

I HAVE COLLECTED over the years an impressive file of tough workouts to review. You see, in forty years I've rarely missed one, and not one was easy. Training all-out with meticulous form and mild sound effects always defined my style.

My most vivid tough workouts are set against the backdrop of the Muscle Beach Gym in the early 1960s. This famous, beloved relic, once located on the unspoiled shores of Santa Monica, was relocated by the encouragement of the city council to the underground basement of a collapsing retirement hotel four blocks inland.

A very long, steep and unsure staircase took me to a cavernous hole in the ground with crumbling plaster walls and a ceiling that bulged and leaked diluted beer from the old-timer's tavern above. Puddles of the stuff added charm to the dim atmosphere, where three strategically placed forty-watt light bulbs gave art deco shadows to the rusting barbells, dumbbells and splintery handcrafted two by four benches and sagging milk crates.

You have no idea how proud I am to have this theater and the real-life plays that unfolded day after day as part of my experience. It's pure gold.

The magic didn't come from the pharmacist; it came from the soul, the era, the history in the making, the presence of uncompromised originality yet to be imitated.

Those years I got to the gym between 5:30 and 6:00 AM while the city slept, curiously content in getting a head start. By the time I left, perhaps three or four other creatures had descended the lonely steps to reluctantly take up arms.

I like the company I keep when I'm alone. I like the sounds of silence; I like the uncluttered space. With a crowd of one there's no one to complain or groan, no self-consciousness, no dividing of attention, no one to impress.

My workouts today bear a striking resemblance to that hardcore iron locomotion of years ago. Achievement and age instruct me to limit my workouts to five per week instead of six. Three days on, one off; two days on, one off is quite satisfying. Hammered joints and insertions convincingly suggest I use lighter weights and discard a pocketful of somehow replaceable exercises. I'm doin' fine.

It was in The Dungeon in '63, '64, '65 and '66 when those tough workouts took place. What kept me going without missing a beat is another story.

There was no glory except a rumor of respect and reputation among the underground bodybuilders and weightlifters. People in the real world sincerely frowned at us . . . a musclehead, misfit, a bewildered loser who's harming himself and isn't doing us any good either.

Man, has that concept taken a spin.

My toughest workouts took place in the middle of those formidable years way back when. I had training partners from time to time, and one in particular, Dick Sweet, pushed, encouraged and goaded me to those otherwise unapproached limits.

There existed on the far end of the caving rack a set of 150-pound dumbbells, awesome in length with pipe handles and suicide welds on the ends. These unwieldy contraptions could be further enlarged by strapping five-pound plates on either end with strips of inner tube. You got it—giant rubber bands. Getting them together took two guys, some muscle and engineering. Getting them overhead took temporary insanity.

We won't talk about the sixty-degree incline bench of wood and ten-penny nails wedged against the wall. Never did get a good look at it in the dark. On the third rep of the third set, the rubber band snapped and slapped me in the face.

Some guy standing in the shadows snickered.

Shortly thereafter a five-pounder bounced off my forehead; I saw it coming. This made me serious. I had two sets to go and no more rubber bands. A short length of rope got me through the last two sets.

Did I tell you I was supersetting?

Workouts without supersets were not workouts at all. I was doing bent-over lateral raises with the sixties. The welds this time were on the inside of the dumbbells and were cracked, not dangerous but sloppy. Every third or fourth rep the web of my left hand between the thumb and the index finger got pinched in the crack. This, too, made me serious.

Good thing there's not much nerve ending and the blood flow was light, or I'd have never finished my workout.

All I had left was upright rows with that rusty, comfortably bent bar over by the beer puddle, and side-arm laterals with the fifty-pound weights. The fifties were tight and balanced like trophies, the best in the house.

69

Bomber Affordable Health Care—Bombercare

WE ON THE CENTRAL COAST of California are enjoying the greatest weather anywhere on the planet Earth since its discovery at least a thousand years ago. A month of sunny, warm and humidity-free days with a stroke of breeze has invigorated the lethargic and calmed the restless. Oh, look there's a puffy white cloud on the azure-blue horizon.

I don't say this without anxiously imagining an imminent 7.9 earthquake lurking in the rock formations just beneath the glorious landscape.

Wait . . . ! Did you feel that?!

Yes, that's a week's supply of rations and emergency supplies in my backpack in case you were wondering. It weighs just over seventy-five pounds with my Bomber Blend protein, rubber exertube, handgrips, tank tops and posing trunks.

And to think they're firing cannons at each other in the Middle East and in Washington, DC. What's that all about? You'd think natural disasters, acts of God and basic survival would be entertaining enough. Get some barbells, dumbbells and benches to resolve your disagreements, people. Life's too short.

The left pulls and the right pushes; the right pulls and the left pushes. All together now—curls and presses, squats and deadlifts. What's so hard about that? You spot me, I spot you. Whatever you do, don't close the gym.

Exercise is good for your health, too.

Weight training is not only cooperative and unifying, it reduces frustration, soothes the soul and is known to fix, mend, heal and restore things that hurt or are broken. Thus, and this is a biggie, it almost eliminates the need for costly, confusing and impossible health care plans.

Major added attraction: Lifting weights offers universal relief.

Dumbbell inclines supersetted with stiff-arm pullovers have solved just about every problem this world traveler has ever encountered. Throw in some standing barbell curls with lying triceps extensions and we have universal energy, abundance and enduring peace.

For laughs, press-behind-necks combined with side-arm lateral raises in superset fashion are a knee-slapping, gut-wrenching riot. Wrist curls with an Olympic bar and thumbs-up curls are good for a smile. Combined, they'll tickle your funny bone as no other multi-set ever.

The lusty among you, those who never seem to get enough, can always count on squats and deadlifts to satisfy your cravings. In the past I performed the exercises on separate days using my reliable 5 × 12, 10, 8, 6, 4 reps approach. Life was simple, as I recall. If lust is problematic, do both exercises on the same day.

Should the problem persist, superset the movements and be done with it. Lust no more.

What's cool about lifting is you don't need a team or fields or courts or mountain slopes or expanses of sky or masses of water to perform. You can lift with friends in a gym or alone in a corner. All you require is a stack of iron, a heap of steel and a bench to lean on.

Oh, and you need some guts, a little madness and a hard head—a nose to follow, a fistful of instincts to guide and strong goals to pursue.

I sometimes lift weights blindfolded while wearing ear plugs. They don't call me the Silent and Masked Bomber Obliterator for nothing.

Note: I lied about the blindfold.

70
For the Ladies and Gentlemen in the Bleachers

I PLOPPED DOWN ON A deck chair in the late-morning sun, knowing the precious rays that give life, stir healing and provide relief for the oft-distressed heart were the last ones of the year. Still and at peace, I basked in warm, tranquil silence. I heard no one, nothing, not a whisper.

The madness dragged on till I twitched like a sack of fleas, every bodyache magnified and throbbed, and the deafening silence gave way to a forest full of clamor.

Woodpeckers persistently hammered and pummeled the trees, and brazen blue jays—like police defending their community—called, warned and chided in demanding shrieks. A hillside swale a mile from the ocean's shore provided the background score, the din of sundry vehicles, industry and population in motion.

Undaunted, my contemplations continued as I sat, observed and twitched. Were they recorded and unedited, they, my bell-tone thoughts, would sound something like this:

I don't get many email questions (wheeze, gag) asking me how to build twenty-inch arms or barn-door lats these days. I suspect (cough-cough) it's because I have all that priceless information recorded in black and white somewhere or another (snorf)—pads, books, magazines, computer files, sweaty palms, paper napkins or walls of tenement halls (sniff).

Nowadays, I receive requests from guys—they've gotta be over sixty (yerp)—asking how on earth (snivel, snort) do they lose their bellies, butts and baldness. Peculiar! In a way it's fascinating and one step short of bizarre (gurgle-glerp). Mysterious, even. I wonder what the devil the world is coming to (burp).

I tell them, look, when you were a kid, you did what kids did. You ran like a gazelle, lifted weights like a gorilla and ate like a prize-winning hog; you'd rest, smile and gleam. Now, as an over-grown grown-up, you do the same things, only more and less.

That is, less gazelle, gorilla and pig, and more rest, smile and gleam.

At three-score years and eleven, the essential quandary I confront is simply this: When am I using up—exhausting, wasting, abusing—my physical stores and strength and my impetus in seeking long-term fitness? When am I being excessive in my physical output and, thus, endangering, sabotaging, violating my health and long life? Or when am I engaged sufficiently and satisfactorily to aspire and be happy?

Really, when is training for an old warship too much, not enough or just right?

That's easy (nothing's easy). I'm heading for the gym and will decide my workout on the way. Zipping down the coast I ask myself a few basic questions, like what hurts (everything hurts), what's safe 'n sound (muffled muttering), what's neglected (feeble glances) and what's hungry for action (complete silence).

Hmmm . . . I've seen this motley group before. Guess I'll have to fake it when I get to the gym. Or, as it is known to my achy body and reluctant mind, the bad Iron Torture Chamber of Horrors (the bad ITCH). On really bad days, the BITCH. I didn't say that.

This is what I did: Arrived and entered, major achievement. Then:

> Wide-grip Cybex machine press supersetted
> with wide-grip pulldown before neck
> *Increment weight each set (3 sets × 12, 10, 8 reps)*
> Engages shoulder and pectoral regions, bis, tris and lats

> Close-grip machine press supersetted with
> wide-grip pulldown behind neck
> *Increment weight each set (3 sets × 12, 10, 8 reps)*
> Recruits shoulder and pectoral muscle,
> bis and tris, lats and upper back

> Close-grip, over-grip pulldown supersetted
> with triceps pulley pushdown
> *Increment weight each set (3 sets × 12 reps)*
> Works lats, bis, tris

These were smooth, well-paced sets with the advantage of light to moderate weight to assure focus and form every rep, maximum exertion the last rep and the good sense to avoid joint injury, muscle overload and system damage.

Heavy weights and extensive workouts have done their muscle and strength building in the past. Now I stimulate, oxygenize and agreeably, desirably and wisely employ, work and play.

Good luck with that.

71

No Knuckle-Dragging Allowed

SHOULD YOU BE A serious-minded ironhead (classy oxymoron), you know the value of a clear mission statement. Composing a simple yet thoughtful personal avowal not only intelligently reviews, sorts and defines your training goals, it roots them in both your conscious and your sub-conscious. You therefore enact them double-strength, inside and out, as if they were facts. I am certain it is this practice engaged nearly sixty years ago that accounts for my hearty achievements today.

Pen in hand one evening in a Secaucus summer, 1960, as a single lifter daring to represent many, I offhandedly jotted down the words that follow.

Take nothing for granted, neither set nor rep nor course of the iron. We have not arrived at gravity's feet unwittingly, by accident or by default. The time is now, the load is upon our yet-narrow shoulders. Force upon the articles of steel the unborn might of our hands, and reward our structures, our characters with almighty goodness. Maximum exertion is our quest; well-formed and stone-hard sinew our mission and a burn hotter than a smithy's fire our charge.

Get lost, kid, or I'll smack ya one!

Two years later I was on a beach in sunny California begging, borrowing and stealing. Go, young people; follow your dreams. Never quit. Never let go. Don't drag your knuckles.

After a delicious night's sleep and a cascade of delectable proteins, carbs and fats and a delirious peek at world affairs, I can think of nothing more desirable than a workout at the local bar—barbell, that is.

Were I a young rascal standing before an Olympic bar for the first time, assuming I didn't have the presence of mind to turn and run like a scalded-arse ape, I'd act on four separate impulses: grasp and lift the beastie bar off the ground, press the bar overhead, curl the bar from my waist to my chin and, finally, repeatedly squat with the bar on my shoulders.

Right about then a knuckle-dragger from out of nowhere—snickering, "I'll show you how it's done"—would no doubt lie on a convenient bench and press the bar from his chest to an overhead position, after which he'd sit upright and complain about the pain in his shoulder. How obtuse. I'd suggest, of course, he use dumbbells next time and put a milk crate under one end of the bench to give it an incline.

"Resist shoulder injury and prevent undesirable development of low, hangy pecs."

Which brings me to my latest attempt to serve, reserve and preserve my lingering muscle and might. I call it Salvaging Remnants (SR).

Just showing up is not enough, as some old-timers like to say. You must move the iron from here to there and back again, the distance, weight and manner of movement dependent upon multiple factors—including luck, the stars and moon-risings, oxygen reserves, efficiency of tattered wraps, degrees of swelling, memory, level of consciousness and God's grace.

This is what I did.

Showed up Monday, mid-afternoon. Don't laugh: I was daydreaming and speeding (bad combo) and missed my exit, forcing me to the next exit five miles down the freeway and killing fifteen minutes retracing my way through foreign territory to the gym's welcoming doors. I counted the lost time and frustration as my daily aerobics.

After scanning the well-populated workout area, I stealthily made my way to a five-foot-square spot where two lusty pieces of equipment were located back to back, a pressing machine and a multi-cable unit. I would train there for the next thirty minutes, sorta nonstop. I'd expend seventy-five percent of my energy in concentrated motion, engaging the various upper-body muscles—chest, back, shoulders, bis and tris—in close harmony.

You know my drill: presses, wide-grip pulldowns before and behind the neck—under-grip, close-grip pulldowns and triceps extensions. Old wineskins, old wine.

Heavy weight (good luck, good riddance) is a thing of the past. Now I accentuate maximum exertion with precise form. In other words, any form that feels really good, loads the muscle, is nonthreatening and doesn't exact unrighteous pain, no matter what it looks like. I can live with that.

I will ache from head to toe on Wednesday and Thursday, like I was beat with a stick, but there'll be no throbbing elbow or immobile shoulder from hostile training. With verve and good sense, I eradicate those demons.

Did I mention I apply absolute, undiluted focus to every set, rep, breath, action and non-action? Probably did since I always do.

One more thing, I prefer four sets of six to fifteen repetitions, unless we're talkin' torso, which sometimes requires forty or fifty reps.

The remaining twenty-five percent of my stores—the last steely fibers and vanishing fifteen minutes—I devise a dedicated superset to drive the spike home. Seated bent-bar curls, straight-arm pullovers and lying triceps extensions, a tri-set for three sets, gives me peace and steals my breath away.

Take this one out back and prop him up against the telephone pole. Use Velcro if you have to. He's done.

72
Without Propellers or a Plan

I JUST RETURNED FROM my first workout after a long layoff. I didn't choose the layoff, it chose me. Those bumps in the road, cracks in the foundation and snags along the way—life's personal traveling companions—presented themselves generously and concurrently early this year. I could gripe under the circumstances, but everywhere I look, people, places and things have it worse, much worse, than I.

If I squint and imagine that which sags is mass and that which wrinkles is ripped, and that gasping is a deep-breathing technique, I'm in darn good shape.

Something I noted upon my recent exercise recess: Having trained steadily and conscientiously for a very long time, the muscle formation and density I have acquired is established. That is to say, it's there for good, not some pumpy stuff that recedes or becomes mushy unless constantly pursued, worshipped, coddled and fawned over. Who knew? It's not like there are a lot of references I can refer to.

The best, wisest and most enjoyable life action I can apply today is to retain my splendid health . . . gasp, gag, groan . . . spare myself of injury (no sleeping on railroad tracks, gnawing on a loaded Glock or jumping from ascending helium-filled dirigibles) and serve my remaining muscle with two tough and tight workouts a week.

Daily physical busyness on days off—Check!

Always eat right—Check!

Don't watch the news—Check!

The return workout was the first after a couple of months of laying low and licking my wounds like one of them mangy, salivating junkyard dogs missing patches of hair. You know the workouts of which I so affectionately speak, often referred to as the UGHS—Utterly Grim Horror Stories.

Everything is heavy, the muscles are stiff, I tire quickly and the groove is hard to find.

The anticipation of the workout is unnerving, the guilt is devastating, no one remembers my name, the equipment has been updated, the floor plan redesigned and my membership has lapsed.

One time, as I recall, the gym was gone and a shopping mall had been erected in its place. You bet I was bummed, but I bought socks and underwear on sale at the new Wal-Mart instead.

Time has rolled over us like a monster truck and looking back and forward are equally divine and exasperating. Where'd time go, where's it been and where's it going? The biggest question, not a question at all: Where are we now? Tell me I'm not the only one confused.

Thank God for the gym, the iron and the nutcases (whack jobs, bizarros and crazies) with whom we share the cold, hard implements. Here's to the vast variety of exercises and movements, the command they have over us and the command we have over them.

No one knows what sets and reps really are unless they've passionately persuaded and powerfully urged a rep and a set to completion.

It—the gym, the quest, the whole catastrophe—begins with the obvious desire for a strong and lean body. We're simple people with simple thoughts. Who doesn't want to look good and feel better? Should the clinking and clanking survive a few weeks, a subtle, almost undetectable relationship begins to form.

You sly devil! You know exactly what I'm talking about.

The gym and the journey to it, the time set aside for the workout and the workout itself apart from each other, are a non-linear experience. Connect the ingredients and a colorless and substance-free multidimensional pattern is produced. And no part of it is separate from the whole, no more separate than you and your subconscious.

And herein we discover truth, integrity and commitment.

Push plus pull equal pump and burn (fulfillment squared).

73
Iron-Age Proverbs

THE LAST TIME I WENT bowling I was twelve years old. Seems like only sixty-some years ago. Time flies when you sit still and stare.

It was at the Secaucus Bowlarama. I bowled 200 if you add up my scores for both games. Never went back. Too social: people, beer, balls and shoes for rent, slipping and sliding, boisterous laughter, confusion, little pencils and score keeping and costly.

I had a quarter and a dime in my pocket and a hole in my sneakers.

Heck, I can play for free where there are no crowds or balls or beers or score cards—downstairs in the basement with my weights and a milk crate. See ya later . . . clank, clank, clank.

Much, much later I'm still at it, which says a lot or very little. I'm either highly committed and disciplined or just plain dumb. Hmm . . . gives me something to ponder between sets.

My workouts are as important as ever. The heavy lifting has been done, the earth moving and plowing, the clearing and leveling, the construction and development. Now to attend the maintenance and repairs. We don't want to allow weeds to grow, leaks to go unchecked or faulty wiring to threaten the electrical system. Once decline begins and repairs are ignored, the interior and exterior quickly fade.

Got caught up in my dopey metaphor and pictured myself as an old tenement building on the rundown eastside, crawling with drug addicts and deadbeats and rats . . . broken windows, forty-watt light bulbs, graffiti and stink. Big belly, hanging butt, sloping shoulders, soft arms . . . yipes, stripes, let me outta here.

I admit I don't know much, but I do know I'm due to train arms today, with a touch of legs to stimulate the system and burn some loose calories. Biceps and triceps comprise a small muscle group (that has not always been the case) and don't require lots of energy. Hard work, burn and focus, yes, but not a big drain on the heart and lungs. Thus, a reserve for some friendly leg work to keep the foundations from failing and crabgrass from cropping up along the walkway.

I intend to arrange my workouts, henceforth, with particular attention to robustness and good cheer, function and wholeness. No longer shall I seek mass and power, huge and ripped, marathon workouts, the last rep, and one more set before they lock the doors and turn the lights out.

I shall train sensibly, wisely and productively.

Time has not caught up with me; I have overtaken time. What was once necessary yesterday or a year ago is too much today. I expect I'll be playing this intricate balancing game from now on: exercises, sets and reps, pace and intensity of performance, ability and purpose.

Just when I thought I knew what I was doing, along come the same old variables disguised in different clothing.

I'll customize my workouts, rotate and alternate the muscle groups and train according to on-the-spot, at-the-moment needs.

"Have to," "ought to" and "supposed to" will not guide me; guilt will not be my judge. "More is better" will no longer rule my hauling and tossing of metal, and beyond my ability will remain beyond my ability.

I recognize you as sober and serious lifters with whom I share similar training precepts. A powerful alliance, I thought we might examine ten post-Stone Age sayings found etched on the walls of ancient cave dwellings and dungeons.

Iron-Age Proverbs

Train hard and eat right, my son;
Be strong, be wise and live long.

Curls for strong arms and presses for mighty shoulders;
The rod for the back that refuses.

The wise man seeks muscle and might daily;
Perseverance and patience are his companions.
Not every day is fruitful and a delight;
Satisfaction comes at a great cost.

Better to sleep in a bed of thorns,
Than to share a house with a drunken scoundrel.
Such a mate is destructive,
Apart from barbells, there is no hope for him or her.

I saw a man walking to ruin and death,
His hands were without iron and steel.
No fresh fruit or greens of the earth entered his belly,
No protein or essential fats satisfied his languishing body.

The foolish choose the easy way,
The wicked the way where evil lurks.
But the courageous fear not toil and pain,
And the devoted delight in loaded bars both long and short.

Listen to the words of wisdom, my child;
Let not health and strength drain from your body.
Serve your muscle and might always,
And they will serve you forevermore.

Worship the heavy bench press and it will take you down;
Treat your body to its rewards and damage will not visit
your house.

A good pump and a stinging burn are the joys of a solid
workout;
Pursue them with diligence and long suffering.
Dullness in spirit and sluggishness in body assure defeat;
Avoid them like poisonous snakes.

Weights that go unattended build up rust,
While the lax attendee builds up no good.
Sluggard is his name,
Frail is his frame.

Early bombers resorted to jumping off cliffs and peaks to gain air; we have wings and propellers, ailerons, rudders and flaps. Yet, some things never change, bombers: Once a dumbbell, always a dumbbell.

A little reassurance goes a long way, and we have a long way to go.

And finally, for all my puffing and advice, I have one thing to say that is true:

> *Trust in the Lord with all your heart,*
>
> *And lean not on your own understanding;*
>
> *In all your ways acknowledge him*
>
> *And he will make your paths straight.*
>
> ~ Proverbs 3:16, 17

About the Author

DAVE DRAPER is the author of the motivational book *Iron on My Mind*, the weight-training instructional book, *Brother Iron, Sister Steel*, and a nutritional guidebook for weight loss called *Your Body Revival*. He also wrote the extended captions in Dick Tyler's *West Coast Bodybuilding Scene*.

These books are available at the On Target Publications website, *otpbooks.com*. You can learn more about Dave on his website, *davedraper.com*.